DEFINING
BIBLICAL HOLINESS

DEFINING BIBLICAL HOLINESS
Two Views Of Christian Perfection

Edited and compiled by
Jeffrey L. Wallace

ISBN-13: 978-0615444048
ISBN-10: 0615444040

Published by:

Apprehending Truth Publishers
Woodville, Mississippi
2011

Apprehending Truth Publishers is a division of Apprehending Truth Ministry.
http://www.ApprehendingTruth.net

This book is dedicated to:

Britt Williams
The man who taught me practical application of
Christian Perfection, not only by Biblical
instruction but by example as well.

My wife-
Stephanie, who is a daily example of Christ to me
and our children

And to-
The Lord Jesus Christ, who for no apparent
reason plucked me out of the fire, hating even
the garment spotted by the flesh.

Defining Biblical Holiness

Two Views Of Christian Perfection

Heritage of Truth Series
Volume I

A Plain Account	Scriptural Doctrine
John Wesley	Asa Mahan

With an introduction
"The Fear of Perfection"
by
J. L. Wallace

DEFINING BIBLICAL HOLINESS
TWO VIEWS OF CHRISTIAN PERFECTION

A PLAIN ACCOUNT OF CHRISTIAN PERFECTION

by

JOHN WESLEY

SCRIPTURE DOCTRINE OF CHRISTIAN PERFECTION

by

ASA MAHAN

Editor's Note:

The following writings by John Wesley and Asa Mahan are a comparison and revision of various editions of their respective works here presented lightly edited and reformatted. However, where minor revision has been applied, the actual words remain Wesley's and Mahan's, and no meaning or intent has been altered in any way. We have limited revisions to updated spelling and minor adjustments to the text where deemed necessary for this edition. The reader is referred to other extant editions for comparison, where these may be found. Wesley's *A Plain Account* can be found in various and multiple venues, while a adequate copy of Mahan's *Scripture Doctrine* is much more difficult to locate in print.

John Fletcher's dissertation on Christian perfection, *The Last Check to Antinomianism*, was originally considered for this volume. The editor has elected to reserve that work for a future project.

CONTENTS

FORWARD

*Mark the perfect man, and behold the upright: for the
end of that man is peace.* ~ *Psalm 37:37*

The question may be asked, why republish books that were
written over one and two hundred years ago?

The prevailing attitude of the professing church is one ranging
from indifference to stark animosity toward the doctrines of
holiness. There is no need to "reinvent the wheel" in order to
demonstrate the spiritual neglect of the professing church of
this day. The treatises here presented are as significant and
relevant to the problems of antinomianism today as they were
when written.

John Wesley's *A Plain Account of Christian Perfection* is a classic
discourse on the subject and is included to provide foundational
clarity and establish the tenets of the doctrine at hand.

Asa Mahan's *Scripture Doctrine of Christian Perfection*, Fletcher
notwithstanding, is possibly the most systematic defense of
holiness available.

In a sense, Wesley sets the nail while Mahan drives it home.
Consequently, to set these two dissertations together in
juxtaposition has the potential to deliver the quintessential

definition of Biblical Holiness and present a clear defense of this doctrine to a generation which has been hoodwinked by the antinomian philosophy of the hour. The works here presented are unanswerable, the presentations intrinsically Biblical, reasonable and logical, nevertheless most will reject them having laid aside the commandment of God that they may keep their own tradition.

I realize in the overall scope of things, that while the intended target of this work is unto all men, the actual target is very small. Not many will in reality read this book, fewer will accept its Biblical veracity, and fewer still will seize hold of this ever more evident possibility of holiness in life and practice. This does not negate the importance of proclaiming the Truth in this hour of deception, of presenting light to the minions of darkness.

We here present the demands of God according to Scripture, it is the decision of the reader to submit and walk in the Light. We have blown the trumpet. Our hands are clean.

J L Wallace
Woodville, Mississippi
January 2011

The Fear of Perfection
And the Perversion of Grace

Nothing is more desperately needed in this hour and yet so vehemently rejected as is the Biblical teaching of Christian perfection; surely the most misunderstood, misrepresented, and maligned doctrine of Scripture, and this by those who call themselves after His name. The word perfection does truly alarm many a professing Christian. All too often this is not because the word has been improperly defined, but because if this doctrine be true, they fall woefully short of the basic requirements of Biblical Christianity.

Hebrews 12:14 states, "*Follow peace with all men, and holiness, without which no man shall see the Lord*". No man lacking holiness of life, no man short of moral perfection, will see the Lord. Such an emphatic statement demands scrupulous and fastidious attention, and yet this is not the only Scriptural admonition to perfection. The Bible is replete with commands of obedience, perfection, and holiness; and speaks of our responsibility to God, to our fellow man, and to ourselves. It is the contention of the proponents of this great doctrine of perfection that man is to strive toward a certain state of excellence whereby God, our brethren, and this world will know of our firm dedication to all things pious, and of our steadfast resistance to all things evil, showing forth the wisdom that is from above, without hypocrisy.

And so the question must inevitably be asked, is man called to be perfect in the eyes of God, and if so, what does that mean?

> *Be ye therefore perfect, even as your Father which is in heaven is perfect. ~ Matthew 5:48*

> *Sanctify yourselves therefore, and <u>be ye holy</u>: for I am the LORD your God. ~ Leviticus 20:7*

> *As obedient children, not fashioning yourselves according to the former lusts in your ignorance: But as he which hath called you is holy, so be ye holy in all manner of conversation; Because it is written, <u>Be ye holy</u>; for I am holy. ~ 1 Peter 1:14-16*

These passages are written in the form of a command. Clearly Christians *"are to be holy in all behavior!"* Because God is holy any who claim to be His disciples must of necessity be holy as well.

> *Nevertheless the foundation of God standeth sure, having this seal, The Lord knoweth them that are his. And, Let every one that nameth the name of Christ depart from iniquity. ~ 2 Timothy 2:19*

Noah Webster's 1828 Dictionary defines holy:

> Properly, whole, entire or perfect, in a moral sense. Hence, pure in heart, temper or dispositions; free from sin and sinful affections. Applied to the Supreme Being, holy signifies perfectly pure, immaculate and complete in moral character; and man is more or less holy, as his heart is more or less sanctified, or purified from evil dispositions. We call a man holy, when

his heart is conformed in some degree to the image of God, and his life is regulated by the divine precepts. Hence, holy is used as nearly synonymous with good, pious, godly *and dare we add, perfect.* (Italics added)

The dictionary references 1 Peter 1 in this definition.

Albert Barnes' note on 1 Peter 1:16 is here interesting.

This command was addressed at first to the Israelites, but it is with equal propriety addressed to Christians, as the professed people of God. The foundation of the command is, that they professed to be his people, and that as his people they ought to be like their God. (Compare *Micah 4:5*) It is a great truth, that people everywhere will imitate the God whom they worship. They will form their character in accordance with his. They will regard what he does as right. They will attempt to rise no higher in virtue than the God whom they adore, and they will practice freely what he is supposed to do or approve. Hence, by knowing what are the characteristics of the gods which are worshipped by any people, we may form a correct estimate of the character of the people themselves; and, hence, as the God who is the object of the Christian's worship is perfectly holy, the character of His worshipers should also be holy. And hence, also, we may see that the tendency of true religion is to make people pure. As the worship of the impure gods of the pagan moulds the character of the worshippers into their image, so the worship of Yahweh moulds the character of His professed friends into His image, and they become like him.

And thus, most will stoop to imperfection because the 'god' they have formed in their own imaginations has overruled the Scriptures and replaced it with individual autonomy. Since their 'god' lightly esteems the Scriptures they too have rejected the implicit demands therein, including the call to holiness. They do not pursue holiness simply because their 'god' does not require it. But the Christian, who can say with the psalmist "*The law of thy mouth is better unto me than thousands of gold and silver*" (Psalms 119:72), searches for no loop hole in Holy Writ, but rather stands in agreement with God and against himself, his experiences and predilections of the flesh.

While it must be conceded that no one is perfect as God is perfect, i.e. in attribute and without defect, there is an obvious Biblical moral perfection to which God holds every man accountable, because it is attainable through grace which He has granted to every man.

> *For the grace of God that bringeth salvation hath appeared to all men, Teaching us that, denying ungodliness and worldly lusts, we should live soberly, righteously, and godly, in this present world;* ~ *Titus 2:11-12*

In fact, God Himself, has declared several men in Scripture to be perfect. Noah (Genesis 6:9), Asa (2 Chronicles 15:17), Job (Job 1:8, 2:3) and David (1 Kings 11:4) are all referred to as being perfect before God. In Genesis 17:1, He commanded Abram personally "walk before me and be thou perfect." And to each and every Christian He has commanded as well, "*Be perfect, be of good comfort, be of one mind, live in peace; and the God of love and peace shall be with you.*" (2 Corinthians 13:11)

Who could dare say that men are not therefore under Divine obligation to perfection? Particularly in light of the fact that God has made provision for such by the atonement, through His grace and Scriptural instruction.

All scripture is given by inspiration of God, and is profitable for doctrine, for reproof, for correction, for instruction in righteousness: That the man of God may be perfect, throughly furnished unto all good works.
~ *2 Timothy 3:16-17*

As has been Biblically affirmed, man is commanded to perfection, to holiness. Being as how Scripture commands and expects perfection, it would be incumbent upon all men to determine what that admonition entails and what the proper response as followers of Christ should be.

Has God instituted a command that is impossible to be obeyed? Many would answer in the affirmative.

And herein lay the crisis. Moral perfection _is_ impossible and cannot be found solely within the constitution of man. However, with God all things are possible. (Matt 19:26) If thou canst believe, all things *are* possible to him that believeth. (Mark 9:23) He has given provision through Himself.

The Bible declares that he who hungers and thirsts after righteousness shall be filled. Most who reject this doctrine do so simply because they do not want to be holy. The desire of their hearts is set on earthly things and not on things above. This is cloaked by vain attempts of piety and claims of humility. "Surely," they contend, "anyone who claims to be perfect is proud, while those who condescend to sin every day are the epitome of the humble. Perfection is impossible, even through grace, because after all, God gives grace to the humble who sin everyday in thought, word and deed, and resists the proud who think they can be perfect."

Be not deceived, dear reader, it is not humility to claim to remain in sin; it is an accusation against God. *That* is pride. It is the deification of self. In an attempt to sound humble this claim only fuels the fires of human pride and the motions of sins revealing the interworking of the flesh and is blasphemy against God; making the commands of God of none effect by tradition.

Oswald Chambers has stated:

> Humility before men may be unconscious blasphemy before God. Why are you not a saint? It is either that you do not want to be a saint, or that you do not believe God can make you one.

No, Jesus didn't die to make holiness unnecessary, but to make it possible. And what greater blasphemy can there be than to suggest that the efficacious blood of the perfect Lamb of God is incapable of cleansing those who cling to Him and His promises by faith, through grace?

> *And she shall bring forth a son, and thou shalt call his name JESUS: for he shall save his people from their sins. ~ Matthew 1:21*

> *But if we walk in the light, as he is in the light, we have fellowship one with another, and the blood of Jesus Christ his Son cleanseth us from all sin. ~ 1 John 1:7*

Abraham told Isaac, God will provide *Himself* a sacrifice.

In providing Himself as a sacrifice He has given man the victory over sin, the flesh and the devil and given him the grace whereby he may live perfect and holy before Him in this life; a truth that is not lost on the unbeliever who diligently watches the Christian for any excuse to confidently remain in his own rebellion against his Creator. Sadly, many who profess the name of Christ have rejected this all important provision, and provided a ready-made excuse to them, turning the grace of God into lasciviousness, continuing in sin, and thinking grace to abound to their accounts. While shunning those who teach the more excellent way, "they shew the work of the law written in

12

their hearts, their conscience also bearing witness, and *their* thoughts the mean while accusing or else excusing one another" (Romans 2:15); all the while attempting to sear their own conscience in the light of His ever probing and revealing Word. And thus, they reveal not Christ to the world, but their own idols of silver and of gold.

> *For where your treasure is, there will your heart be also.*
> ~ *Luke 12:34*

The importance of Christian testimony in a world gone mad with sin is obvious to those who love Christ and His Word. Jesus said you will know them by their fruits. Every man is known by his fruits, whether of evil or of good. And His disciples shall be known by their love one to another. Love has been referred to by Jesus Christ, Himself as the highest form of obedience unto holiness.

> *Master, which is the great commandment in the law?*
> *Jesus said unto him, Thou shalt love the Lord thy God*
> *with all thy heart, and with all thy soul, and with all thy*
> *mind. This is the first and great commandment. And the*
> *second is like unto it, Thou shalt love thy neighbour as*
> *thyself. On these two commandments hang all the law*
> *and the prophets.* ~ *Matthew 22:36-40*
> (See also, Romans 13:8-10, Galatians 5:14, James 2:8)

In examination of a particular passage of Scripture, many have thought to use God's own words against Him in order to bolster the claim that all must remain in sin.

> *That I may know him, and the power of his*
> *resurrection, and the fellowship of his sufferings, being*
> *made conformable unto his death; If by any means I*
> *might attain unto the resurrection of the dead.* **Not as**
> **though I had already attained, either were already**
> **perfect**: *but I follow after, if that I may apprehend that*

*for which also I am apprehended of Christ Jesus. Brethren, I count not myself to have apprehended: but this one thing I do, forgetting those things which are behind, and reaching forth unto those things which are before, I press toward the mark for the prize of the high calling of God in Christ Jesus. **Let us therefore, as many as be perfect**, be thus minded: and if in any thing ye be otherwise minded, God shall reveal even this unto you. Nevertheless, whereto we have already attained, let us walk by the same rule, let us mind the same thing. ~ Philippians 3:10-16*

Those who would use verse 12 to defend the antinomian position have indeed turned plain reason upon its ear and do wrest the Scriptures to their own destruction.

In verse 12 the apostle testifies, "Not as though I had already attained, either were already perfect" yet in verse 15 he declares, "Let us therefore, as many as be perfect."

Adam Clarke adequately addresses the passage.

> St. Paul, therefore, is not speaking here of any *deficiency* in his own grace, or spiritual state; he does not mean by not being yet *perfect*, that he had a *body of sin and death* cleaving to him, and was still polluted with *indwelling sin*, as some have most falsely and dangerously imagined; he speaks of his not having terminated his course by martyrdom, which he knew would sooner or later be the case. This he considered as the *perfection*, of his whole career, and was led to view everything as *imperfect* or *unfinished* till this had taken place.

The implication of the word "perfect" used by Paul in verse 12 is obviously one of completion and not of moral rectitude.

Clarke says of the word in verse 15: "as many as have entered fully into the spirit and design of the Gospel".

The description here is of one given over to Christ, one who earnestly strives for holiness, who hungers and thirst after righteousness and seeks the maximum amount of grace available to live in accord with the Word of God.

What Christian Perfection is Not

The distinction is here made between the false accusation of "sinless" perfection and that of Biblical Christian perfection. It is very apparent and quite obvious through Biblical precept and universal experience that "sinless perfection" is never something attainable by human endeavor. And yet the strawman built by the opponents of Christian perfection, is presented as the standard position of its adherents.[1]

The opponents of holiness continuously construct these erroneous arguments by misappropriating the Scriptures and misrepresenting the Biblical position of perfection as held by its proponents.

True Biblical Christian Perfection does not, nor ever has presented the proposition that man ever has or ever will live holy apart from the propitiation established on the cross. Nor has the doctrine ever posited that once justified it is impossible to ever again transgress the Law of God. On the contrary, the position only establishes the Biblical Truth that is it possible, by grace to refrain from all known infractions of Scripture and conscience.

> *If we say that we have no sin, we deceive ourselves, and the truth is not in us. If we confess our sins, he is faithful and just to forgive us our sins, and to cleanse*

---

[1] While we acknowledge that there are those who teach the error of "sinless perfection" we vehemently deny any association therewith and relegate the group under the umbrella of antinomian. This is addressed in the dissertation which follows.

us from all unrighteousness. If we say that we have not
sinned, we make him a liar, and his word is not in us.
~ 1 John 1:8-10

To say that we have reached a sinless state in which we no longer need the blood of Christ to cleanse us is a deception; which is the implication of the term "sinless perfection" and is the building blocks of the façade used by the opponents of Christian Perfection.

For a clear understanding of the principles that are here being applied, Adam Clarke is again consulted, concerning 1 John 1:8.

> **If we say that we have no sin** - This is tantamount to 1 John 1:10: If we say that we have not sinned. All have sinned, and come short of the glory of God; and therefore every man needs a Savior, such as Christ is. It is very likely that the heretics, against whose evil doctrines the apostle writes, denied that they had any sin, or needed any Savior. In deed, the Gnostics even denied that Christ suffered: the Aeon, or Divine Being that dwelt in the man Christ Jesus, according to them, left him when he was taken by the Jews; and he, being but a common man, his sufferings and death had neither merit nor efficacy.
> **We deceive ourselves** - By supposing that we have no guilt, no sinfulness, and consequently have no need of the blood of Christ as an atoning sacrifice: this is the most dreadful of all deceptions, as it leaves the soul under all the guilt and pollution of sin, exposed to hell, and utterly unfit for heaven.
> **The truth is not in us** - We have no knowledge of the Gospel of Jesus, the whole of which is founded on this most awful truth - all have sinned, all are guilty, all are unholy; and none can redeem himself. Hence it is as necessary

that Jesus Christ should become incarnated, and suffer and die to bring men to God.

What Christian Perfection Is

In short Christian Perfection is striving for holiness and continuing in all the light and understanding that God has provided. "He is perfect in holiness whose love toward God at each successive moment corresponds with the extent of his powers." So it is not assumed that everyone is at the same level or degree of perfection but we are all of the same nature, i.e. partakers of the very nature of God and thus perfect as we walk in the light as he is in the light.

All men are under a divine obligation to fear and reverence God.

Noah Webster defines reverence:

> Fear mingled with respect and esteem; veneration.

> The fear acceptable to God, is a filial fear, an awful reverence of the divine nature, proceeding from a just esteem of his perfections, which produces in us an inclination to his service and an unwillingness to offend him.

Within the heart of the moral agent who chooses to fear God and walk in holiness is an unwillingness to offend God or to violate his own conscience in any way. The key word here is "unwilling".

It has been said that no man will rise above his theology. This is a true proverb. No man sets his will to live holy who believes it is neither possible nor necessary to do so. And yet the Bible emphatically teaches not only the possibility through grace, but also the necessity by the command to live holy.

What is being implied here?

> A full and perfect discharge of our entire duty, of
> all existing obligations in respect to God and all
> other beings. It is perfect obedience to the
> moral law. It is "loving the Lord our God with
> all our heart, and with all our soul, and with all
> our strength, and our neighbor as ourselves." It
> implies the entire absence of all selfishness, and
> the perpetual presence and all prevading
> influence of pure and perfect love. "Love is the
> fulfilling of the Law". ~ Asa Mahan

Most have devised their own sense of morality, restraining
themselves in social acceptability and since in their experience
no one is perfect they concoct an aberrant theology to coincide
with their experiences. This is *antinomianism* in the sense that
there exists a dullness to righteousness, a carelessness toward
obedience, and a haphazard treatment of Scripture.

No longer is there a healthy fear of God in society because the
professing church has replaced reverence for God with a
"friendship gospel" and turned the Just and Holy One of Israel
into an eccentric old man wringing his hands over whether or
not people will like him. They have redefined Scripture and
relegated holiness to a prudish and antiquated scheme of "cultic
legalists" designed to deprive them of their newfound "liberty"
in Christ. Indeed, perfection has been undermined and
rejected and grace perverted by moral relativism and the
autonomous proclivities of the flesh. And the people love to
have it so.

By surrendering their will to their experience instead of the
Scripture, they usurp the law of God and because there is no
such thing as a legal vacuum, they replace God's perfect law of
liberty with a law of their own autonomous reasoning.

With all of the striving toward holiness, attention must not be allowed to drift from Christ. In the moment this takes place holiness has been lost, for He **is** holiness.

Christ must be the center, the focal point of all efforts toward holiness.   Seek Christ and holiness will be found.   Emulate Christ and holiness will be achieved.   The Bible says to put on the Lord Jesus Christ.

When it is remembered that the first thing that ever died, was killed by God, Himself in order to clothe Adam and Eve, in order to cover their transgression, the magnitude of this doctrine becomes evident.   This Biblical example is displayed in the fact that the more barbaric the culture, the less clothing that society will deem as acceptable.   The application?

When we refuse to put on light, regardless how much religion we retain, we will become spiritually naked before God. Holiness is a person.   His name is Jesus, and all must of necessity be clothed with Christ.

> *And that ye put on the new man, which after God is created in righteousness and true holiness.   ~ Ephesians 4:24*

Perfection in holiness is attained in the same manner as every other promise and provision of God, i.e. by faith.   Although faith is mandatory, faith alone is not meritorious.   There is no merit of reward in faith or in believing God, to obedience; no more than a citizen deserves special acknowledgment for keeping the laws of his country.   The obedience of faith is expected, yeah, even a very obligation.

> *But which of you, having a servant plowing or feeding cattle, will say unto him by and by, when he is come from the field, Go and sit down to meat? And will not rather say unto him, Make ready wherewith I may sup, and gird thyself, and serve me, till I have eaten and*

drunken; and afterward thou shalt eat and drink? Doth he thank that servant because he did the things that were commanded him? I trow not. So likewise ye, when ye shall have done all those things which are commanded you, say, We are unprofitable servants: we have done that which was our duty to do.
~ Luke 17:7-10

But there remains great benefit in obedience to God.

The Bible alone makes civilized people differ from the barbarian. Without it we should soon be like them ignorant, superstitious, impure and cruel. What greater incentive to holiness and perfection than the want of that very attribute in the culture at large. Unfortunately, that want has had the exact opposite effect upon the professing Christian. When men are taught that they cannot live holy, the once great chasm between good and evil becomes a narrow trench easily stepped over. Hence the want of holiness in society is no longer of any great concern for the same want has migrated to this side the ditch.

Richard Watson explains:

> It is equally a matter of undoubted fact, that, in all questions of morals which restrain the vices, passions, and immediate interests of men, conviction is generally resisted, and the rule is brought down to the practice, rather than the practice raised to the rule; so that the most flimsy sophisms are admitted as arguments, and principles the most lax displace those of rigid rectitude and virtue. (Theological Institutes)

Christ must remain the object of faith. Faith cannot be had in holiness itself, or morality, or modesty, or ethics. He alone must be the focus, the author and finisher of every man's faith. When the object of faith is Jesus, all the aspects of holiness will indelibly fall into place. Our nature is His.

Standing on the promises, I now can see
Perfect present cleansing in the blood for me;
Standing in the liberty where Christ makes free,
Standing on the promises of God.

Standing on the promises, I cannot fall,
Listening every moment to the Spirit's call,
Resting in my Savior as my all I all,
Standing on the promises of God.

As Paul the Apostle once penned on another subject, "if any man seem to be contentious, we have no such custom, neither the churches of God."

JLW.

Do you hear them coming, brother,
Thronging up the steeps of light,
Clad in glorious shining garments,
Blood washed, garments pure and white?

Do you hear the stirring anthems,
Filling all the earth and sky,
'Tis a grand, victorious army,
Lift its banner up on high!

Never fear the clouds of sorrow,
Never fear the storms of sin.
We shall triumph on the morrow,
Even now our joys begin.

Wave the banner, shout His praises,
For our victory is nigh!
We shall join our conqu'ring Savior,
We shall reign with Him on high!

'Tis a glorious church without spot or wrinkle,
Washed in the blood of the Lamb;
'Tis a glorious church without spot or wrinkle,
Washed in the blood of the Lamb.

Ralph E. Hudson
1892

PART ONE:

A PLAIN ACCOUNT OF CHRISTIAN PERFECTION

by

JOHN WESLEY

A Plain Account of Christian Perfection

As Believed and Taught by The Reverend Mr. John Wesley, From the Year 1725, to the Year 1777

1. What I purpose in the following papers is, to give a plain and distinct account of the steps by which I was led, during a course of many years, to embrace the doctrine of Christian perfection. This I owe to the serious part of mankind, those who desire to know all "the truth as it is in Jesus." And these only are concerned in questions of this kind. To these I would nakedly declare the thing as it is, endeavoring all along to show, from one period to another, both what I thought, and why I thought so.

2. In the year 1725, being in the twenty-third year of my age, I met with Bishop Taylor's "Rule and Exercises of Holy Living and Dying." In reading several parts of this book, I was exceedingly affected; that part in particular which relates to purity of intention. Instantly I resolved to dedicate all my life to God, all my thoughts, and words, and actions; being thoroughly

convinced, there was no medium; but that every part of my life (not some only) must either be a sacrifice to God, or myself, that is, in effect, to the devil.

Can any serious person doubt of this, or find a medium between serving God and serving the devil?

3. In the year 1726, I met with Kempis's "Christian's Pattern."[2] The nature and extent of inward religion, the religion of the heart, now appeared to me in a stronger light than ever it had done before. I saw, that giving even all my life to God (supposing it possible to do this, and go no farther would profit me nothing, unless I gave my heart, yea, all my heart, to him.

I saw, that "simplicity of intention, and purity of affection," one *design* in all we speak or do, and one *desire* ruling all our tempers, are indeed "the wings of the soul," without which she can never ascend to the mount of God.

4. A year or two after, Mr. Law's "Christian Perfection" and "Serious Call"[3] were put into my hands. These convinced me, more than ever, of the absolute impossibility of being half a Christian; and I determined, through his grace, (the absolute necessity of which I was deeply sensible of;) to be all-devoted to God, to give him all my soul, my body, and my substance

Will any considerate man say that this is carrying matters too far? Or that anything less is due to Him who has given himself for us, than to give him ourselves, all we have, and all we are?

---

[2] The editor here invokes a strong caution regarding Kempis. Thomas à Kempis was a 12th century Roman Catholic mystic. He is best known for his devotional titled, "Imitation of Christ" here referred to by Wesley as "Christian's Pattern". As F. J. Huegel so adequately pointed out, Christianity is not an *imitation* of Christ but a *participation* of Christ. "The basic idea [of "Imitation of Christ"] is false to the principles that underlie the Christian life." (F. J. Huegel. Bone of His Bone. 6th American Edition. Grand Rapids, MI: Zondervan. pg 19)

[3] Wesley here refers to *A Treatise of Christian Perfection* (1726), and *Serious Call to a Devout and Holy Life* (1728), by William Law.

5. In the year 1729, I began not only to read, but to study, the Bible, as the one, the only standard of truth, and the only model of pure religion. Hence I saw, in a clearer and clearer light, the indispensable necessity of having "*the mind which was in Christ*," and of "*walking as Christ also walked*;" even of having, not some part only, but all the mind which was in him; and of walking as he walked, not only in many or in most respects, but in *all* things. And this was the light, wherein at this time I generally considered religion, as an uniform following of Christ, an entire inward and outward conformity to our Master. Nor was I afraid of anything more, than of bending this rule to the experience of myself; or of other men; of allowing myself in any the least disconformity to our grand Exemplar.

6. On January 1, 1733, I preached before the University in St. Mary's church, on "*The Circumcision of the Heart*;"[4] an account of which I gave in these words: "It is that habitual disposition of soul which, in the sacred writings, is termed holiness; and which directly implies, the being cleansed from sin 'from all filthiness both of flesh and spirit;' and, by consequence the being endued with those virtues which were in Christ Jesus the being so 'renewed in the image of our mind,' as to be 'perfect as our Father in heaven is perfect'"

In the same sermon I observed, "'Love is the fulfilling of the law, the end of the commandment.' It is not only 'the first and great' command, but all the commandments in one. 'Whatsoever things are just, whatsoever things are pure, if there be any virtue, if there be any praise,' they are all comprised in this one word, love. In this is perfection, and glory, and happiness: The royal law of heaven and earth is this, 'Thou shall love the Lord thy God with all thy heart, and with all thy soul, and with all thy mind, and with all thy strength.' The one perfect good shall be your one ultimate end. One thing shall ye desire for its own sake, -- the fruition of Him who is all in all.

---

[4] See: *Sermons of John Wesley; Volume 1* [to be published by Apprehending Truth Publishers in 2011.]

One happiness shall ye propose to your souls, even an union with Him that made them, the having 'fellowship with the Father and the Son,' the being 'joined to the Lord in one spirit.' One design ye are to pursue to the end of time, -- the enjoyment of God in time and in eternity. Desire other things so far as they tend to this; love the creature, as it leads to the Creator. But in every step you take, be this the glorious point that terminates your view. Let every affection, and thought and word, and action, be subordinate to this. Whatever ye desire or fear, whatever ye seek or shun, whatever ye think speak, or do, be it in order to your happiness in God, the sole end, as well as source, of your being."

I concluded in these words: "Here is the sum of the perfect law, the circumcision of the heart. Let the spirit return to God that gave it, with the whole train of its affections. -- Other sacrifices from us he would not, but the living sacrifice of the heart hath he chosen. Let it be continually offered up to God through Christ, in flames of holy love. And let no creature be suffered to share with him; for he is a jealous God. His throne will he not divide with another; he will reign without a rival. Be no design, no desire admitted there, but what has Him for its ultimate object. This is the way wherein those children of God once walked, who being dead still speak to us: 'Desire not to live but to praise his name; let all your thoughts, words, and works tend to his glory.' 'Let your soul be filled with so entire a love to Him that you may love nothing but for his sake.' 'Have a pure intention of heart, a steadfast regard to his glory in all your actions.' For then, and not till then, is that 'mind in us, which was also in Christ Jesus,' when in every motion of our heart, in every word of our tongue, in every work of our hands, we 'pursue nothing but in relation to him, and in subordination to his pleasure;' when we too neither think, nor speak, nor act, to fulfill 'our own will, but the will of Him that sent us;' when, 'whether we eat or drink, or whatever we do,' we do it all 'to the glory of God.'"

It may be observed, this sermon was composed the first of all my writings which have been published. This was the view of religion I then had, which even then I scrupled not to term *perfection*. This is the view I have of it now, without any material addition or diminution. And what is there here, which any man of understanding, who believes the Bible, can object to? What can he deny, without flatly contradicting the Scripture? What retrench, without taking from the word of God?

7. In the same sentiment did my brother and I remain (with all those young gentlemen in derision termed *Methodists*) till we embarked for America, in the latter end of 1735. It was the next year, while I was at Savannah, that I wrote the following lines: --

> Is there a thing beneath the sun,
>> That strives with thee my heart to share?
> Ah! tear it thence, and reign alone,
>> The Lord of every motion there!

In the beginning of the year 1738, as I was returning from thence, the cry of my heart was,

> O grant that nothing in my soul
>> May dwell, but thy pure love alone!
> O may thy love possess me whole,
>> My joy, my treasure, and my crown !
> Strange fires far from my heart remove;
> My every act, word, thought, be love!

I never heard that any one objected to this. And indeed who can object? Is not this the language, not only of every believer, but of every one that is truly awakened? But what have I wrote, to this day, which is either stronger or plainer?

8. In August following, I had a long conversation with Arvid Gradin, in Germany. After he had given me an account of his experience, I desired him to give me, in writing, a definition of "the full assurance of faith," which he did in the following words:

"Repose in the blood of Christ; a firm confidence in God, and persuasion of his favor; the highest tranquility, serenity, and peace of mind, with a deliverance from every fleshly desire, and a cessation of all, even inward sins."

This was the first account I ever heard from any living man, of what I had before learned myself from the oracles of God, and had been praying for, (with the little company of my friends,) and expecting, for several years.

9. In 1739, my brother and I published a volume of "Hymns and Sacred Poems." In many of these we declared our sentiments strongly and explicitly. So, page 24, --

> Turn the fall stream of nature's tide;
>   Let all our actions tend
> To thee, their source; thy love the guide,
>   Thy glory be the end.
>
> Earth then a scale to heaven shall be;
>   Sense shall point out the road;
> The creatures all shall lead to thee,
>   And all we taste be God.

Again, --

> Lord, arm me with thy Spirit's might,
>   Since I am call'd by thy great name:
> In thee my wand'ring thoughts unite,
>   Of all my works be thou the aim:
> Thy love attend me all my days,
> And my sole business be thy praise. (Page 122.)

Again, --

> Eager for thee I ask and pant,

> So strong the principle divine,
> Carries me out with sweet constraint,
> Till all my hallow'd soul be thine;
> Plunged in the Godhead's deepest sea,
> And lost in thine immensity! (Page 125.)

Once more, --

> Heavenly Adam, life divine,
> Change my nature into thine;
> Move and spread throughout my soul,
> Actuate and fill the whole. (Page 153.)

It would be easy to cite many more passages to the same effect. But these are sufficient to show, beyond contradiction, what our sentiments then were.

10. The first tract I ever wrote expressly on this subject was published in the latter end of this year. That none might be prejudiced before they read it, I gave it the indifferent title of "The Character of a Methodist." In this I described a perfect Christian, placing in the front, "Not as though I had already attained." Part of it I subjoin without any alteration: --

"A Methodist is one who loves the Lord his God with all his heart, with all his soul, with all his mind, and with all his strength. God is the joy of his heart, and the desire of his soul, which is continually crying, 'Whom have I in heaven but thee? and there is none upon earth whom I desire besides thee.' My God and my all! 'Thou art the strength of my heart, and my portion for ever.' He is therefore happy in God; yea, always happy, as having in him a well of water springing up unto everlasting life, and over-flowing his soul with peace and joy. Perfect love living now cast out fear, he rejoices evermore. Yea, his joy is full, and all his bones cry out, 'Blessed be the God and Father of our Lord Jesus Christ, who, according to his abundant mercy, hath begotten me again unto a living hope of an inheritance incorruptible and undefiled, reserved in heaven for me.'

"And he, who hath this hope, thus full of immortality, in everything giveth thanks, as knowing this (whatsoever it is) is the will of God in Christ Jesus concerning him. From him therefore he cheerfully receives all, saying, 'Good is the will of the Lord;' and whether he giveth or taketh away, equally blessing the name of the Lord. Whether in ease or pain, whether in sickness or health, whether in life or death, he giveth thanks from the ground of the heart to Him who orders it for good; into whose hands he hath wholly committed his body and soul, 'as into the hands of a faithful Creator.' He is therefore anxiously 'careful for nothing,' as having 'cast all his care on Him that careth for him;' and 'in all things' resting on him, after 'making' his 'request known to him with thanksgiving.'

"For indeed he 'prays without ceasing;' at all times the language of his heart is this, 'Unto thee is my mouth, though without a voice; and my silence speaketh unto thee.' His heart is lifted up to God at all times, and in all places. In this he is never hindered, much less interrupted, by any person or thing. In retirement or company, in leisure, business, or conversation, his heart is ever with the Lord. Whether he lie down, or rise up, 'God is in all his thoughts:' He walks with God continually; having the loving eye of his soul fixed on him, and everywhere 'seeing Him that is invisible.'

"And loving God, he 'loves his neighbour as himself;' he loves every man as his own soul. He loves his enemies, yea, and the enemies of God. And if it be not in his power to 'do good to them that hate' him, yet he ceases not to 'pray for them,' though they spurn his love, and still 'despite, fully use him, and persecute him.'

"For he is 'pure in heart.' Love has purified his heart from envy, malice, wrath, and every unkind temper. It has cleansed him from pride, whereof 'only cometh contention;' and he hath now 'put on bowels of mercies, kindness, humbleness of mind, meekness, long-suffering.' And indeed all possible ground for contention, on his part, is cut off. For none can take from him what he desires, seeing he 'loves not the world, nor any of the things of the world;' but 'all his desire is unto God, and to the remembrance of his name.'

"Agreeable to this his one desire, is this one design of his life; namely, 'to do, not his own will, but the will of Him that sent him.' His one intention at all times and in all places is, not to please himself, but Him whom his soul loveth. He hath a single eye; and because his 'eye is single, his whole body is full of light. The whole is light, as when the bright shining of a candle doth enlighten the house.' God reigns alone; all that is in the soul is 'holiness to the Lord.' There is not a motion in his heart but is according to his will. Every thought that arises points to him, and is in 'obedience to the law of Christ.'

"And the tree is known by its fruits. For, as he loves God, so he 'keeps his commandments;' not only some, or most of them, but all, from the least to the greatest. He is not content to 'keep the whole law and offend in one point,' but has in all points 'a conscience void of offence towards God, and towards man.' Whatever God has forbidden, he avoids; whatever God has enjoined, he does. 'He runs the way of God's commandments,' now He hath set his heart at liberty. It is his glory and joy so to do; it is his daily crown of rejoicing, to 'do the will of God on earth, as it is done in heaven.'

"All the commandments of God he accordingly keeps, and that with all his might; for his obedience is in proportion to his love, the source from whence it flows. And therefore, loving God with all his heart, he serves him with all his strength; he continually presents his soul and 'body a living sacrifice, holy, acceptable to God;' entirely and without reserve devoting himself, all he has, all he is, to his glory. All the talents he has, he constantly employs according to his Master's will; every power and faculty of his soul, every member of his body.

"By consequence, 'whatsoever he doeth, it is all to the glory of God.' In all his employments of every kind, he not only aims at this, which is implied in having a single eye, but actually attains it; his business and his refreshments, as well as his prayers, all serve to this great end. Whether he 'sit in the house, or walk by the way,' whether he lie down, or rise up, he is promoting, in all he speaks or does, the one business of his life. Whether he put on his apparel, or labor, or eat and drink, or divert himself from too wasting labor, it all tends to advance the glory of God, by peace and good-will among men. His one invariable rule is this: 'Whatsoever ye do, in word or deed, do it all in the name of the Lord Jesus, giving thanks to God, even the Father, through him.'

"Nor do the customs of the world at all hinder his 'running the race which is set before him.' He cannot therefore 'lay up treasures upon earth,' no more than he can take fire into his bosom. He cannot speak evil of his neighbor, any more than he can lie either for God or man. He cannot utter an unkind word of any one; for love keeps the door of his lips. He cannot 'speak idle words; no corrupt conversation' ever 'comes out of his mouth;' as is all that is not 'good to the use of edifying,' not fit to 'minister grace to the hearers.' But 'whatsoever things are pure, whatsoever things are lovely, whatsoever things are' justly 'of good report,' he thinks, speaks, and acts, 'adorning the doctrine of God our Savior in all things.'"

These are the very words wherein I largely declared, for the first time, my sentiments of Christian perfection. And is it not easy to see, (1.) That this is the very point at which I aimed all along from the year 1725; and more determinately from the year 1730, when I began to be *homo unius libri*, "*a man of one book*," regarding none, comparatively, but the Bible? Is it not easy to see, (2.) That this is the very same doctrine which I believe and teach at this day; not adding one point, either to that inward or outward holiness which I maintained eight-and-thirty years ago? And it is the same which, by the grace of God, I have continued to teach from that time till now; as will appear to every impartial person from the extracts subjoined below.

11. I do not know that any writer has made any objection against that tract to this day; and for some time, I did not find much opposition upon the head, at least, not from serious persons. But after a time, a cry arose, and, what a little surprised me, among religions men, who affirmed, not that I stated perfection wrong, but that "there is *no perfection on earth*;" nay, and fell vehemently on my brother and me for affirming the contrary. We scarce expected so rough an attack from these; especially as we were clear on justification by faith, and careful to ascribe the whole of salvation to the mere grace of God. But what most surprised us, was, that we were said to "dishonor Christ," by asserting that he "saveth to the uttermost;" by maintaining he will reign in our hearts alone, and subdue all things to himself.

12. I think it was in the latter end of the year 1740, that I had a conversation with Dr. Gibson, then Bishop of London, at Whitehall. He asked me what I meant by perfection. I told him without any disguise or reserve. When I ceased speaking, he said, "Mr. Wesley, if this be all you mean, publish it to all the world. If any one then can confute what you say, he may have free leave." I answered, "My Lord, I will;" and accordingly wrote and published the sermon on Christian perfection.

In this I endeavored to show,

(1.) In what sense Christians are not,
(2.) In what sense they are, perfect.

"(1.) In what sense they are not. They are not perfect in knowledge. They are not free from ignorance, no, nor from mistake. We are no more to expect any living man to be infallible, than to be omniscient. They are not free from infirmities, such as weakness or slowness of understanding, irregular quickness or heaviness of imagination. Such in another kind are impropriety of language, ungracefulness of pronunciation; to which one might add a thousand nameless defects, either in conversation or behavior. From such infirmities as these none are perfectly freed till their spirits return to God; neither can we expect till then to be wholly freed from temptation; for the servant is not above his master. But neither in this sense is there any absolute perfection on earth. There is no perfection of degrees, none which does not admit of a continual increase.

"(2.) In what sense then are they perfect? Observe, we are not now speaking of babes in Christ, but adult Christians But even babes in Christ are so far perfect as not to commit sin. This St. John affirms expressly; and it cannot be disproved by the examples of the Old Testament. For what, if the holiest of the ancient Jews did sometimes commit sin? We cannot infer from hence, that all Christians do and must commit sin as long as they live.

"But does not the Scripture say, 'A just man sinneth seven times a day?' It does not. Indeed it says, 'A just man falleth seven times.' But this is quite another thing; for, First, the words, a day, are not in the text. Secondly, here is no mention of falling into sin at all. What is here mentioned, is, falling into temporal affliction.

"But elsewhere Solomon says, 'There is no man that sinneth not.' Doubtless thus it was in the days of Solomon; yea, and from Solomon to Christ there was then no man that sinned not. But whatever was the case of those under the law, we may safely affirm, with St. John, that, since the gospel was given, 'he that is born of God sinneth not.'

"The privileges of Christians are in nowise to be measured by what the Old Testament records concerning those who were under the Jewish dispensation; seeing the fulness of time is now come, the Holy Ghost is now given, the great salvation of God is now brought to men by the revelation of Jesus Christ. The kingdom of heaven is now set up on earth, concerning which the Spirit of God declared of old time, (so far is David from being the pattern or standard of Christian perfection,) 'He that is feeble among them, at that day, shall be as David, and the house of David shall be as the angel of the Lord before them.' (Zech. 12:8.)

But the Apostles themselves committed sin; Peter by dissembling, Paul by his sharp contention with Barnabas. Suppose they did, will you argue thus: 'If two of the Apostles once committed sin, then all other Christians, in all ages, do and must commit sin as long as they live?' Nay, God forbid we should thus speak. No necessity of sin was laid upon them; the grace of God was surely sufficient for them. And it is sufficient for us at this day.

"But St. James says, 'In many things we offend all.' True; but who are the persons here spoken of? Why, those 'many masters' or teachers whom God had not sent; not the Apostle himself, nor any real Christian. That in the word we, used by a figure of speech, common in all other as well as the inspired writings, the Apostle could not possibly include himself, or any other true believer, appears, First, from the ninth verse, 'Therewith bless we God, and therewith curse we men.' Surely not we Apostles! not we believers! Secondly, from the words preceding the text: 'My brethren, be not many masters,' or teachers, 'knowing that we shall receive the greater condemnation. For in many things we offend all.' *We!* Who? Not the Apostles nor true believers, but they who were to 'receive the greater condemnation,' because of those many offences. Nay, Thirdly, the verse itself proves, that 'we offend all,' cannot be spoken either of all men or all Christians. For in it immediately follows the mention of a man who 'offends not,' as the *we* first mentioned did; from whom therefore he is professedly contradistinguished, and pronounced a 'perfect man.'

"But St. John himself says, 'If we say that we have no sin, we deceive ourselves;' and, 'If we say we have not sinned, we make him a liar, and his word is not in us.'

"I answer, (1.) The tenth verse fixes the sense of the eighth: 'If we say we have no sin,' in the former, being explained by, 'If we say we have not sinned,' in the latter, verse. (2.) The point under consideration is not, whether we have or have not sinned heretofore; and neither of these verses asserts that we do sin, or commit sin now. (3.) The ninth verse explains both the eighth and tenth: 'If we confess our sins, he is faithful and just to forgive us our sins, and to cleanse us from all unrighteousness.' As if he had said, 'I have before affirmed, The blood of Christ cleanseth from all sin.' And no man can say, 'I need it not; I have no sin to be cleansed, from.' 'If we say, we have no sin, that 'we have not sinned, we deceive ourselves,' and make God a liar: But 'if we confess our sins, he is faithful and just,' not only 'to forgive us our sins,' but also 'to cleanse us from all unrighteousness,' that we may 'go and sin no more.' In conformity, therefore, both to the doctrine of St. John, and the whole tenor of the New Testament, we fix this conclusion: A Christian is so far perfect, as not to commit sin.

"This is the glorious privilege of every Christian, yea, though he be but a babe in Christ. But it is only of grown Christians it can be affirmed, they are in such a sense perfect, as, Secondly, to be freed from evil thoughts and evil tempers. First, from evil or sinful thoughts. Indeed, whence should they spring? 'Out of the heart of man,' if at all, 'proceed evil thoughts.' If, therefore, the heart be no longer evil, then evil thoughts no longer proceed out of it: For 'a good tree cannot bring forth evil fruit.'

"And as they are freed from evil thoughts, so likewise from evil tempers. Every one of these can say, with St. Paul, 'I am crucified with Christ; nevertheless I live; yet not I, but Christ liveth in me;' -- words that manifestly describe a deliverance from inward as well as from outward sin. This is expressed both negatively, 'I live not,' my evil nature, the body of sin, is destroyed; and positively, 'Christ liveth in me,' and therefore all that is holy, and just, and good. Indeed, both these, 'Christ liveth in me,' and, 'I live not,' are inseparably connected. For what communion hath light with darkness, or Christ with Belial?

"He, therefore, who liveth in these Christians hath 'purified their hearts by faith;' insomuch that every one that has Christ in him, 'the hope of glory, purifieth himself even as he is pure.' He is purified from pride; for Christ was lowly in heart: He is pure from desire and self-will; for Christ desired only to do the will of his Father: And he is pure from anger, in the common sense of the word; for Christ was meek and gentle. I say, *in the common sense of the word;* for he is angry at sin, while he is grieved for the sinner. He feels a displacency at every offence against God, but only tender compassion to the offender.

"Thus doth Jesus save his people from their sins, not only from outward sins, but from the sins of their hearts. 'True,' say some, 'but not till death, not in this world.' Nay, St. John says, 'Herein is our love made perfect, that we may have boldness in the day of judgment; because, as he is, so are we in this world.' The Apostle here, beyond all contradiction, speaks of himself and other living Christians, of whom he flatly affirms, that, not only at or after death, but 'in this world,' they are 'as their Master.'

"Exactly agreeable to this are his words in the first chapter: 'God is light, and in him is no darkness at all. If we walk in the light, as he is in the light, we have fellowship one with another, and the blood of Jesus Christ his Son cleanseth us from all sin.' And again: 'If we confess our sins, he is faithful and just to forgive us our sins, and to cleanse us from all unrighteousness.' Now, it is evident, the Apostle here speaks of a deliverance wrought in this world: For he saith not, The blood of Christ will cleanse, (at the hour of death, or in the day of judgment,) but it *'cleanseth,'* at the time present, us living Christians 'from *all* sin.' And it is equally evident, that if any sin remain, we are not cleansed from *'all'* sin. If any unrighteousness remain in the soul, it is not cleansed from 'all', unrighteousness. Neither let any say that this relates to justification only, or the cleansing us from the *guilt* of sin: First, because this is confounding together what the Apostle clearly distinguishes, who mentions, first, 'to forgive us our sins,' and then 'to cleanse us from all unrighteousness.' Secondly, because this is asserting justification by works, in the strongest sense possible; it is making all inward, as well as all outward, holiness, necessarily previous to justification. For if the cleansing here spoken of is no other than the cleansing us from the guilt of sin, then we are not cleansed from guilt, that is, not justified, unless on condition of walking 'in the light, as he is in the light.' It remains, then, that Christians are saved in this world from all sin, from all unrighteousness; that they are now in such a sense perfect, as not to commit sin, and to be freed from evil thoughts and evil tempers."

It could not be, but that a discourse of this kind, which directly contradicted the favorite opinion of many, who were esteemed by others, and possibly esteemed themselves, some of the best of Christians, (whereas, if these things were so, they were not Christians at all,) should give no small offence. Many answers or animadversions, therefore, were expected; but I was agreeably disappointed. I do not know that any appeared; so I went quietly on my way.

13. Not long after, I think in the spring, 1741, we published a second volume of Hymns. As the doctrine was still much misunderstood, and consequently misrepresented, I judged it needful to explain yet farther upon the head; which was done in the preface to it as follows : --

"This great gift of God, the salvation of our souls, is no other than the image of God fresh stamped on our hearts. It is a 'renewal of believers in the spirit of their minds, after the likeness of Him that created them.' God hath now laid 'the axe unto the root of the tree, purifying their hearts by faith,' and 'cleansing all the thoughts of their hearts by the inspiration of his Holy Spirit.' Having this hope, that they shall see God as he is, they 'purify themselves even as he is pure,' and are 'holy, as he that hath called them is holy, in all manner of conversation.' Not that they have already attained all that they shall attain, either are already in this sense perfect. But they daily 'go on from strength to strength; beholding' now, 'as in a glass, the glory of the Lord, they are changed into the same image, from glory to glory, by the Spirit of the Lord.'

"And 'where the Spirit of the Lord is, there is liberty;' such liberty 'from the law of sin and death,' as the children of this world will not believe, though a man declare it unto them. 'The Son hath made them free' who are thus 'born of God,' from that great root of sin and bitterness, pride. They feel that all their 'sufficiency is of God,' that it is He alone who 'is in all their thoughts,' and 'worketh in them both to will and to do of his good pleasure.' They feel that 'it is not they' that speak, but the Spirit of their Father who speaketh in them, and that whatsoever is done by their hands, the Father who is in them, he doeth the works. So that God is to them all in all, and they are nothing in his sight. They are freed from self-will, as desiring nothing but the holy and perfect will of God; not supplies in want, not ease in pain, *[This is too strong. Our Lord himself desired ease in pain. He asked for it, only with resignation: "Not as I will," I desire, "but as thou wilt."]* nor life, or death, or any creature; but continually crying in their Inmost soul, Father, thy will be done. They are freed from evil thoughts, so that they cannot enter into them, no, not for a moment. Aforetime, when an evil thought came in, they hooked up, and it vanished away. But now it does not come in, there being no room for this, in a soul which is full of God. They are free from wanderings in prayer. Whensoever they pour out their hearts in a more immediate manner before God, they have no thought of anything past, *[This is far too strong. See the sermon "On Wandering Thoughts."]* or absent, or to come, but of God alone. In times past, they had wandering thoughts darted in, which yet fled away like smoke; but now that smoke does not rise at all. They have no fear or doubt, either as to their state in general, or as to any particular action. *[Frequently this is the case; but only for a time.]* The unction from the Holy One teacheth them every hour what they shall do, and what they shall speak; *[For a time it may be so; but not always.]* nor therefore have they any need to reason concerning it. *[Sometimes they have no need; at other times they have.]* They are in one sense freed from temptations; for though numberless temptations fly about them, yet they trouble them not. *[Sometimes they do not; at other times they do, and that grievously.]* At all times their souls are even and calm, their hearts are steadfast and unmovable. Their peace, flowing as a river, passeth all understanding, and they rejoice with joy unspeakable and full of glory. For they are sealed by the Spirit unto the day of redemption, having the witness in themselves, that there is laid up for them a crown of righteousness which the Lord will give them in that day. *[Not all who are saved from sin; many of them have not attained it yet.]*

"Not that every one is a child of the devil, till he is thus renewed in love: On the contrary, whoever has a sure confidence in God, that through the merits of Christ, his sins are forgiven, he is a child of God, and, if he abide in him, an heir of all the promises. Neither ought he in anywise to cast away his confidence, or to deny the faith he has received, because it is weak, or because it is tried with fire, so that his soul is in heaviness through manifold temptations.

"Neither dare we affirm, as some have done, that all this salvation is given at once. There is indeed an instantaneous, as well as a gradual, work of God in his children; and there wants not, we know, a cloud of witnesses, who have received, in one moment, either a clear sense of the forgiveness of their sins, or the abiding witness of the Holy Spirit. But we do not know a single instance, in any place, of a person's receiving, in one and the same moment, remission of sins, the abiding witness of the Spirit, and a new, a clean heart.

"Indeed, how God may work, we cannot tell; but the general manner wherein he does work is this: Those who once trusted in themselves that they were righteous, that they were rich, and increased in goods, and had need of nothing, are, by the Spirit of God applying his word, convinced that they are poor and naked. All the things that they have done are brought to their remembrance and set in array before them, so that they see the wrath of God hanging over their heads, and feel that they deserve the damnation of hell. In their trouble they cry unto the Lord, and he shows them that he hath taken away their sins, and opens the kingdom of heaven in their hearts, righteousness, and peace, and joy in the Holy Ghost. Sorrow and pain are fled away, and sin has no more dominion over them. Knowing they are justified freely through faith in his blood, they have peace with God *through Jesus Christ;* they rejoice in hope of the glory of God, and the love of God is shed abroad in their hearts.

"In this peace they remain for days, or weeks, or months, and commonly suppose they shall not know war any more; till some of their old enemies, their bosom sins, or the sin which did most easily beset them, (perhaps anger or desire,) assault them again, and thrust sore at them, that they may fall. Then arises fear, that they shall not endure to the end; and often doubt, whether God has not forgotten them, or whether they did not deceive themselves in thinking their sins were forgiven. Under these clouds, especially if they reason with the devil, they go mourning all the day long. But it is seldom long before their Lord answers for himself, sending them the Holy Ghost to comfort them, to bear witness continually with their spirits that they are the children of God. Then they are indeed meek and gentle and teachable, even as a little child. And now first do they see the ground of their heart; *[Is it not astonishing, that while this book is extant, which was published four-and-twenty years ago, any one should face me down, that this is a new doctrine, and what I never taught before? -- [This note was first published in the year 1765.]]* which God before would not disclose unto them, lest the soul should fail before him, and the spirit which he had made. Now they see all the hidden abominations there, the depths of pride, self-will, and hell; yet leaving the witness in themselves, Thou art an heir of God, a joint heir with Christ, even in the midst of this fiery trial; which continually heightens both the strong sense they then have of their inability to help themselves, and the inexpressible hunger they feel after a full renewal in his image, in righteousness and true holiness. Then God is mindful of the desire of them that fear him, and gives them a single eye, and a pure heart; he stamps upon them his own image and superscription; He createth them anew in Christ Jesus; he cometh unto them with his Son and blessed Spirit, and, fixing his abode in their souls, bringeth them into the rest which remaineth for the people of God.

Here I cannot but remark, (1.) That this is the strongest account we ever gave of Christian perfection; indeed too strong in more than one particular, as is observed in the notes annexed. (2.) That there is nothing which we have since advanced upon the subject, either in verse or prose, which is not either directly or indirectly contained in this preface. So that whether our present doctrine be right or wrong, it is however the same which we taught from the beginning.

14. I need not give additional proofs of this, by multiplying quotations from the volume itself. It may suffice, to cite part of one hymn only the last in that volume: --

> Lord, I believe a rest remains,
>   To all thy people known;
> A rest where pure enjoyment reigns,
>   And thou art loved alone;
>
> A rest where all our soul's desire
>   Is fix'd on things above;
> Where doubt and pain and fear expire,
>   Cast out by perfect love.
>
> From every evil motion freed,
>   (The Son hath made us free,)
> On all the powers of hell we tread,
>   In glorious liberty.

Safe in the way of life, above
    Death, earth, and hell we rise;
We find, when perfected in love,
    Our long-sought paradise.

O that I now the rest might know,
    Believe, and enter in!
Now, Saviour, now the power bestow,
    And let me cease from sin!

Remove this hardness from my heart,
    This unbelief remove:
To me the rest of faith impart,
    The sabbath of thy love.

Come, O my Saviour, come away
    Into my soul descend!
No longer from thy creature stay,
    My author and my end.

The bliss thou hast for me prepared,
    No longer be delay'd:
Come, my exceeding great reward,
    For whom I first was made.

Come, Father, Son, and Holy Ghost,
    And seal me thine abode!
Let all I am in thee be lost:
    Let all be lost in God!

Can anything be more clear, than:
(1.) That here also is as full and high a salvation as we have ever spoken of? (2.) That this is spoken of as receivable by mere faith, and as hindered only by unbelief? (3.) That this faith, and consequently the salvation which it brings, is spoken of as given in an instant? (4.) That it is supposed that instant may be now? that we need not stay another moment? that "now," the very

"now, is the accepted time? now is the day of" this full "salvation?" And, Lastly, that, if any speak otherwise, he is the person that brings new doctrine among us?

15. About a year after, namely, in the year 1742, we published another volume of Hymns. The dispute being now at the height, we spoke upon the head more largely than ever before. Accordingly abundance of the hymns in this volume treat expressly on this subject. And so does the preface, which, as it is short, it may not be amiss to insert entire :

"(1.) Perhaps the general prejudice against Christian perfection may chiefly arise from a misapprehension of the nature of it. We willingly allow, and continually declare, there is no such perfection in this life, as implies either a dispensation from doing good, and attending all the ordinances of God, or a freedom from ignorance, mistake, temptation, and a thousand infirmities necessarily connected with flesh and blood.
"(2.) First. We not only allow, but earnestly contend, that there is no perfection in this life, which implies any dispensation from attending all the ordinances of God, or from doing good unto all men while we have time, though especially unto the household of faith. We believe, that not only the babes in Christ, who have newly found redemption in his blood, but those also who are grown up into perfect men, are indispensably obliged, as often as they have opportunity, to eat bread and drink wine in remembrance of Him, and to search the Scriptures; by fasting, as well as temperance, to keep their bodies under, and bring them into subjection; and, above all, to pour out their souls in prayer, both secretly, and in the great congregation.
"(3.) We Secondly believe, that there is no such perfection in this life, as implies an entire deliverance, either from ignorance, or mistake, in things not essential to salvation, or from manifold temptations, or from numberless infirmities, wherewith the corruptible body more or less presses down the soul. We cannot find any ground in Scripture to suppose, that any inhabitant of a house of clay is wholly exempt either from bodily infirmities,

or from ignorance of many things; or to imagine any is incapable of mistake, or falling into divers temptations.

"(4.) But whom then do you mean by one that is perfect? We mean one in whom is the mind which was in Christ, and who so walketh as Christ also walked; a man that hath clean hands and a pure heart, or that is cleansed from all filthiness of flesh and spirit; one in whom is no occasion of stumbling, and who, accordingly, does not commit sin. To declare this a little more particularly: We understand by that scriptural expression, *a perfect man*, one in whom God hath fulfilled his faithful word, "From all your filthiness and from all your idols I will cleanse you: I will also save you from all your uncleannesses." We understand hereby, one whom God lath *sanctified* throughout in body, soul, and spirit; one who walketh in the light as He is in the light, in whom is no darkness at all; the blood of Jesus Christ his Son having cleansed him from all sin.

"(5.) This man can now testify to all mankind, I am crucified with Christ: Nevertheless I live; yet not I, but Christ liveth in me. He is *holy* as God who called him is holy, both in heart and in all manner of conversation. He loveth the Lord his God with all his heart, and serveth him with all his strength. He loveth his neighbor, every man, as himself; yea, as Christ loveth us; them, in particular, that despitefully use him and persecute him, because they know not the Son, neither the Father. Indeed his soul is all love, filled with bowels of mercies, kindness, meekness, gentleness, longsuffering. And his life agreeth thereto, full of the work of faith, the patience of hope, the labor of love. And whatsoever he doeth either in word or deed, he doeth it all in the name, in the love and power, of the Lord Jesus. In a word, he doeth the will of God on earth, as it is done in heaven.

"(6.) This it is to be a perfect man, to be *sanctified* throughout; even to have a heart so all-flaming with the love of God, (to use Archbishop Usher's words,) as continually to offer up every thought, word, and work, as a spiritual sacrifice, acceptable to God through Christ. In every thought of our hearts, in every word of our tongues, in every work of our hands, to show forth his praise, who hath called us out of darkness into his marvelous light. O that both we, and all who seek the Lord Jesus in sincerity, may thus be made perfect in one!"

This is the doctrine which we preached from the beginning, and which we preach at this day. Indeed, by viewing it in every point of light, and comparing it again and again with the word of God on the one hand, and the experience of the children of God on the other, we saw farther into the nature and properties of Christian perfection. But still there is no contrariety at all between our first and our last sentiments. Our first conception of it was, It is to have "the mind which was in Christ," and to "walk as He walked;" to have all the mind that was in Him, and always to walk as he walked: In other words, to be inwardly and outwardly devoted to God; all devoted in heart and life. And we have the same conception of it now, without either addition or diminution.

16. The hymns concerning it in this volume are too numerous to transcribe. I shall only cite a part of three :

> Saviour from sin, I wait to prove
>   That Jesus is thy healing name;
> To lose, when perfected in love,
>   Whate'er I have, or can, or am;
> I stay me on thy faithful word,
> "The servant shall be as his Lord."
>
> Answer that gracious end in me
>   For which thy precious life was given;
> Redeem from all iniquity,
>   Restore, and make me meet for heaven.
> Unless thou purge my every stain,
> Thy suffering and my faith is vain.
>
> Didst thou not die, that I might live,
>   No longer to myself but thee?
> Might body, soul, and spirit give
>   To Him who gave himself for me?

Come then, my Master and my God,
Take the dear purchase of thy blood.

Thy own peculiar servant claim,
  For thy own truth and mercy's sake;
Hallow in me thy glorious name;
  Me for thine own this moment take;
And change and throughly purify;
Thine only may I live and die. (Page 80.)

Chose from the world, if now I stand,
  Adorn'd with righteousness divine;
If, brought into the promised land,
  I justly call the Saviour mine;

The sanctifying Spirit pour,
  To quench my thirst and wash me clean,
Now, Saviour let the gracious shower
  Descend, and make me pure from sin.

Purge me from every sinful blot:
  My idols all be cast aside:
Cleanse me from every evil thought,
  From all the filth of self and pride.

The hatred of the carnal mind
  Out of my flesh at once remove:
Give me a tender heart, resign'd,
  And pure, and fall of faith and love.

O that I now, from sin released,
  Thy word might to the utmost prove,
Enter into thy promised rest;
  The Canaan of thy perfect love!

Now let me gain perfection's height!
  Now let me into nothing fall;
Be less than nothing in my sight,

And feel that Christ is all in all. (Page 258.)

Lord, I believe, thy work of grace
 Is perfect in the soul;
His heart is pure who sees thy face,
 His spirit is made whole.

From every sickness, by thy word,
 From every foul disease,
Saved, and to perfect health restored,
 To perfect holiness:

He walks in glorious liberty,
 To sin entirely dead:
The Truth, the Son hath made him free,
 And he is free indeed.

Throughout his soul thy glories shine,
 His soul is all renew'd,
And deck'd in righteousness divine,
 And clothed and fill'd with God.

This is the rest, the life, the peace,
 Which all thy people prove;
Love is the bond of perfectness,
 And all their soul is love.

O joyful sound of gospel grace!
 Christ shall in me appear;
I, even I, shall see his face,
 I shall be holy here!

He visits now the house of clay,
 He shakes his future home; --
O would'st thou, Lord, on this glad day,
 Into thy temple come!

Come, O my God, thyself reveal,

Fill all this mighty void;
Thou only canst my spirit fill:
Come, O my God, my God!

Fulfil, fulfil my large desires,
Large as infinity!
Give, give me all my soul requires,
All, all that is in thee ! (Page 298.)

17. On Monday, June 25, 1744, our First Conference began; six Clergymen and all our Preachers being present. The next morning we seriously considered the doctrine of sanctification, or perfection. The questions asked concerning it, and the substance of the answers given, were as follows: --

"QUESTION. What is it to be sanctified?
"ANSWER. To be renewed in the image of God, in righteousness and true holiness.

"Q. What is implied in being a perfect Christian?
"A. The loving God with all our heart, and mind, and soul. (Deut. 6:5.)

"Q. Does this imply, that all inward sin is taken away?
"A. Undoubtedly; or how can we be Said to be saved from all our uncleannesses? (Ezek. 36:29.)"

Our Second Conference began August 1, 1745. The next morning we spoke of sanctification as follows :

"Q. When does inward sanctification begin?
"A. In the moment a man is justified. (Yet sin remains in him, yea, the seed of all sin, till he is sanctified throughout.) From that time a believer gradually dies to sin, and grows in grace.

"Q. Is this ordinarily given till a little before death?
"A. It is not, to those who expect it no sooner.

"Q. But may we expect it sooner?

"A. Why not? For, although we grant,

(1.) That the generality of believers, whom we have hitherto known, were not so sanctified till near death;

(2.) That few of those to Whom St. Paul wrote his Epistles were so at that time; nor,

(3.) He himself at the time of writing his former Epistles; yet all this does not prove, that we may not be so to-day.

"Q. In what manner should we preach sanctification?

"A. Scarce at all to those who are not pressing forward: To those who are, always by way of promise; always drawing, rather than driving."

Our Third Conference began Tuesday, May 13, 1746.

In this we carefully read over the Minutes of the two preceding Conferences, to observe whether anything contained therein might be retrenched or altered on more mature consideration. But we did not see cause to alter in any respect what we had agreed upon before.

Our Fourth Conference began on Tuesday, June the 16th, 1747. As several persons were present, who did not believe the doctrine of perfection, we agreed to examine it from the foundation.

In order to this, it was asked,

"How much is allowed by our brethren who differ from us with regard to entire sanctification?

"A. They grant, (1.) That every one must be entirely sanctified in the article of death. (2.) That till then a believer daily grows in grace, comes nearer and nearer to perfection. (3.) That we ought to be continually pressing after it, and to exhort all others so to do.

"Q. What do we allow them?

"A. We grant, (1.) That many of those who have died in the faith, yea, the greater part of those we have known, were not perfected in love till a little before their death. (2.) That the term *sanctified* is continually applied by St. Paul to all that were justified. (3.) That by this term alone, he rarely, if ever, means saved from all sin. (4.) That, consequently, it is not proper to use it in that sense, without adding the word *wholly, entirely,* or the like. (5.) That the inspired writers almost continually speak of or to those who were justified, but very rarely of or to those who were wholly sanctified. [That is, unto those alone, exclusive of others; but they speak to them, jointly with others, almost continually.] (6.) That, consequently, it behooves us to speak almost continually of the state of justification; but more rarely, [More rarely, I allow; but yet in some places very frequently, strongly, and explicitly.] at least in full and explicit terms, concerning entire sanctification.

"Q. What then is the point where we divide?
"A. It is this: Should we expect to be saved from all sin before the article of death?

"Q. Is there any clear Scripture promise of this, -- that God will save us from all sin?
"A. There is: "He shall redeem Israel from all his sins." (Psalm 130:8.)

"This is more largely expressed in the prophecy of Ezekiel: 'Then will I sprinkle clean water upon you, and ye shall be clean; from all your filthiness and from all your idols will I cleanse you: I will also save you from all your uncleannesses.' (Ezek. 36:25, 29.) No promise can be more clear. And to this the Apostle plainly refers in that exhortation: 'Having these promises, let us cleanse ourselves from all filthiness of flesh and spirit, perfecting holiness in the fear of God.' (2 Cor. 7:1.) Equally clear and express is that ancient promise: 'The Lord thy God will circumcise thy heart, and the heart of thy seed, to love the Lord thy God with all thy heart and with all thy soul.' (Deut. 30:6.)

"Q. But does any assertion answerable to this occur in the New Testament?

"A. There does, and that laid down in the plainest terms. So 1 John 3:8: 'For this purpose the Son of God was manifested, that he might destroy the works of the devil;' the works of the devil, without any limitation or restriction; but all sin is the work of the devil. Parallel to which is the assertion of St. Paul: 'Christ loved the Church, and gave himself for it, that he might present it to himself a glorious Church, not having spot or wrinkle, or any such thing, but that it might be holy and without blemish.' (Eph. 5:25-27.)

"And to the same effect is his assertion in the eighth of the Romans, verses 3, 4: 'God sent his Son, that the righteousness of the law might be fulfilled in us, who walk not after the flesh, but after the spirit.' [Rom. 8:3, 4]

"Q. Does the New Testament afford any farther ground for expecting to be saved from all sin?

"A. Undoubtedly it does; both in those prayers and commands, which are equivalent to the strongest assertions.

"Q. What prayers do you mean?

"A. Prayers for entire sanctification; which, were there no such thing, would be mere mockery of God. Such in particular are,

(1.) 'Deliver us from evil.' Now, when this is done, when we are delivered from all evil, there can be no sin remaining.

(2.) 'Neither pray I for these alone, but for them also who shall believe on me through their word; that they all may be one; as thou, Father, art in me and I in thee, that they also may be one in us; I in them, and thou in me, that they may be made perfect in one.' (John 17:20-23.)

(3.) 'I bow my knees unto the God and Father of our Lord Jesus Christ, that he would grant you, that ye, being rooted and grounded in love, may be able to comprehend, with all saints, what is the breadth, and length, and depth, and height, and to know the love of Christ, which passeth knowledge; that ye may be filled with all the fulness of God.' (Eph. 3:14, &c.)

(4.) 'The very God of peace sanctify you wholly. And I pray God, your whole spirit, soul, and body, may be preserved blameless unto the coming of our Lord Jesus Christ.' (1 Thess. 5:23.)

"Q. What command is there to the same effect?

"A. (1.) 'Be ye perfect, as your Father who is in heaven is perfect.' (Matt. 5:48.)

(2.) 'Thou shalt love the Lord thy God with all thy heart, and with all thy soul, and with all thy mind.' (Matt. 12:37.) But if the love of God fill all the heart, there can be no sin therein.

"Q. But how does it appear that this is to be done before the article of death?

"A. (1.) From the very nature of a command, which is not given to the dead, but to the living. Therefore, 'Thou shalt love God with all thy heart,' cannot mean, Thou shalt do this when thou diest; but, while thou livest.

"(2.) From express texts of Scripture:

> (i.) 'The grace of God, that bringeth salvation, hath appeared to all men; teaching us that, having renounced ungodliness and worldly lusts, we should live soberly, righteously, and godly in this present world; looking for the glorious appearing of our Lord Jesus Christ, who gave himself for us, that he might redeem us from all iniquity, and purify unto himself a peculiar people, zealous of good works. (Titus 2:11-14.)
>
> (ii.) He hath raised up an horn of salvation for us, to perform the mercy promised to our fathers; the oath which he sware to our father Abraham, that he would grant unto us, that we, being delivered out of the hands of our enemies, should serve him without fear, in holiness and righteousness before him, all the days of our life. (Luke 1:69, &c.)

"Q. Is there any example in Scripture of persons who had attained to this?

"A. Yes; St. John, and all those of whom he says, 'Herein is our love made perfect, that we may have boldness in the day of judgment; because, as he is, so are we in this world.' (1 John 4:17.)

"Q. Can you show one such example now? Where is he that is thus perfect?

"A. To some that make this inquiry one might answer, If I knew one here, I would not tell you; for you do not inquire out of love. You are like Herod; you only seek the young child to slay it.

"But more directly we answer: There are many reasons why there should be few, if any, indisputable examples. What inconveniences would this bring on the person himself, set as a mark for all to shoot at! And how unprofitable would it be to gainsayers! 'For if they hear not Moses and the Prophets,' Christ and his Apostles, 'neither would they be persuaded though one rose from the dead.'

"Q. Are we not apt to have a secret distaste to any who say they are saved from all sin?

"A. It is very possible we may, and that upon several grounds; partly from a concern for the good of souls, who may be hurt if these are not what they profess; partly from a kind of implicit envy at those who speak of higher attainments than our own; and partly from our natural slowness and unreadiness of heart to believe the works of God.

"Q,. Why may we not continue in the joy of faith till we are perfected in love?

"A. Why indeed? since holy grief does not quench this joy; since even while we are under the cross, while we deeply partake of the sufferings of Christ, we may rejoice with joy unspeakable."

From these extracts it undeniably appears, not only what was mine and my brother's judgment, but what was the judgment of all the Preachers in connection with us, in the years 1744, 45, 46 and 47. Nor do I remember that, in any one of these Conferences, we had one dissenting voice; but whatever doubts any one had when we met, they were all removed before we parted.

18. In the year 1749, my brother printed two volumes of "Hymns and Sacred Poems." As I did not see these before they were published, there were some things in them which I did not approve of. But I quite approved of the main of the hymns on this head; a few verses
of which are subjoined : --

> Come, Lord, be manifested here,
>   And all the devil's works destroy;
> Now, without sin, in me appear,
>   And fill with everlasting joy:
> Thy beatific face display;
> Thy presence is the perfect day. (Vol. I., p. 203.)

> Swift to my rescue come,
> Thy own this moment seize;
> Gather my wand'ring spirit home,
>   And keep in perfect peace.

> Suffer'd no more to rove
> O'er all the earth abroad,
> Arrest the pris'ner of thy love,
>   And shut me up in God! (Page 247.)

> Thy pris'ners release, Vouchsafe us thy peace;
> And our sorrows and sins in a moment shall cease.
> That moment be now! Our petition allow,
>   Our present Redeemer and Comforter thou! (Vol.
> II., p. 124.)

From this inbred sin deliver;
Let the yoke Now be broke;
    Make me thine for ever.

    Partner of thy perfect nature,
Let me be Now in thee
    A new, sinless creature. (Page 156.)

Turn me, Lord, and turn me now,
To thy yoke my spirit bow;
Grant me now the pearl to find
Of a meek and quiet mind.

Calm, O calm my troubled breast;
Let me gain that second rest:
From my works for ever cease,
Perfected in holiness. (Page 162.)

Come in this accepted hour,
    Bring thy heavenly kingdom in!
Fill us with the glorious power;
    Rooting out the seeds of sin. (Page 168.)

Come, thou dear Lamb, for sinners slain,
    Bring in the cleansing flood;
Apply, to wash out every stain,
    Thine efficacious blood.

O let it sink into our soul
    Deep as the inbred sin:
Make every wounded spirit whole,
    And every leper clean! (Page 171.)

    Pris'ners of hope arise,
    And see your Lord appear:
Lo! on the wings of love he flies,
    And brings redemption near.

Redemption in his blood
He calls you to receive:
"Come unto me, the pard'ning God:
Believe," he cries, "believe!"

Jesus, to thee we look,
Till saved from sin's remains,
Reject the inbred tyrant's yoke,
And cast away his chains.

Our nature shall no more
O'er us dominion have:
By faith we apprehend the power,
Which shall for ever save. (Page 188.)

Jesus, our life, in us appear,
Who daily die thy death:
Reveal thyself the finisher;
Thy quick'ning Spirit breathe!

Unfold the hidden mystery,
The second gift impart;
Reveal thy glorious self in me,
In every waiting heart. (Page 195.)

In Him we have peace, In Him we have power!
Preserved by his grace Throughout the dark hour,
In all our temptation He keeps us, to prove
His utmost salvation, His fulness of love.

Pronounce the glad word, And bid us be free!
Ah, hast thou not, Lord, A blessing for me?
The peace thou hast given, This moment impart,
And open thy heaven, O Love, in my heart! (Page
324.)

A second edition of these hymns was published in the year 1752; and that without any other alteration, than that of a few literal mistakes.

I have been the more large in these extracts, because hence it appears, beyond all possibility of exception, that to this day both my brother and I maintained,
(1.) That Christian perfection is that love of God and our neighbor, which implies deliverance from all sin.
(2.) That this is received merely by faith.
(3.) That it is given instantaneously, in one moment.
(4.) That we are to expect it, not at death, but every moment; that now is the accepted time, now is the day of this salvation.

19. At the Conference in the year 1759, perceiving some danger that a diversity of sentiments should insensibly steal in among us, we again largely considered this doctrine; and soon after I published "Thoughts on Christian Perfection," prefaced with the following advertisement: --

"The following tract is by no means designed to gratify the curiosity of any man. It is not intended to prove the doctrine at large, in opposition to those who explode and ridicule it; no, nor to answer the numerous objections against it, which may be raised even by serious men. All I intend here is, simply to declare what are my sentiments on this head; what Christian perfection does, according to my apprehension, include, and what it does not; and to add a few practical observations and directions relative to the subject.

"As these thoughts were at first thrown together by way of question and answer, I let them continue in the same form. They are just the same that I have entertained for above twenty years.

"QUESTION. What is Christian perfection?
"ANSWER. The loving God with all our heart, mind, soul, and strength. This implies, that no wrong temper, none contrary to

love, remains in the soul; and that all the thoughts, words, and actions, are governed by pure love.

"Q. Do you affirm, that this perfection excludes all infirmities, ignorance, and mistake?
"A. I continually affirm quite the contrary, and always have done so.

"Q. But how can every thought, word, and work, be governed by pure love, and the man be subject at the same time to ignorance and mistake?
"A. I see no contradiction here: A man may be filled with pure love, and still be liable to mistake. Indeed I do not expect to be freed from actual mistakes, till this mortal puts on immortality. I believe this to be a natural consequence of the soul's dwelling in flesh and blood. For we cannot now think at all, but by the mediation of those bodily organs which have suffered equally with the rest of our frame. And hence we cannot avoid sometimes thinking wrong, till this corruptible shall have put on incorruption.

"But we may carry this thought farther yet. A mistake in judgment may possibly occasion a mistake in practice. For instance: Mr. De Renty's mistake touching the nature of mortification, arising from prejudice of education, occasioned that practical mistake, his wearing an iron girdle. And a thousand such instances there may be, even in those who are in the highest state of grace. Yet, Where every word and action springs from love, such a mistake is not properly a sin. However, it cannot bear the rigor of God's justice, but needs the atoning blood.

"Q. What was the judgment of all our brethren who met at Bristol in August, 1758, on this head?
"A. It was expressed in these words:
(1.) Every one may mistake as long as he lives.
(2.) A mistake in opinion may occasion a mistake in practice.

(3.) Every such mistake is a transgression of the perfect law. Therefore,

(4.) Every such mistake, were it not for the blood of atonement, would expose to eternal damnation.

(5.) It follows, that the most perfect have continual need of the merits of Christ, even for their actual transgressions, and may say for themselves, as well as for their brethren, 'Forgive us our trespasses.'

"This easily accounts for what might otherwise seem to be utterly unaccountable; namely, that those who are not offended when we speak of the highest degree of love, yet will not hear of living without sin. The reason is, they know all men are liable to mistake, and that in practice as well as in judgment. But they do not know, or do not observe, that this is not sin, if love is the sole principle of action.

"Q. But still, if they live without sin, does not this exclude the necessity of a Mediator? At least, is it not plain that they stand no longer in need of Christ in his priestly office ?

"A. Far from it. None feel their need of Christ like these; none so entirely depend upon him. For Christ does not give life to the soul separate from, but in and with, himself. Hence his words are equally true of all men, in whatsoever state of grace they are: 'As the branch cannot bear fruit of itself, except it abide in the vine; no more can ye, except ye abide in me: Without' (or separate from) 'me ye can do nothing.'

"In every state we need Christ in the following respects

(1.) Whatever grace we receive, it is a free gift from him.

(2.) We receive it as his purchase, merely in consideration of the price he paid.

(3.) We have this grace, not only from Christ, but in him. For our perfection is not like that of a tree, which flourishes by the sap derived from its own root, but, as was said before, like that of a branch which, united to the vine, bears fruit; but, severed from it, is dried up and withered.

(4.) All our blessings, temporal, spiritual, and eternal, depend on his intercession for us, which is one branch of his priestly office, whereof therefore we have always equal need.

(5.) The best of men still need Christ in his priestly office, to atone for their omissions, their short-comings, (as some not improperly speak,) their mistakes in judgment and practice, and their defects of various kinds. For these are all deviations from the perfect law, and consequently need an atonement. Yet that they are not properly sins, we apprehend may appear from the words of St. Paul, 'He that loveth, hath fulfilled the law; for love is the fulfilling of the law.' (Rom. 13:10.) Now, mistakes, and whatever infirmities necessarily flow from the corruptible state of the body, are no way contrary to love; nor therefore, in the Scripture sense, sin.

"To explain myself a little farther on this head:

(1.) Not only sin, properly so called, (that is, a voluntary transgression of a known law,) but sin, improperly so called, (that is, an involuntary transgression of a divine law, known or unknown,) needs the atoning blood.

(2.) I believe there is no such perfection in this life as excludes these involuntary transgressions which I apprehend to be naturally consequent on the ignorance and mistakes inseparable from mortality.

(3.) Therefore sinless perfection is a phrase I never use, lest I should seem to contradict myself.

(4.) I believe, a person filled with the love of God is still liable to these involuntary transgressions.

(5.) Such transgressions you may call sins, if you please: I do not, for the reasons above-mentioned.

"Q. What advice would you give to those that do, and those that do not, call them so?

"A. Let those that do not call them sins, never think that themselves or any other persons are in such a state as that they can stand before infinite justice without a Mediator. This must argue either the deepest ignorance, or the highest arrogance and presumption.

"Let those who do call them so, beware how they confound these defects with sins, properly so called.

"But how will they avoid it? How will these be distinguished from those, if they are all promiscuously called sins? I am much afraid, if we should allow any sins to be consistent with perfection, few would confine the idea to those defects concerning which only the assertion could be true.

"Q. But how can a liableness to mistake consist with perfect love? Is not a person who is perfected in love every moment under its influence? And can any mistake flow from pure love?
"A. I answer,
(1.) Many mistakes may consist with pure love;
(2.) Some may accidentally flow from it: I mean, love itself may incline us to mistake. The pure love of our neighbor, springing from the love of God, thinketh no evil, believeth and hopeth all things. Now, this very temper, unsuspicious, ready to believe and hope the best of all men, may occasion our thinking some men better than they really are. Here then is a manifest mistake, accidentally flowing from pure love.

"Q. How shall we avoid setting perfection too high or too low?
"A. By keeping to the Bible, and setting it just as high as the Scripture does. It is nothing higher and nothing lower than this, --the pure love of God and man; the loving God with all our heart and soul, and our neighbor as ourselves. It is love governing the heart and life, running through all our tempers, words, and actions.

"Q. Suppose one had attained to this, would you advise him to speak of it?
"A. At first perhaps he would scarce be able to refrain, the fire would be so hot within him; his desire to declare the loving-kindness of the Lord carrying him away like a torrent. But afterwards he might; and then it would be advisable, not to speak of it to them that know not God; (it is most likely, it would only provoke them to contradict and blaspheme;) nor to others,

without some particular reason, without some good in view. And then he should have especial care to avoid all appearance of boasting; to speak with the deepest humility and reverence, giving all the glory to God.

"Q. But would it not be better to be entirely silent, not to speak of it at all?
"A. By silence, he might avoid many crosses, which will naturally and necessarily ensue, if he simply declare, even among believers, what God has wrought in his soul. If, therefore, such a one were to confer with flesh and blood he would be entirely silent. But this could not be done with a clear conscience; for undoubtedly he ought to speak. Men do not light a candle to put it under a bushel; much less does the all-wise God. He does not raise such a monument of his power and love, to hide it from all mankind. Rather, he intends it as a general blessing to those who are simple of heart. He designs thereby, not barely the happiness of that individual person, but the animating and encouraging others to follow after the same blessing. His will is, that many shall see it and rejoice, and put their trust in the Lord. Nor does anything under heaven more quicken the desires of those who are justified, than to converse with those whom they believe to have experienced a still higher salvation. This places that salvation full in their view, and increases their hunger and thirst after it; an advantage which must have been entirely lost, had the person so saved buried himself in silence.

"Q. But is there no way to prevent these crosses which usually fall on those who speak of being thus saved?
"A. It seems they cannot be prevented altogether, while so much of nature remains even in believers. But something might be done, if the Preacher in every place would,
(1.) Talk freely with all who speak thus; and,
(2.) Labor to prevent the unjust or unkind treatment of those in favor of whom there is reasonable proof.

"Q. What is reasonable proof? How may we certainly know one that is saved from all sin?

"A. We cannot infallibly know one that is thus saved, (no, nor even one that is justified,) unless it should please God to endow us with the miraculous discernment of spirits[5]. But we apprehend those would be sufficient proofs to any reasonable man, and such as would leave little room to doubt either the truth or depth of the work:

(1.) If we had clear evidence of his exemplary behavior for some time before this supposed change. This would give us reason to believe, he would not 'lie for God,' but speak neither more nor less than he felt;

(2.) If he gave a distinct account of the time and manner wherein the change was wrought, with sound speech which could not be reproved; and,

(3.) If it appeared that all his subsequent words and actions were holy and unblamable.

"The short of the matter is this:

(1.) I have abundant reason to believe, this person will not lie;

(2.) He testifies before God, 'I feel no sin, but all love; I pray, rejoice, and give thanks without ceasing; and I have as clear an inward witness, that I am fully renewed, as that I am justified.' Now, if I have nothing to oppose to this plain testimony, I ought in reason to believe it.

"It avails nothing to object, 'But I know several things wherein he is quite mistaken.' For it has been allowed, that all who are in the body are liable to mistake; and that a mistake in judgment may sometimes occasion a mistake in practice; though great care is to be taken that no ill use be made of this concession. For instance: Even one that is perfected in love may mistake with regard to another person, and may think him, in a particular case, to be more or less faulty than he really is. And hence he may speak to him with more or less severity than the truth requires. And in this sense, (though that be not the primary

---

[5] Wesley here refers to one of the gifts of the Spirit with the apparent assumption that these gifts at least in some cases remain extant.

meaning of St. James,) 'in many things we offend all.' This therefore is no proof at all, that the person so speaking is not perfect.

"Q. But is it not a proof, if he is surprised or fluttered by a noise, a fall, or some sudden danger?
"A. It is not; for one may start, tremble, change color, or be otherwise disordered in body, while the soul is calmly stayed on God, and remains in perfect peace. Nay, the mind itself may be deeply distressed, may be exceeding sorrowful, may be perplexed and pressed down by heaviness and anguish, even to agony, while the heart cleaves to God by perfect love, and the will is wholly resigned to him. Was it not so with the Son of God himself? Does any child of man endure the distress, the anguish, the agony, which he sustained? And yet he knew no sin.

"Q. But can any one who has a pure heart prefer pleasing to unpleasing food; or use any pleasure of sense which is not strictly necessary? If so, how do they differ from others?
"A. The difference between these and others in taking pleasant food is,
(1.) They need none of these things to make them happy; for they have a spring of happiness within. They see and love God. Hence they rejoice evermore, and in everything give thanks.
(2.) They may use them, but they do not seek them.
(3.) They use them sparingly, and not for the sake of the thing itself. This being premised, we answer directly, -- Such a one may use pleasing food, without the danger which attends those who are not saved from sin. He may prefer it to unpleasing, though equally wholesome, food, as a means of increasing thankfulness, with a single eye to God, who giveth us all things richly to enjoy: On the same principle, he may smell to a flower, or eat a bunch of grapes, or take any other pleasure which does not lessen but increase his delight in God. Therefore, neither can we say that one perfected in love would be incapable of marriage, and of worldly business: If he were called thereto, he would be more capable than ever; as being able to do all things without hurry or carefulness, without any distraction of spirit.

"Q. But if two perfect Christians had children, how could they be born in sin, since there was none in the parents?

"A. It is a possible, but not a probable, case; I doubt whether it ever was or ever will be. But waving this, I answer, Sin is entailed upon me, not by immediate generation, but by my first parent. 'In Adam all died; by the disobedience of one, all men were made sinners;' all men, without exception, who were in his loins when he ate the forbidden fruit.

"We have a remarkable illustration of this in gardening: Grafts on a crab-stock bear excellent fruit; but sow the kernels of this fruit, and what will be the event? They produce as mere crabs as ever were eaten.

"Q. But what does the perfect one do more than others? more than the common believers?

"A. Perhaps nothing; so may the providence of God have hedged him in by outward circumstances. Perhaps not so much; though he desires and longs to spend and be spent for God; at least, not externally: He neither speaks so many words, nor does so many works. As neither did our Lord himself speak so many words, or do so many, no, nor so great works, as some of his Apostles. (John 14:12.) But what then? This is no proof that he has not more grace; and by this God measures the outward work. Hear ye Him: 'Verily, I say unto you, this poor widow has cast in more than them all.' Verily, this poor man, with his few broken words, hath spoken more than them all. Verily, this poor woman, that hath given a cup of cold water, hath done more than them all. O cease to judge according to appearance, and learn to judge righteous judgment!

"Q. But is not this a proof against him, -- I feel no power either in his words or prayer?

"A. It is not; for perhaps that is your own fault. You are not likely to feel any power therein, if any of these hindrances lie in the way:

(1.) Your own deadness of soul. The dead Pharisees felt no power even in His words who 'spake as never man spake.'

(2.) The guilt of some unrepented sin lying upon the conscience.

(3.) Prejudice toward him of any kind.

(4.) Your not believing that state to be attainable wherein he professes to be.

(5.) Unreadiness to think or own he has attained it.

(6.) Overvaluing or idolizing him.

(7.) Overvaluing yourself and your own judgment.

If any of these is the case, what wonder is it that you feel no power in anything he says? But do not others feel it? If they do, your argument falls to the ground. And if they do not, do none of these hindrances lie in their way too? You must be certain of this before you can build any argument thereon; and even then your argument will prove no more than that grace and gifts do not always go together.

"'But he does not come up to my idea of a perfect Christian.' And perhaps no one ever did, or ever will. For your idea may go beyond, or at least beside, the scriptural account. It may include more than the Bible includes therein, or, however, something which that does not include. Scripture perfection is, pure love filling the heart, and governing all the words and actions. If your idea includes anything more or anything else, it is not scriptural; and then no wonder, that a scripturally perfect Christian does not come up to it.

"I fear many stumble on this stumbling-block. They include as many ingredients as they please, not according to Scripture, but their own imagination, in their idea of one that is perfect; and then readily deny any one to be such, who does not answer that imaginary idea.

"The more care should we take to keep the simple, scriptural account continually in our eye. Pure love reigning alone in the heart and life, -- this is the whole of scriptural perfection.

"Q. When may a person judge himself to have attained this?

"A. When, after having been fully convinced of inbred sin, by a far deeper and clearer conviction than that he experienced before justification, and after having experienced a gradual mortification of it, he experiences a total death to sin, and an entire renewal in the love and image of God, so as to rejoice evermore, to pray without ceasing, and in everything to give thanks. Not that 'to feel all love and no sin' is a sufficient proof. Several have experienced this for a time, before their souls were fully renewed. None therefore ought to believe that the work is done, till there is added the testimony of the Spirit, witnessing his entire sanctification, as clearly as his justification.

"Q. But whence is it, that some imagine they are thus sanctified, when in reality they are not?

"A. It is hence; they do not judge by all the preceding marks, but either by part of them, or by others that are ambiguous. But I know no instance of a person attending to them all, and yet deceived in this matter. I believe, there can be none in the world. If a man be deeply and fully convinced, after justification, of inbred sin; if he then experience a gradual mortification of sin, and afterwards an entire renewal in the image of God; if to this change, immensely greater than that wrought when he was justified, be added a clear, direct witness of the renewal; I judge it as impossible this man should be deceived herein, as that God should lie. And if one whom I know to be a man of veracity testify these things to me, I ought not, without some sufficient reason, to reject his testimony.

"Q. Is this death to sin, and renewal in love, gradual or instantaneous?

"A. A man may he dying for some time; yet he does not, properly speaking, die, till the instant the soul is separated from the body; and in that instant he lives the life of eternity. In like manner, he may be dying to sin for some time; yet he is not dead to sin, till sin is separated from his soul; and in that instant he lives the full life of love. And as the change undergone, when the body dies, is of a different kind, and infinitely greater than any we had known before, yea, such as till then it is impossible to conceive; so the change wrought, when the soul dies to sin, is of a different kind, and infinitely greater than any before, and than any can conceive till he experiences it. Yet he stills grows in grace, in the knowledge of Christ, in the love and image of God; and will do so, not only till death, but to all eternity.

"Q. How are we to wait for this change?
"A. Not in careless indifference, or indolent inactivity; but in vigorous, universal obedience, in a zealous keeping of all the commandments, in watchfulness and painfulness, in denying ourselves, and taking up our cross daily; as well as in earnest prayer and fasting and a close attendance on all the ordinances of God. And if any man dream of attaining it any other way, (yea, or of keeping it when it is attained, when he has received it even in the largest measure,) he deceive his own soul. It is true, we receive it by simple faith: But God does not, will not, give that faith, unless we seek it with all diligence, in the way which he hath ordained.

"This consideration may satisfy those who inquire, why so few have received the blessing. Inquire, how many are seeking it in this way; and you have a sufficient answer.

"Prayer especially is wanting. Who continues instant therein? Who wrestles with God for this very thing? So, 'ye have not, because ye ask not; or because ye ask amiss,' namely, that you may be renewed before you die. *Before you die!* Will that content you? Nay, but ask that it may be done now; to-day, while it is called to-day. Do not call this 'setting God a time.' Certainly, to-day is his time as well as to-morrow.
Make haste, man, make haste! Let

> Thy soul break out in strong desire
> The perfect bliss to prove;
> Thy longing heart be all on fire
> To be dissolved in love!

"Q. But may we not continue in peace and joy till we are perfected in love?

"A. Certainly we may; for the kingdom of God is not divided against itself; therefore, let not believers be discouraged from 'rejoicing in the Lord always.' And yet we may be sensibly pained at the sinful nature that still remains in us. It is good for us to have a piercing sense of this, and a vehement desire to be delivered from it. But this should only incite us the more zealously to fly every moment to our strong Helper, the more earnestly to 'press forward to the mark, the prize of our high calling in Christ Jesus.' And when the sense of our *sin* most abounds, the sense of his *love* should much more abound.

"Q. How should we treat those who think they have attained?

"A. Examine them candidly, and exhort them to pray fervently, that God would show them all that is in their hearts. The most earnest exhortations to abound in every grace, and the strongest cautions to avoid all evil, are given throughout the New Testament, to those who are in the highest state of grace. But this should be done with the utmost tenderness; and without any harshness, sternness or sourness. We should carefully avoid the very appearance of anger, unkindness, or contempt. Leave it to Satan thus to tempt, and to his children to cry out, 'Let us examine him with despitefulness and torture, that we may know his meekness and prove his patience.' If they are faithful to the grace given, they are in no danger of perishing thereby; no, not if they remain in that mistake till their spirit is returning to God.

"Q. But what hurt can it do to deal harshly with them?

"A. Either they are mistaken, or they are not. If they are, it may destroy their souls. This is nothing impossible, no, nor improbable. It may so enrage or so discourage them, that they will sink and rise no more. If they are not mistaken, it may grieve those whom God has not grieved, and do much hurt unto our own souls. For undoubtedly he that toucheth them, toucheth, as it were, the apple of God's eye. If they are indeed full of his Spirit, to behave unkindly or contemptuously to them is doing no little despite to the Spirit of grace. Hereby, likewise, we feed and increase in ourselves evil surmising, and many wrong tempers. To instance only in one: What self-sufficiency is this, to set ourselves up for inquisitors-general, for peremptory judges in these deep things of God! Are we qualified for the office? Can we pronounce, in all cases, how far infirmity reaches? what may, and what may not, be resolved into it? what may in all circumstances, and what may not, consist with perfect love? Can we precisely determine, how it will influence the look, the gesture, the tone of voice? If we can, doubtless we are 'the men, and wisdom shall die with us.'

"Q. But if they are displeased at our not believing them, is not this a full proof against them?
"A. According as that displeasure is: If they are angry, it is a proof against them; if they are grieved, it is not. They ought to be grieved, if we disbelieve a real work of God, and thereby deprive ourselves of the advantage we might have received from it. And we may easily mistake this grief for anger, as the outward expressions of both are much alike.

"Q. But is it not well to find out those who fancy they have attained when they have not?
"A. It is well to do it by mild, loving examination. But it is not well to triumph even over these. It is extremely wrong, if we find such an instance, to rejoice as if we had found great spoils. Ought we not rather to grieve, to be deeply concerned, to let our eyes run down with tears? Here is one who seemed to be a living proof of God's power to save to the uttermost; but, alas, it is not as we hoped. He is weighed in the balance, and found wanting! And is this matter of joy? Ought we not to rejoice a thousand times more, if we can find nothing but pure love?

"'But he is deceived.' What then? It is a harmless mistake, while he feels nothing but love in his heart. It is a mistake which generally argues great grace, an high degree both of holiness and happiness. This should be a matter of real joy to all that are simple of heart; not the mistake itself, but the height of grace which for a time occasions it. I rejoice that this soul is always happy in Christ, always full of prayer and thanksgiving. I rejoice that he feels no unholy temper, but the pure love of God continually. And I will rejoice, if sin is suspended till it is totally destroyed.

"Q. Is there no danger then in a man's being thus deceived?
"A. Not at the time that he feels no sin. There was danger before, and there will be again when he comes into fresh trials. But so long as he feels nothing but love animating all his thoughts, and words, and actions, he is in no danger; he is not only happy, but safe, under the shadow of the Almighty; and, for God's sake, let him continue in that love as long as he can. Meantime, you may do well to warn him of the danger that will be, if his love grow cold and sin revive; even the danger of casting away hope, and supposing, that, because he hath not attained yet, therefore he never shall.

"Q. But what, if none have attained it yet? What, if all who think so are deceived?
"A. Convince me of this, and I will preach it no more. But understand me right: I do not build any doctrine on this or that person. This or any other man may be deceived, and I am not moved. But, if there are none made perfect yet, God has not sent me to preach perfection.

"Put a parallel case: For many years I have preached, There is a peace of God which passeth all understanding? Convince me that this word has fallen to the ground; that in all these years none have attained this peace; that there is no living witness of it at this day; and I will preach it no more.

"'O, but several persons have died in that peace.' Perhaps so; but I want living witnesses. I cannot indeed be infallibly certain that this or that person is a witness; but if I were certain there are none such, I must have done with this doctrine.

"'You misunderstand me. I believe some who died in this love, enjoyed it long before their death. But I was not certain that their former testimony was true till some hours before they died.'

"You had not an infallible certainty then: And a reasonable certainty you might have had before; such a certainty as might have quickened and comforted your own soul, and answered all other Christian purposes. Such a certainty as this, any candid person may have, suppose there be any living witness, by talking one hour with that person in the love and fear of God.

"Q. But what does it signify, whether any have attained it or no, seeing so many scriptures witness for it?
"A. If I were convinced that none in England had attained what has been so clearly and strongly preached by such a number of Preachers, in so many places, and for so long a time, I should be clearly convinced that we had all mistaken the meaning of those scriptures; and therefore, for the time to come, I too must teach that sin will remain till death."

20. In the year 1762, there was a great increase of the work of God in London. Many, who had hitherto cared for none of these things, were deeply convinced of their lost estate; many found redemption in the blood of Christ; not a few backsliders were healed; and a considerable number of persons believed that God had saved them from all sin. Easily foreseeing that Satan would be endeavoring to sow tares among the wheat, I took much pains to apprize them of the danger, particularly with regard to pride and enthusiasm. And while I stayed in town, I had reason to hope they continued both humble and sober-minded. But almost as soon as I was gone enthusiasm broke in. Two or three began to take their own imaginations for impressions from God, and thence to suppose that they should never die; and these, laboring to bring others into the same opinion, occasioned much noise and confusion. Soon after, the same persons, with a few more, ran into other extravagances; fancying they could not be tempted; that they should feel no more pain; and that they had the gift of prophecy, and of discerning of spirits. At my return to London, in autumn, some

of them stood reproved; but others were got above instruction. Meantime, a flood of reproach came upon me almost from every quarter; from themselves, because I was checking them on all occasions; and from others, because, they said, I did not check them. However, the hand of the Lord was not stayed, but more and more sinners were convinced; while some were almost daily converted to God, and others enabled to love him with all their heart.

21. About this time, a friend at some distance from London wrote to me as follows: --

"Be not over alarmed that Satan sows tares among the wheat of Christ. It ever has been so, especially on any remarkable outpouring of his Spirit; and ever will be so, till he is chained up for a thousand years. Till then he will always ape, and endeavor to counteract, the work of the Spirit of Christ.

"One melancholy effect of this has been, that a world, who is always asleep in the arms of the evil one, has ridiculed every work of the Holy Spirit.

"But what can real Christians do? Why, if they would act worthy of themselves, they should,
(1.) Pray that every deluded soul may be delivered;
(2.) Endeavour to reclaim them in the spirit of meekness; and,
Lastly, take the utmost care, both by prayer and watchfulness, that the delusion of others may not lessen their zeal in seeking after that universal holiness of soul, body, and spirit, 'without which no man shall see the Lord.'

"Indeed this complete new creature is mere madness to a mad world. But it is, notwithstanding, the will and wisdom of God. May we all seek after it!

"But some who maintain this doctrine in its full extent are too often guilty of limiting the Almighty. He dispenses his gifts just as he pleases; therefore, it is neither wise nor modest to affirm that a person must be a believer for any length of time before he is capable of receiving a high degree of the Spirit of holiness.

"God's usual method is one thing, but his sovereign pleasure is another. He has wise reasons both for hastening and retarding his work. Sometimes he comes suddenly and unexpected; sometimes, not till we have long looked for him.

"Indeed it has been my opinion for many years, that one great cause why men make so little improvement in the divine life is their own coldness, negligence, and unbelief. And yet I here speak of believers.

"May the Spirit of Christ give us a right judgment in all things, and fill us with all the fulness of God; that so we may be perfect and entire, wanting nothing."

22. About the same time, five or six honest enthusiasts foretold the world was to end on the 28th of February. I immediately withstood them, by every possible means, both in public and private. I preached expressly upon the subject, both at West-Street and Spitalfields. I warned the society, again and again, and spoke severally to as many as I could; and I saw the fruit of my labor. They made exceeding few converts: I believe scarce thirty in our whole society. Nevertheless, they made abundance of noise, gave huge occasion of offence to those who took care to improve to the uttermost every occasion against me, and greatly increased both the number and courage of those who opposed Christian perfection.

23. Some questions, now published by one of these, induced a plain man to write the following --

"QUERIES, humbly proposed to those who deny perfection to be attainable in this life.
"(1.) Has there not been a larger measure of the Holy Spirit given under the Gospel, than under the Jewish dispensation? If

not, in what sense was the Spirit not given before Christ was glorified? (John 7:39.)

"(2.) Was that glory which followed the sufferings of Christ, (1 Peter 1:11,) an external glory, or an internal, viz., the glory of holiness?

"(3.) Has God anywhere in Scripture commanded us more than he has promised to us?

"(4.) Are the promises of God respecting holiness to be fulfilled in this life, or only in the next?

"(5.) Is a Christian under any other laws than those which God promises to write in our hearts? (Jer. 31:31, &c.; Heb. 8:10.)

"(6.) In what sense is the righteousness of the law fulfilled in those who walk not after the flesh, but after the Spirit? (Rom. 8:4.)

"(7.) Is it impossible for any one in this life to love God with all his heart, and mind, and soul, and strength? And is the Christian under any law which is not fulfilled in this love?

"(8.) Does the soul's going out of the body effect its purification from indwelling sin?

"(9.) If so, is it not something else, not the blood of Christ which cleanseth it from all sin?

"(10.) If his blood cleanseth us from all sin, while the soul and body are united, is it not in this life?

"(11.) If when that union ceases, is it not in the next? And is not this too late?

"(12.) If in the article of death; what situation is the soul in, when it is neither in the body nor out of it?

"(13.) Has Christ anywhere taught us to pray for what he never designs to give?

"(14.) Has he not taught us to pray, 'Thy will be done on earth, as it is done in heaven?' And is it not done perfectly in heaven?

"(15.) If so, has he not taught us to pray for perfection on earth? Does he not then design to give it?

"(16.) Did not St. Paul pray according to the will of God, when he prayed that the Thessalonians might be sanctified wholly, and preserved (in this world, not the next, unless he was praying for the dead) blameless in body, soul, and spirit, unto the coming of Jesus Christ?

"(17.) Do you sincerely desire to be freed from indwelling sin in this life?

"(18.) If you do, did not God give you that desire?

"(19.) If so, did he not give it you to mock you, since it is impossible it should ever be fulfilled?

"(20.) If you have not sincerity enough even to desire it, are you not disputing about matters too high for you?

"(21.) Do you ever pray God to cleanse the thoughts of your heart, that you may perfectly love him?

"(22.) If you neither desire what you ask, nor believe it attainable, pray you not as a fool prayeth?

"God help thee to consider these questions calmly and impartially!"

24. In the latter end of this year, God called to himself that burning and shining light, Jane Cooper. As she was both a living and a dying witness of Christian perfection, it will not be at all foreign to the subject to add a short account of her death; with one of her own letters, containing a plain and artless relation of the manner wherein it pleased God to work that great change in her soul:

"May 2, 1761.

"I believe while memory remains in me, gratitude will continue. From the time you preached on Gal. 5:5, I saw clearly the true state of my soul. That sermon described my heart, and what it wanted to be; namely, truly happy. You read Mr. M---'s letter, and it described the religion which I desired. From that time the prize appeared in view, and I was enabled to follow hard after it. I was kept watching unto prayer, sometimes in much distress, at other times in patient expectation of the blessing. For some days before you left London, my soul was stayed on a promise I had applied to me in prayer: 'The Lord whom ye seek shall suddenly come to his temple.' I believed he would, and that he would sit there as a refiner's fire. The Tuesday after you went, I thought I could not sleep, unless he fulfilled his word that night. I never knew as I did then the force of these words: 'Be still, and know that I am God.' I became nothing before Him, and enjoyed perfect calmness in my soul. I knew not whether he had destroyed my sin; but I desired to know, that I might praise Him. Yet I soon found the return of unbelief, and groaned, being burdened. On Wednesday I went to London, and sought the Lord without ceasing. I promised, if he would save me from sin, I would praise him. I could part with all things, so I might win Christ. But I found all these pleas to be nothing worth; and that if He saved me, it must be freely, for his own name's sake. On Thursday I was so much tempted, that I thought of destroying myself, or never conversing more with the people of God: And yet I had no doubt of his pardoning love; but,

> 'Twas worse than death my God to love,
> And not my God alone.

On Friday my distress was deepened. I endeavored to pray, and could not. I went to Mrs. D., who prayed for me, and told me it was the death of nature. I opened the Bible, on, 'The fearful and unbelieving shall have their part in the lake which burneth with fire and brimstone.' I could not bear it. I opened again, on Mark 16:6, 7: 'Be not affrighted; ye seek Jesus of Nazareth. Go your way; tell his disciples he goeth before you into Galilee; there ye shall see him.' I was encouraged, and enabled to pray, believing I should see Jesus at home. I returned that night, and found Mrs. G. She prayed for me; and the Predestinarian had no plea, but, 'Lord, thou art no respecter of persons.' He proved he was not, by blessing me. I was in a moment enabled to lay hold on Jesus Christ, and found salvation by simple faith. He assured me, the Lord, the King, was in the midst of me, and that I should see evil no more. I now blessed Him who had visited and redeemed me, and was become my 'wisdom, righteousness, sanctification, and redemption.' I saw Jesus altogether lovely; and knew he was mine in all his offices. And, glory be to Him, He now reigns in my heart without a rival. I find no will but his. I feel no pride; nor any affection but what is placed on Him. I know it is by faith I stand; and that watching unto prayer must be the guard of faith. I am happy in God this moment, and I believe for the next. I have often read the chapter you mention, (1 Cor. 13.,) and compared my heart and life with it. In so doing, I feel my shortcomings, and the need I have of the atoning blood. Yet I dare not say, I do not feel a measure of the love there described, though I am not all I shall be. I desire to be lost in that 'love which passeth knowledge.' I see 'the just shall live by faith;' and unto me, who am less than the least of all saints, is this grace given. If I were an archangel, I should veil my face before him, and let silence speak his praise!"

 The following account is given by one who was an eye and ear witness of what she relates: --
"(1.) In the beginning of November, she seemed to have a foresight of what was coming upon her, and used frequently to sing these words: --

> When pain o'er this weak flesh prevails,
> With lamb-like patience arm my breast.

And when she sent to me, to let me know she was ill, she wrote in her note, 'I suffer the will of Jesus. All he sends is sweetened by His
love. I am as happy as if I heard a voice say, --

> `For me my elder brethren stay,
> And angels beckon me away,
> And Jesus bids me come!'

"(2.) Upon my telling her, 'I cannot choose life or death for you,' she said, 'I asked the Lord, that, if it was His will I might die first. And he told me, you should survive me, and that you should close my eyes.' When we perceived it was the small-pox, I said to her, 'My dear, you will not be frighted if we tell you what is your distemper.' She said, 'I cannot be frighted at His will.'
"(3.) The distemper was so very heavy upon her; but so much the more was her faith strengthened. Tuesday, November 16,

she said to me, 'I have been worshipping before the throne in a glorious manner; my soul was so let into God!' I said, 'Did the Lord give you any particular promise?' 'No,' replied she; 'it was all

> That sacred awe that dares not move,
> And all the silent heaven of love.'

"(4.) On Thursday, upon my asking, 'What have you to say to me?' she said, 'Nay, nothing but what you know already: God is love.' I asked, 'Have you any particular promise?' She replied, 'I do not seem to want any; I can live without. I shall die a lump of deformity, but shall meet you all-glorious: And, meantime, I shall still have fellowship with your spirit.'

"(5.) Mr. M. asked, what she thought the most excellent way to walk in, and what were its chief hindrances. She answered: 'The greatest hindrance is generally from the natural constitution. It was mine to be reserved, to be very quiet, to suffer much, and to say little. Some may think one way more excellent, and some another: But the thing is to live in the will of God. For some months past, when I have been particularly devoted to this, I have felt such a guidance of his Spirit, and the unction which I have received from the Holy One has so taught me of all things, that I needed not any man should teach me, save as this anointing teacheth.'

"(6.) On Friday morning she said, 'I believe I shall die.' She then sat up in her bed and said, 'Lord, I bless thee, that thou art ever with me, and all thou hast is mine. Thy love is greater than my weakness, greater than my helplessness, greater than my unworthiness. Lord, thou sayest *to corruption, Thou art my sister!* And glory be to thee, O Jesus, thou art my Brother. Let me comprehend, with all saints, the length, and breadth, and depth, and height of thy love! Bless these;' (some that were present;) 'let them be every moment exercised in all things as thou wouldest have them to be.'

"(7.) Some hours after, it seemed as if the agonies of death were just coming upon her; but her face was full of smiles of triumph, and she clapped her hands for joy. Mrs. C. said, 'My dear, you are more than conqueror through the blood of the Lamb.' She answered: 'Yes, O yes, sweet Jesus! O death, where is thy sting?' She then lay as in a doze for some time. Afterwards, she strove to speak, but could not: However, she testified her love, by shaking hands with all in the room.

"(8.) Mr. W. then came. She said, 'Sir, I did not know that I should live to see you. But I am glad the Lord has given me this opportunity, and likewise power to speak to you. I love you. You have always preached the strictest doctrine; and I loved to follow it. Do so still, whoever is pleased or displeased.' He asked, 'Do you now believe you are saved from sin?' She said, 'Yes; I have had no doubt of it for many months. That I ever had, was, because I did not abide in the faith. I now feel I have kept the faith; and perfect love casteth out all fear. As to you, the Lord promised me, your latter works should exceed your former, though I do not live to see it. I have been a great enthusiast, as they term it, these six months; but never lived so near the heart of Christ in my life. You, Sir, desire to comfort the hearts of hundreds by following that simplicity your soul loves.'

"(9.) To one who had received the love of God under her prayer, she said, 'I feel I have not followed a cunningly-devised fable; for I am as happy as I can live. Do you press on, and stop not short of the mark.' To Miss M---s she said, 'Love Christ; he loves you. I believe I shall see you at the right hand of God: But *as one star differs from another star in glory, so shall it be in the resurrection.* I charge you, in the presence of God, meet me in that day all-glorious within. Avoid all conformity to the world. You are robbed of many of your privileges. I know I shall be found blameless. Do you labor to be found of him *in peace, without spot.*

"(10.) Saturday morning, she prayed nearly as follows: 'I know, my Lord, my life is prolonged only to do thy will. And though I should never eat or drink more,' (she had not swallowed anything for near eight-and-twenty hours,) 'thy will be done. I am willing to be kept so a twelvemonth: *Man liveth not by bread alone.* I praise thee that there is not a shadow of complaining in our streets. In that sense we know not what sickness means. Indeed, Lord, *neither life, nor death, nor things present, nor things to come, no, nor any creature, shall separate us from thy love* one moment. Bless these, that there may be no lack in their souls. I believe there shall not. I pray in faith.'

"On Sunday and Monday she was light-headed, but sensible at times. It then plainly appeared, her heart was still in heaven. One said to her, 'Jesus is our mark.' She replied: 'I have but one mark; I am all spiritual.' Miss M. said to her, 'You dwell in God.' She answered: 'Altogether.' A person asked her: 'Do you love me?' She said, 'O, I love Christ; I love my Christ.' To another she said, 'I shall not long be here; Jesus is precious, very precious indeed.' She said to Miss M., 'The Lord is very good; he keeps my soul above all.' For fifteen hours before she died, she was in strong convulsions: Her sufferings were extreme. One said, 'You are made perfect through sufferings.' She said, 'More and more so.' After lying quiet some time, she said, 'Lord, thou art strong!' Then pausing a considerable space, she uttered her last words, 'My Jesus is all in all to me: Glory be to him through time and eternity.' After this, she lay still for about half an hour, and then expired without a sigh or groan."

25. The next year, the number of those who believed they were saved from sin still increasing, I judged it needful to publish, chiefly for their use, "Farther Thoughts on Christian Perfection:" –

"QUESTION 1. How is Christ the end of the law for righteousness to every one that believeth? (Rom. 10:4.)
"ANSWER. In order to understand this, you must understand what law is here spoken of; and this, I apprehend, is,
(1.) The Mosaic law, the whole Mosaic dispensation; which St. Paul continually speaks of as one, though containing three parts, the political, moral, and ceremonial.
(2.) The Adamic law, that given to Adam in innocence, properly called 'the law of works.' This is in substance the same with the angelic law, being common to angels and men. It required that man should use, to the glory of God, all the powers with which he was created. Now, he was created free from any defect, either

in his understanding or his affections. His body was then no clog to the mind; it did not hinder his apprehending all things clearly, judging truly concerning them, and reasoning justly, if he reasoned at all. I say, *if he reasoned;* for possibly he did not. Perhaps he had no need of reasoning, till his corruptible body pressed down the mind, and impaired its native faculties. Perhaps, till then, the mind saw every truth that offered as directly as the eye now sees the light.

"Consequently, this law, proportioned to his original powers, required that he should always think, always speak, and always act precisely right, in every point whatever. He was well able so to do: And God could not but require the service he was able to pay.

"But Adam fell; and his incorruptible body became corruptible; and ever since, it is a clog to the soul, and hinders its operations. Hence, at present, no child of man can at all times apprehend clearly, or judge truly. And where either the judgment or apprehension is wrong, it is impossible to reason justly. Therefore, it is as natural for a man to mistake as to breathe; and he can no more live without the one than without the other: Consequently, no man is able to perform the service which the Adamic law requires.

"And no man is obliged to perform it; God does not require it of any man: For Christ is the end of the Adamic, as well as the Mosaic, law. By his death, he hath put an end to both; he hath abolished both the one and the other, with regard to man; and the obligation to observe either the one or the other is vanished away. Nor is any man living bound to observe the Adamic more than the Mosaic law. [I mean, it is not the condition either of present or future salvation.]

"In the room of this, Christ hath established another, namely, the law of faith. Not every one that doeth, but every one that believeth, now receiveth righteousness, in the full sense of the word; that is, he is justified, sanctified, and glorified.[6]

"Q. 2. Are we then dead to the law?
"A. We are dead to the law, by the body of Christ given for us; (Rom. 7:4;) to the Adamic as well as Mosaic law. We are wholly freed therefrom by his death; that law expiring with him.

"Q. 3. How, then, are we not without law to God, but under the law to Christ? (1 Cor. 9:21.)
"A. We are without that law; but it does not follow that we are without any law: For God has established another law in its place, even the law of faith: And we are all under this law to God and to Christ; both our Creator and our Redeemer require us to observe it.

"Q. 4. Is love the fulfilling of this law?
"A. Unquestionably it is. The whole law under which we now are, is fulfilled by love. (Rom. 13:9, 10.) Faith working or animated by love is all that God now requires of man. He has substituted (not sincerity, but) love, in the room of angelic perfection.

"Q. 5. How is love the end of the commandment? (1 Tim. 1:5.)
"A. It is the end of every commandment of God. It is the point aimed at by the whole and every part of the Christian institution. The foundation is faith, purifying the heart; the end love, preserving a good conscience.

"Q. 6. What love is this?
"A. The loving the Lord our God with all our heart, mind, soul, and strength; and the loving our neighbor, every man, as ourselves, as our own souls.

"Q. 7. What are the fruits or properties of this love?

---

[6] Wesley is not here distinguishing works from faith, but expressing the Biblical principle that without faith it is impossible to please God (Hebrews 11:6).

"A. St. Paul informs us at large, love is long-suffering. It suffers all the weaknesses of the children of God, all the wickedness of the children of the world; and that not for a little time only, but as long as God pleases. In all, it sees the hand of God, and willingly submits thereto. Meantime, it is kind. In all, and after all, it suffers, it is soft, mild, tender, benign. 'Love envieth not;' it excludes every kind and degree of envy out of the heart: 'love acteth not rashly,' in a violent, headstrong manner, nor passes any rash or severe judgment: It 'doth not behave itself indecently;' is not rude, does not act out of character: 'Seeketh not her own' ease, pleasure, honor, or profit: 'Is not provoked;' expels all anger from the heart: 'Thinketh no evil;' casteth out all jealousy, suspiciousness, and readiness to believe evil: 'Rejoiceth not in iniquity;' yea, weeps at the sin or folly of its bitterest enemies: 'But rejoiceth in the truth;' in the holiness and happiness of every child of man. 'Love covereth all things,' speaks evil of no man; 'believeth all things' that tend to the advantage of another's character. It 'hopeth all things,' whatever may extenuate the faults which cannot be denied; and it 'endureth all things' which God can permit, or men and devils inflict. This is 'the law of Christ, the perfect law, the law of liberty.'

"And this distinction between the 'law of faith' (or love) and 'the law of works,' is neither a subtle nor an unnecessary distinction. It is plain, easy, and intelligible to any common understanding. And it is absolutely necessary, to prevent a thousand doubts and fears, even in those who do 'walk in love.'

"Q. 8. But do we not in many things offend all, yea, the best of us, even against this law?
"A. In one sense we do not, while all our tempers, and thoughts, and words, and works, spring from love. But in another we do, and shall do, more or less, as long as we remain in the body. For neither love nor the unction of the Holy One makes us infallible: Therefore, through unavoidable defect of understanding, we cannot but mistake in many things. And these mistakes will frequently occasion something wrong, both

in our temper, and words, and actions. From mistaking his character, we may love a person less than he really deserves. And by the same mistake we are unavoidably led to speak or act, with regard to that person, in such a manner as is contrary to this law, in some or other of the preceding instances.

"Q. 9. Do we not then need Christ, even on this account?
"A. The holiest of men still need Christ, as their Prophet, as the light of the world. For he does not give them light, but from moment to moment: The instant he withdraws, all is darkness. They still need Christ as their King; for God does not give them a stock of holiness. But unless they receive a supply every moment, nothing but unholiness would remain. They still need Christ as their Priest, to make atonement for their holy things. Even perfect holiness is acceptable to God only through Jesus Christ.

Q. 10. May not, then, the very best of men adopt the dying Martyr's confession: 'I am in myself nothing but sin, darkness, hell; but thou art my light, my holiness, my heaven?'
"A. Not exactly. But the best of men may say, 'Thou art my light, my holiness, my heaven. Through my union with thee, I am full of light, of holiness, and happiness. But if I were left to myself, I should be nothing but sin, darkness, hell.'

"But to proceed: The best of men need Christ as their Priest, their Atonement, their Advocate with the Father; not only as the continuance of their every blessing depends on his death and intercession, but on account of their coming short of the law of love. For every man living does so. You who feel all love, compare yourselves with the preceding description. Weigh yourselves in this balance, and see if you are not wanting in many particulars.

"Q. 11. But if all this be consistent with Christian perfection, that perfection is not freedom from all sin; seeing sin is the transgression of the law: And the perfect transgress the very law they are under. Besides, they need the atonement of Christ; and he is the atonement of nothing but sin. Is, then, the term *sinless perfection,* proper?

"A. It is not worth disputing about. But observe in what sense the persons in question need the atonement of Christ. They do not need him to reconcile them to God afresh; for they are reconciled. They do not need him to restore the favor of God, but to continue it. He does not procure pardon for them anew, but 'ever liveth to make intercession for them;' and 'by one offering he hath perfected for ever them that are sanctified.' (Heb. 10:14.)

"For want of duly considering this, some deny that they need the atonement of Christ. Indeed, exceeding few; I do not remember to have found five of them in England. Of the two, I would sooner give up perfection; but we need not give up either one or the other. The perfection I hold, 'Love rejoicing evermore, praying without ceasing, and in everything giving thanks,' is well consistent with it; if any hold a perfection which is not, they must look to it.

"Q. 12. Does then Christian perfection imply any more than sincerity?

"A. Not if you mean by that word, love filling the heart, expelling pride, anger, desire, self-will; rejoicing evermore, praying without ceasing, and in everything giving thanks. But I doubt, few use sincerity in this sense. Therefore, I think the old word is best.

"A person may be sincere who has all his natural tempers, pride, anger, lust, self-will. But he is not perfect till his heart is cleansed from these, and all its other corruptions.

"To clear this point a little farther: I know many that love God with all their heart. He is their one desire, their one delight, and they are continually happy in him. They love their neighbor as themselves. They feel as sincere, fervent, constant a desire for the happiness of every man, good or bad, friend or enemy, as for their own. They rejoice evermore, pray without ceasing, and in everything give thanks. Their souls are continually streaming up to God, in holy joy, prayer, and praise. This is a point of fact; and this is plain, sound, scriptural experience.

"But even these souls dwell in a shattered body, and are so pressed down thereby, that they cannot always exert themselves as they would, by thinking, speaking, and acting precisely right. For want of better bodily organs, they must times think, speak, or act wrong; not indeed through a defect of love, but through a defect of knowledge. And while this is the case, notwithstanding that defect, and its consequences, they fulfil the law of love.

"Yet as, even in this case, there is not a full conformity to the perfect law, so the most perfect do, on this very account, need the blood of atonement, and may properly for themselves, as well as for their brethren, say, 'Forgive us our trespasses.'

"Q. 13. But if Christ has put an end to that law, what need of any atonement for their transgressing it?
"A. Observe in what sense he has put an end to it, and the difficulty vanishes. Were it not for the abiding merit of his death, and his continual intercession for us, that law would condemn us still. These, therefore, we still need for every transgression of it.

"Q. 14. But can one that is saved from sin be tempted?
"A. Yes; for Christ was tempted.

"Q. 15. However, what you call temptation, I call the corruption of my heart. And how will you distinguish one from the other?
"A. In some cases it is impossible to distinguish, without the direct witness of the Spirit. But in general one may distinguish thus:

"One commends me. Here is a temptation to pride. But instantly my soul is humbled before God. And I feel no pride; of which I am as sure, as that pride is not humility.

"A man strikes me. Here is a temptation to anger. But my heart overflows with love. And I feel no anger at all; of which I can be as sure, as that love and anger are not the same.

"A woman solicits me. Here is a temptation to lust. But in the instant I shrink back. And I feel no desire or lust at all; of which I can be as sure, as that my hand is cold or hot.

"Thus it is, if I am tempted by a present object; and it is just the same, if; when it is absent, the devil recalls a commendation, an injury, or a woman, to my mind. In the instant the soul repels the temptation, and remains filled with pure love.

"And the difference is still plainer, when I compare my present state with my past, wherein I felt temptation and corruption too.

"Q. 16. But how do you know, that you are sanctified, saved from your inbred corruption?
"A. I can know it no otherwise than I know that I am justified. Hereby know we that we are of God, in either sense, by the Spirit that he hath given us.

"We know it by the witness and by the fruit of the Spirit. And, First, by the witness. As, when we were justified, the Spirit bore witness with our spirit, that our sins were forgiven; so, when we were sanctified, he bore witness, that they were taken away. Indeed, the witness of sanctification is not always clear at first; (as neither is that of justification;) neither is it afterward always the same, but, like that of justification, sometimes stronger and sometimes fainter. Yea, and sometimes it is withdrawn. Yet, in general, the latter testimony of the Spirit is both as clear and as steady as the former.

"Q. 17. But what need is there of it, seeing sanctification is a real change, not a relative only, like justification?
"A. But is the new birth a relative change only? Is not this a real change? Therefore, if we need no witness of our sanctification,

because it is a real change, for the same reason we should need none, that we are born of or are the children of God.

"Q. 18. But does not sanctification shine by its own light?
"A. And does not the new birth too? Sometimes it does; and so does sanctification; at others it does not. In the hour of temptation Satan clouds the work of God, and injects various doubts and reasonings, especially in those who have either very weak or very strong understandings. At such times there is absolute need of that witness; without which the work of sanctification not only could not be discerned, but could no longer subsist. Were it not for this, the soul could not then abide in the love of God; much less could it rejoice evermore, and in everything give thanks. In these circumstances, therefore, a direct testimony that we are sanctified is necessary in the highest degree.

'But I have no witness that I am saved from sin. And yet I have no doubt of it.' Very well: As long as you have no doubt, it is enough; when you have, you will need that witness.

"Q. 19. But what scripture makes mention of any such thing, or gives any reason to expect it?
"A. That scripture, 'We have received, not the spirit that is of the world, but the Spirit which is of God; that we may know the things which are freely given us of God.' (1 Cor. 2:12.)

"Now surely sanctification is one of the things which are freely given us of God. And no possible reason can be assigned why this should be excepted, when the Apostle says, 'We receive the Spirit' for this very end, 'that we may know the things which are' thus 'freely given us.'

"Is not the same thing implied in that well-known scripture, 'The Spirit itself witnesseth with our spirit, that we are the children of God?' (Romans 8:16.) Does he witness this only to those who are children of God in the lowest sense? Nay, but to those also who are such in the highest sense. And does he not witness, that they are such in the highest sense? What reason have we to doubt it?

"What, if a man were to affirm, (as indeed many do,) that this witness belongs only to the highest class of Christians? Would not you answer, The Apostle makes no restriction; therefore doubtless it belongs to all the children of God? And will not the same answer hold, if any affirm, that it belongs only to the lowest class?

"Consider likewise 1 John 5:19: 'We know that we are of God.' How? 'By the Spirit that he hath given us.' Nay, 'hereby we know that He abideth in us.' And what ground have we, either from Scripture or reason, to exclude the witness, any more than the fruit, of the Spirit, from being here intended? By this then also 'we know that we are of God,' and in what sense we are so; whether we are babes, young men, or fathers, we know in the same manner.

"Not that I affirm that all young men, or even fathers, have this testimony every moment. There may be intermissions of the direct testimony that they are thus born of God; but those intermissions are fewer and shorter as they grow up in Christ; and some have the testimony both of their justification and sanctification, without any intermission at all; which I presume more might have, did they walk humbly and closely with God.

"Q. 20. May not some of them have a testimony from the Spirit, that they shall not finally fall from God?
"A. They may. And this persuasion, that neither life nor death shall separate them from Him, far from being hurtful, may in some circumstances be extremely useful. These therefore we should in nowise grieve, but earnestly encourage them to hold the beginning of their confidence steadfast to the end.

"Q. 21. But have any a testimony from the Spirit that they shall never sin?

"A. We know not what God may vouchsafe to some particular persons; but we do not find any general state described in Scripture, from which a man cannot draw back to sin. If there were any state wherein this was impossible, it would be that of these who are sanctified, who are fathers in Christ, who rejoice evermore, pray without ceasing, and in every thing give thanks; but it is not impossible for these to draw back. They who are sanctified, yet may fall and perish. (Heb. 10:29.) Even fathers in Christ need that warning: 'Love not the world.' (1 John 2:15.) They who rejoice, pray, and give thanks without ceasing, may, nevertheless, quench the Spirit. (1 Thess. 5:16, &c.) Nay, even they who are sealed unto the day of redemption, may yet grieve the Holy Spirit of God. (Ephesians 4:30.)

"Although, therefore, God may give such a witness to some particular persons, yet it is not to be expected by Christians in general; there being no scripture whereon to ground such an expectation.

"Q. 22. By what 'fruit of the Spirit' may we know that we are of God, even in the highest sense?
"A. By love, joy, peace, always abiding; by invariable long-suffering, patience, resignation; by gentleness, triumphing over all provocation; by goodness, mildness, sweetness, tenderness of spirit; by fidelity, simplicity, godly sincerity; by meekness, calmness, evenness of spirit; by temperance, not only in food and sleep, but in all things natural and spiritual.

"Q. 23. But what great matter is there in this? Have we not all this when we are justified?
"A. What, total resignation to the will of God, without any mixture of self-will? gentleness, without any touch of anger, even the moment we are provoked? love to God, without the least love to the creature, but in and for God, excluding all pride? love to man, excluding all envy, all jealousy, and rash judging? meekness, keeping the whole soul inviolably calm? and temperance in all things? Deny that any ever came up to this, if you please; but do not say, all who are justified do.

"Q. 24. But some who are newly justified do. What then will you say to these?

"A. If they really do, I will say they are sanctified; saved from sin in that moment; and that they never need lose what God has given, or feel sin any more.

"But certainly this is an exempt case. It is otherwise with the generality of those that are justified: They feel in themselves more or less pride, anger, self-will, a heart bent to backsliding. And, till they have gradually mortified these, they are not fully renewed in love.

"Q. 25. But is not this the case of all that are justified? Do they not gradually die to sin and grow in grace, till at, or perhaps a little before, death God perfects them in love?

"A. I believe this is the case of most, but not all. God usually gives a considerable time for men to receive light, to grow in grace, to do and suffer his will, before they are either justified or sanctified; but he does not invariably adhere to this; sometimes he cuts short his work: he does the work of many years in a few weeks; perhaps in a week, a day, an hour. He justifies or sanctifies both those who have done or suffered nothing, and who have not had time for a gradual growth either in light or grace. And may he not do what he will with his own? Is thine eye evil, because he is good?

"It need not, therefore, be affirmed over and over, and proved by forty texts of Scripture, either that most men are perfected in love at last, that there is a gradual work of God in the soul, or that, generally speaking, it is a long time, even many years, before sin is destroyed. All this we know: But we know likewise, that God may, with man's good leave, cut short his work, in whatever degree he pleases, and do the usual work of many years in a moment. He does so in many instances; and yet there is a gradual work, both before and after that moment: So that one may affirm the work is gradual, another, it is instantaneous, without any manner of contradiction.

"Q. 26. Does St. Paul mean any more by being 'sealed with the Spirit,' than being 'renewed in love?'

"A. Perhaps in one place, (2 Cor. 1:22,) he does not mean so much; but in another, (Eph. 1:13,) he seems to include both the fruit and the witness; and that in a higher degree than we experience even when we are first 'renewed in love;' God 'sealeth us with the Spirit of promise,' by giving us the full assurance of hope; such a confidence of receiving all the promises of God, as excludes the possibility of doubting; with that Holy Spirit, by universal holiness, stamping the whole image of God on our hearts.

"Q. 27. But how can those who are thus sealed grieve the Holy Spirit of God?

"A. St. Paul tells you very particularly,

(1.) By such conversation as is not profitable, not to the use of edifying, not apt to minister grace to the hearers.

(2.) By relapsing into bitterness or want of kindness.

(3.) By wrath, lasting displeasure, or want of tender-heartedness.

(4.) By anger, however soon it is over; want of instantly forgiving one another.

(5.) By clamour or bawling, loud, harsh, rough speaking.

(6.) By evil-speaking, whispering, tale-bearing; needlessly mentioning the fault of an absent person, though in ever so soft a manner.

"Q. 28. What do you think of those in London, who seem to have been lately 'renewed in love?'

"A. There is something very peculiar in the experience of the greater part of them. One would expect that a believer should first be filled with love, and thereby emptied of sin; whereas these were emptied of sin first, and then filled with love. Perhaps it pleased God to work in this manner, to make his work more plain and undeniable; and to distinguish it more clearly from that overflowing love, which is often felt even in a justified state.

"It seems likewise most agreeable to the great promise: 'From all your filthiness I will cleanse you; a new heart also will I give you, and a new spirit will I put within you.' (Ezek. 36:25, 26.)

"But I do not think of them all alike: There is a wide difference between some of them and others. I think most of them with whom I have spoken, have much faith, love, joy, and peace. Some of these I believe are renewed in love, and have the direct witness of it; and they manifest the fruit above described, in all their words and actions. Now, let any man call this what he will; it is what I call perfection.

"But some who have much love, peace, and joy, yet have not the direct witness; and others who think they have, are, nevertheless, manifestly wanting in the fruit. How many I will not say; perhaps one in ten; perhaps more or fewer. But some are undeniably wanting in longsuffering, Christian resignation. They do not see the hand of God in whatever occurs, and cheerfully embrace it. They do not in everything give thanks, and rejoice evermore. They are not happy; at least, not always happy; for sometimes they complain. They say, this or that is hard!

"Some are wanting in gentleness. They resist evil, instead of turning the other cheek. They do not receive reproach with gentleness; no, nor even reproof. Nay, they are not able to bear contradiction, without the appearance, at least, of resentment. If they are reproved or contradicted, though mildly, they do not take it well; they behave with more distance and reserve than they did before. If they are reproved or contradicted harshly, they answer it with harshness; with a loud voice, or with an angry tone, or in a sharp and surly manner. They speak sharply or roughly, when they reprove others; and behave roughly to their inferiors.

"Some are wanting in goodness. They are not kind, mild, sweet, amiable, soft, and loving at all times, in their spirit, in their words, in their look and air, in the whole tenor of their behavior; and that to all, high and low, rich and poor, without respect of persons; particularly to them that are out of the way, to opposers, and to those of their own household. They do not long, study, endeavor by every means, to make all about them happy. They can see them uneasy, and not be concerned; perhaps they make them so; and then wipe their mouths and say, 'Why, they deserve it; it is their own fault.'

"Some are wanting in fidelity, a nice regard to truth, simplicity, and godly sincerity. Their love is hardly without dissimulation; something like guile is found in their mouth. To avoid roughness, they lean to the other extreme. They are smooth to an excess, so as scarce to avoid a degree of fawning, or of seeming to mean what they do not.

"Some are wanting in meekness, quietness of spirit, composure, evenness of temper. They are up and down, sometimes high, sometimes low; their mind is not well balanced. Their affections are either not in due proportion; they have too much of one, too little of another; or they are not duly mixed and tempered together, so as to counterpoise each other. Hence there is often a jar. Their soul is out of tune, and cannot make the true harmony.

"Some are wanting in temperance. They do not steadily use that kind and degree of food, which they know, or might know, would most conduce to the health strength, and vigor of the body: Or they are not temperate in sleep; they do not rigorously adhere to what is best both for body and mind; otherwise they would constantly go to bed and rise early, and at a fixed hour: Or they sup late, which is neither good for body nor soul: Or they use neither fasting nor abstinence: Or they prefer (which are so many sorts of intemperance) that preaching, reading, or conversation, which gives them transient joy and comfort, before that which brings godly sorrow, or instruction in righteousness. Such joy is not sanctified; it doth not tend to, and terminate in, the crucifixion of the heart. Such faith doth not centre in God, but rather in itself.

"So far all is plain. I believe you have faith, and love, and joy, and peace. Yet you who are particularly concerned know each for yourself, that you are wanting in the respects above-mentioned. You are wanting either in long-suffering, gentleness, or goodness; either in fidelity, meekness, or temperance. Let us not, then, on either hand, fight about words. In the thing we clearly agree.

"You have not what I call perfection; if others will call it so, they may. However, hold fast what you have, and earnestly pray for what you have not.

"Q. 29. Can those who are perfect grow in grace?
"A. Undoubtedly they can; and that not only while they are in the body, but to all eternity.

"Q. 30. Can they fall from it?
"A. I am well assured they can; matter of fact puts this beyond dispute. Formerly we thought, one saved from sin could not fall; now we know the contrary. We are surrounded with instances of those who lately experienced all that I mean by perfection. They had both the fruit of the Spirit, and the witness; but they have now lost both. Neither does any one stand by virtue of anything that is implied in the nature of the state. There is no such height or strength of holiness as it is impossible to fall from. If there be any that cannot fall, this wholly depends on the promise of God.

"Q. 31. Can those who fall from this state recover it?
"A. Why not? We have many instances of this also. Nay, it is an exceeding common thing for persons to lose it more than once, before they are established therein.

"It is therefore to guard them who are saved from sin, from every occasion of stumbling, that I give the following advices. But first I shall speak plainly concerning the work itself.

"I esteem this late work to be of God; probably the greatest now upon earth. Yet, like all others, this also is mixed with much human frailty. But these weaknesses are far less than might have been expected; and ought to have been joyfully borne by all that loved and followed after righteousness. That there have been a few weak, warm-headed men, is no reproach to the work itself, no just ground for accusing a multitude of sober-minded men, who are patterns of strict holiness. Yet (just the contrary to what ought to have been) the opposition is great; the helps few. Hereby many are hindered from seeking faith and holiness by the false zeal of others; and some who at first began to run well are turned out of the way.

"Q. 32. What is the First advice[7] that you would give them?
"A. Watch and pray continually against pride. If God has cast it out, see that it enter no more: It is full as dangerous as desire. And you may slide back into it unawares; especially if you think there is no danger of it. 'Nay, but I ascribe all I have to God.' So you may, and be proud nevertheless. For it is pride, not only to ascribe anything we have to ourselves, but to think we have what we really have not. Mr. L---, for instance, ascribed all the light he had to God, and so far he was humble; but then he thought he had more light than any man living; and this was palpable pride. So you ascribe all the knowledge you have to God; and in this respect you are humble. But if you think you

---

[7] The advices which follow were published in a separate tract in the year 1762, under the title of "Cautions and Directions given to the Greatest Professors in the Methodist Societies," with the following motto: --

"Set the false witnesses aside,
Yet hold the truth for ever fast."

It was evidently intended to guard the people against the mischievous extravagances of George Bell and his friends, a particular account of whom is given in Mr. Wesley's Journal about that period.

have more than you really have; or if you think you are so taught of God, as no longer to need man's teaching; pride lieth at the door. Yes; you have need to be taught, not only by Mr. Morgan, by one another, by Mr. Maxfield, or me, but by the weakest Preacher in London; yea, by all men. For God sendeth by whom he will send.

"Do not therefore say to any who would advise or reprove you, 'You are blind; you cannot teach me.' Do not say, 'This is your wisdom, your carnal reason;' but calmly weigh the thing before God.

"Always remember, much grace does not imply much light. These do not always go together. As there may be much light where there is but little love, so there may be much love where there is little light. The heart has more heat than the eye; yet it cannot see. And God has wisely tempered the members of the body together, that none may say to another, 'I have no need of thee.'

"To imagine none can teach you, but those who are themselves saved from sin, is a very great and dangerous mistake. Give not place to it for a moment; it would lead you into a thousand other mistakes, and that irrecoverably. No; dominion is not founded in grace, as the madmen of the last age talked. Obey and regard them that are over you in the Lord, and do not think you know better than them. Know their place and your own; always remembering, much love does not imply much light.

"The not observing this has led some into many mistakes, and into the appearance, at least, of pride. O beware of the appearance, and the thing! Let there be in you that lowly mind which was in Christ Jesus. And. be ye likewise clothed with humility. Let it not only fill, but cover you all over. Let modesty and self-diffidence appear in all your words and actions. Let all you speak and do show that you are little, and base, and mean, and vile in your own eyes.

"As one instance of this, be always ready to own any fault you have been in. If you have at any time thought, spoke, or acted wrong, be not backward to acknowledge it. Never dream that this will hurt the cause of God; no, it will further it. Be therefore open and frank, when you are taxed with anything; do not seek either to evade or disguise it; but let it appear just as it is, and you will thereby not hinder, but adorn, the gospel.

"Q. 33. What is the Second advice which you would give them?
"A. Beware of that daughter of pride, enthusiasm. O keep at the utmost distance from it! Give no place to a heated imagination. Do not hastily ascribe things to God. Do not easily suppose dreams, voices, impressions, visions, or revelations to be from God. They may be from him. They may be from nature. They may be from the devil. Therefore, 'believe not every spirit, but try the spirits whether they be of God.' Try all things by the written word, and let all bow down before it. You are in danger of enthusiasm every hour, if you depart ever so little from Scripture; yea, or from the plain, literal meaning of any text, taken in connection with the context. And so you are, if you despise or lightly esteem reason, knowledge, or human learning; every one of which is an excellent gift of God, and may serve the noblest purposes.

"I advise you, never to use the words, wisdom, reason, or knowledge, by way of reproach. On the contrary, pray that you yourself may abound in them more and more. If you mean worldly wisdom, useless knowledge, false reasoning, say so; and throw away the chaff, but not the wheat.

"One general inlet to enthusiasm is, expecting the end without the means; the expecting knowledge, for instance, without searching the Scriptures, and consulting the children of God; the expecting spiritual strength without constant prayer, and steady watchfulness; the expecting any blessing without hearing the word of God at every opportunity.

"Some have been ignorant of this device of Satan. They have left off searching the Scriptures. They said, 'God writes all the Scriptures on my heart. Therefore, I have no need to read it.' Others thought they had not so much need of hearing, and so grew slack in attending the morning preaching. O take warning, you who are concerned herein! You have listened to the voice of a stranger. Fly back to Christ, and keep in the good old way, which was 'once delivered to the saints;' the way that even a Heathen bore testimony of: 'That the Christians rose early every day to sing hymns to Christ as God.'

"The very desire of growing in grace may sometimes be an inlet of enthusiasm. As it continually leads us to seek new grace, it may lead us unawares to seek something else new, beside new degrees of love to God and man. So it has led some to seek and fancy they had received gifts of a new kind, after a new heart, as,

        (1.) The loving God with all our mind;
        (2.) With all our soul;
        (3.) With all our strength:
        (4.) Oneness with God:
        (5.) Oneness with Christ:
        (6.) Having our life hid with Christ in God:
        (7.) Being dead with Christ:
        (8.) Rising with him:
        (9.) The sitting with him in heavenly places:
        (10.) The being taken up into his throne:
        (11.) The being in the New Jerusalem:
        (12.) The seeing the tabernacle of God come down among men:
        (13.) The being dead to all works:
        (14.) The not being liable to death, pain, or grief, or temptation.

"One ground of many of these mistakes is, the taking every fresh, strong application of any of these scriptures to the heart, to be a gift of a new kind; not knowing that several of these scriptures are not fulfilled yet; that most of the others are fulfilled when we are justified; the rest, the moment we are sanctified. It remains only to experience them in higher degrees. This is all we have to expect.

"Another ground of these, and a thousand mistakes, is, the not considering deeply, that love is the highest gift of God; humble, gentle, patient love; that all visions, revelations, manifestations whatever, are little things compared to love; and that all the gifts above-mentioned are either the same with, or infinitely inferior to, it.

"It were well you should be thoroughly sensible of this, -- 'the heaven of heavens is love.' There is nothing higher in religion; there is, in effect, nothing else; if you look for anything but more love, you are looking wide of the mark, you are getting out of the royal way. And when you are asking others, 'Have you received this or that blessing?' if you mean anything but more love, you mean wrong; you are leading them out of the way, and putting them upon a false scent. Settle it then in your heart, that from the moment God has saved you from all sin, you are to aim at nothing more, but more of that love described in the thirteenth of the Corinthians. You can go no higher than this, till you are carried into Abraham's bosom.

"I say yet again, beware of enthusiasm. Such is, the imagining you have the gift of prophesying, or of discerning of spirits, which I do not believe one of you has; no, nor ever had yet. Beware of judging people to be either right or wrong by your own feelings. This is no scriptural way of judging. O keep close to 'the law and to the testimony!'

"Q. 34. What is the Third?
"A. Beware of Antinomianism; 'making void the law,' or any part of it, 'through faith.' Enthusiasm naturally leads to this; indeed they can scarce be separated. This may steal upon you in a thousand forms, so that you cannot be too watchful against it. Take heed of everything, whether in principle or practice, which has any tendency thereto. Even that great truth, that

'Christ is the end of the law,' may betray us into it, if we do not consider that he has adopted every point of the moral law, and grafted it into the law of love. Beware of thinking, 'Because I am filled with love, I need not have so much holiness. Because I pray always, therefore I need no set time for private prayer. Because I watch always, therefore I need no particular self-examination.' Let us 'magnify the law,' the whole written word, 'and make it honorable.' Let this be our voice: 'I prize thy commandments above gold or precious stones. O what love have I unto thy law! all the day long is my study in it.' Beware of Antinomian books; particularly the works of Dr. Crisp and Mr. Saltmarsh. They contain many excellent things; and this makes them the more dangerous. O be warned in time! Do not play with fire. Do not put your hand on the hole of a cockatrice den. I entreat you, beware of bigotry. Let not your love or beneficence be confined to Methodists, so called, only; much less to that very small part of them who seem to be renewed in love; or to those who believe yours and their report. O make not this your Shibboleth! Beware of stillness; ceasing in a wrong sense from your own works. To mention one instance out of many: 'You have received,' says one, 'a great blessing. But you began to talk of it, and to do this and that; so you lost it. You should have been still.'

"Beware of self-indulgence; yea, and making a virtue of it, laughing at self-denial, and taking up the cross daily, at fasting or abstinence. Beware of censoriousness; thinking or calling them that anyways oppose you, whether in judgment or practice, blind, dead, fallen, or 'enemies to the work.' Once more, beware of Solifidianism[8]; crying nothing but, 'Believe, believe!' and condemning those as ignorant or legal who speak in a more scriptural way. At certain seasons, indeed, it may be right to treat of nothing but repentance, or merely of faith, or altogether of holiness; but, in general, our call is to declare the whole counsel of God, and to prophesy according to the analogy of faith. The written word treats of the whole and every

---

[8] Solifidianism: The belief that faith alone, without works, is sufficient for justification.

particular branch of righteousness, descending to its minutest branches; as to be sober, courteous, diligent, patient, to honor all men. So, likewise, the Holy Spirit works the same in our hearts, not merely creating desires after holiness in general, but strongly inclining us to every particular grace, leading us to every individual part of 'whatsoever is lovely.' And this with the greatest propriety: For as by works faith is made perfect; so the completing or destroying the work of faith, and enjoying the favor, or suffering the displeasure, of God, greatly depends on every single act of obedience or disobedience.

"Q. 35. What is the Fourth?
"A. Beware of sins of omission; lose no opportunity of doing good in any kind. Be zealous of good works; willingly omit no work, either of piety or mercy. Do all the good you possibly can to the bodies and souls of men. Particularly, 'thou shalt in anywise reprove thy neighbour, and not suffer sin upon him.' Be active. Give no place to indolence or sloth; give no occasion to say, 'Ye are idle, ye are idle.' Many will say so still; but let your whole spirit and behavior refute the slander. Be always employed; lose no shred of time; gather up the fragments, that nothing be lost. And whatsoever thy hand findeth to do, do it with thy might. Be 'slow to speak,' and wary in speaking. 'In a multitude of words there wanteth not sin.' Do not talk much; neither long at a time. Few can converse profitably above an hour. Keep at the utmost distance from pious chit-chat, from religious gossiping.

"Q. 36. What is the Fifth?
"A. Beware of desiring anything but God. Now you desire nothing else; every other desire is driven out; see that none enter again. Keep thyself pure; let your eye remain single, and your whole body shall be full of light. Admit no desire of pleasing food, or any other pleasure of sense; no desire of pleasing the eye or the imagination, by anything grand, or new, or beautiful; no desire of money, of praise, or esteem; of happiness in any creature. You may bring these desires back;

but you need not; you need feel them no more. O stand fast in the liberty wherewith Christ hath made you free.

"Be patterns to all, of denying yourselves, and taking up your cross daily. Let them see that you make no account of any pleasure which does not bring you nearer to God, nor regard any pain which does; that you simply aim at pleasing him, whether by doing or suffering; that the constant language of your heart, with regard to pleasure or pain, honor or dishonor, riches or poverty, is,

'All's alike to me, so I
In my Lord may live and die!'

Q. 37. What is the Sixth?
A. Beware of schism, of making a rent in the Church of Christ. That inward disunion, the members ceasing to have a reciprocal love one for another, (1 Cor. 12:25,) is the very root of all contention, and every outward separation. Beware of everything tending thereto. Beware of a dividing spirit; shun whatever has the least aspect that way. Therefore, say not, 'I am of Paul or of Apollos;' the very thing which occasioned the schism at Corinth. Say not, 'This is my Preacher; the best Preacher in England. Give me him, and take all the rest.' All this tends to breed or foment division, to disunite those whom God hath joined. Do not despise or run down any Preacher; do not exalt any one above the rest, lest you hurt both him and the cause of God. On the other hand, do not bear hard upon any by reason of some incoherency or inaccuracy of expression; no, nor for some mistakes, were they really such.

"Likewise, if you would avoid schism, observe every rule of the Society, and of the Bands, for conscience sake. Never omit meeting your Class or Band; never absent yourself from any public meeting. These are the very sinews of our Society; and whatever weakens, or tends to weaken, our regard for these, or our exactness in attending them, strikes at the very root of our community. As one saith, 'That part of our economy, the private weekly meetings for prayer, examination, and particular exhortation, has been the greatest means of deepening and confirming every blessing that was received by the word preached, and of diffusing it to others, who could not attend the public ministry; whereas, without this religious connection and intercourse, the most ardent attempts, by mere preaching, have proved of no lasting use.'

"Suffer not one thought of separating from your brethren, whether their opinions agree with yours or not. Do not dream that any man sins in not believing you, in not taking your word; or that this or that opinion is essential to the work, and both must stand or fall together. Beware of impatience of contradiction. Do not condemn or think hardly of those who cannot see just as you see, or who judge it their duty to contradict you, whether in a great thing or a small. I fear some of us have thought hardly of others, merely because they contradicted what we affirmed. All this tends to division; and, by everything of this kind, we are teaching them an evil lesson against ourselves.

"O beware of touchiness, of testiness, not bearing to be spoken to; starting at the least word; and flying from those who do not implicitly receive mine or another's sayings!

"Expect contradiction and opposition, together with crosses of various kinds. Consider the words of St. Paul: 'To you it is given, in the behalf of Christ,' -- for his sake, as a fruit of his death and intercession for you, -- 'not only to believe, but also to suffer for his sake.' (Phil. 1:29.) *It is given!* God gives you this opposition or reproach; it is a fresh token of his love. And will you disown the Giver; or spurn his gift, and count it a misfortune? Will you not rather say, 'Father, the hour is come, that thou shouldest be glorified: Now thou givest thy child to suffer something for thee: Do with me according to thy will?' Know that these things, far from being hindrances to the work of God, or to your soul, unless by your own fault, are not only unavoidable in the course of Providence, but profitable, yea, necessary, for you. Therefore, receive them from God (not from chance) with willingness, with thankfulness. Receive them from men with humility, meekness, yieldingness, gentleness, sweetness. Why should not even your outward appearance and manner be soft? Remember the character of Lady Cutts: It was said of the Roman Emperor Titus, Never any one came displeased from him. But it might be said of her, Never any one went displeased to her: So secure were all of the kind and favorable reception which they would meet with from her.

"Beware of tempting others to separate from you. Give no offence which can possibly be avoided; see that your practice be in all things suitable to your profession, adorning the doctrine of God our Savior. Be particularly careful in speaking of yourself: You may not, indeed, deny the work of God; but speak of it, when you are called thereto, in the most inoffensive manner possible. Avoid all magnificent, pompous words; indeed, you need give it no general name; neither perfection, sanctification, the second blessing, nor the having attained. Rather speak of the particulars which God has wrought for you. You may say, 'At such a time I felt a change which I am not able to express; and since that time, I have not felt pride, or self-will, or anger, or unbelief; nor anything but a fullness of love to God and to all mankind.' And answer any other plain question that is asked with modesty and simplicity.

"And if any of you should at any time fall from what you now are, if you should again feel pride or unbelief, or any temper from which you are now delivered; do not deny, do not hide, do not disguise it at all, at the peril of your soul. At all events go to one in whom you can confide, and speak just what you feel. God will enable him to speak a word in season, which shall be health to your soul. And surely He will again lift up your head, and cause the bones that have been broken to rejoice.

"Q. 38. What is the last advice that you would give them?

"A. Be exemplary in all things; particularly in outward things, (as in dress,) in little things, in the laying out of your money, (avoiding every needless expense,) in deep, steady seriousness, and in the solidity and usefulness of all your conversation. So shall you be a light shining in a dark place. So shall you daily grow in grace, till an entrance be ministered unto you abundantly into the everlasting kingdom of our Lord Jesus Christ.

"Most of the preceding advices are strongly enforced in the following reflections; which I recommend to your deep and frequent consideration, next to the Holy Scriptures: --

"(1.) The sea is an excellent figure of the fullness of God, and that of the blessed Spirit. For as the rivers all return into the sea; so the bodies, the souls, and the good works of the righteous, return into God, to live there in his eternal repose.

"Although all the graces of God depend on his mere bounty, yet is He pleased generally to attach them to the prayers, the instructions, and the holiness of those with whom we are. By strong though invisible attractions He draws some souls through their intercourse with others.

"The sympathies formed by grace far surpass those formed by nature.

"The truly devout show that passions as naturally flow from true as from false love; so deeply sensible are they of the goods and evils of those whom they love for God's sake. But this can only be comprehended by those who understand the language of love.

"The bottom of the soul may be in repose, even while we are in many outward troubles; just as the bottom of the sea is calm, while the surface is strongly agitated.

"The best helps to growth in grace are the ill usage, the affronts, and the losses which befall us. We should receive them with all thankfulness, as preferable to all others, were it only on this account, that our will has no part therein.

"The readiest way to escape from our sufferings is, to be willing they should endure as long as God pleases.

"If we suffer persecution and affliction in a right manner, we attain a larger measure of conformity to Christ, by a due improvement of one of these occasions, than we could have done merely by imitating his mercy, in abundance of good works.

"One of the greatest evidences of God's love to those that love him is, to send them afflictions, with grace to bear them.

"Even in the greatest afflictions, we ought to testify to God, that, in receiving them from his hand, we feel pleasure in the midst of the pain, from being afflicted by Him who loves us, and whom we love.

"The readiest way which God takes to draw a man to himself is, to afflict him in that he loves most, and with good reason; and to cause this affliction to arise from some good action done with a single eye; because nothing can more clearly show him the emptiness of what is most lovely and desirable in the world.

"(2.) True resignation consists in a thorough conformity to the whole will of God; who wills and does all (excepting sin) which comes to pass in the world. In order to this we have only to embrace all events, good and bad, as His will.

"In the greatest afflictions which can befall the just, either from heaven or earth, they remain immovable in peace, and perfectly submissive to God, by an inward, loving regard to Him, uniting in one all the powers of their souls.

"We ought quietly to suffer whatever befalls us, to bear the defects of others and our own, to confess them to God in secret prayer, or with groans which cannot be uttered; but never to speak a sharp or peevish word, nor to murmur or repine; but thoroughly willing that God should treat you in the manner that pleases him. We are his lambs, and therefore ought to be ready to suffer, even to the death, without complaining.

"We are to bear with those we cannot amend, and to be content with offering them to God. This is true resignation. And since He has borne our infirmities, we may well bear those of each other for His sake.

"To abandon all, to strip one's self of all, in order to seek and to follow Jesus Christ naked to Bethlehem, where he was born; naked to the hall where he was scourged; and naked to Calvary, where he died on the cross, is so great a mercy, that neither the thing, nor the knowledge of it is given to any, but through faith in the Son of God.

"(3.) There is no love of God without patience, and no patience without lowliness and sweetness of spirit.

"Humility and patience are the surest proofs of the increase of love.

"Humility alone unites patience with love; without which it is impossible to draw profit from suffering; or indeed, to avoid complaint, especially when we think we have given no occasion for what men make us suffer.

"True humility is a kind of self-annihilation; and this is the centre of all virtues.

"A soul returned to God ought to be attentive to everything which is said to him, on the head of salvation, with a desire to profit thereby.

"Of the sins which God has pardoned, let nothing remain but a deeper humility in the heart, and a stricter regulation in our words, in our actions, and in our sufferings.

"(4.) The bearing men, and suffering evils in meekness and silence, is the sum of a Christian life.

"God is the first object of our love: Its next office is, to bear the defects of others. And we should begin the practice of this amidst our own household.

"We should chiefly exercise our love towards them who most shock either our way of thinking, or our temper, or our knowledge, or the desire we have, that others should be as virtuous as we wish to be ourselves.

"(5.) God hardly gives his Spirit even to those whom he has established in grace, if they do not pray for it on all occasions, not only once, but many times.

"God does nothing but in answer to prayer; and even they who have been converted to God without praying for it themselves, (which is exceeding rare,) were not without the prayers of others. Every new victory which a soul gains is the effect of a new prayer.

"On every occasion of uneasiness, we should retire to prayer, that we may give place to the grace and light of God and then form our resolutions, without being in any pain about what success they may have.

In the greatest temptations, a single look to Christ, and the barely pronouncing his name, suffices to overcome the wicked one, so it be done with confidence and calmness of spirit.

God's command to "pray without ceasing' is founded on the necessity we have of his grace to preserve the life of God in the soul, which can no more subsist one moment without it, than the body can without air.

Whether we think of; or speak to, God, whether we act or suffer for him, all is prayer, when we have no other object than his love, and the desire of pleasing him.

"All that a Christian does, even in eating and sleeping, is prayer, when it is done in simplicity, according to the order of God, without either adding to or diminishing from it by his own choice.

"Prayer continues in the desire of the heart, though the understanding be employed on outward things.

"In souls filled with love, the desire to please God is a continual prayer.

"As the furious hate which the devil bears us is termed the roaring of a lion, so our vehement love may be termed crying after God.

"God only requires of his adult children, that their hearts be truly purified, and that they offer him continually the wishes and vows that naturally spring from perfect love. For these desires, being the genuine fruits of love, are the most perfect prayers that can spring from it.

(6.) It is scarce conceivable how strait the way is wherein God leads them that follow him; and how dependent on him we must be, unless we are wanting in our faithfulness to him.

"It is hardly credible of how great consequence before God the smallest things are; and what great inconveniences some times follow those which appear to be light faults.

As a very little dust will disorder a clock, and the least sand will obscure our sight, so the least grain of sin which is upon the heart will hinder its right motion towards God.

"We ought to be in the church as the saints are in heaven, and in the house as the holiest men are in the church; doing our work in the house as we pray in the church; worshipping God from the ground of the heart.

"We should be continually laboring to cut off all the useless things that surround us; and God usually retrenches the superfluities of our souls in the same proportion as we do those of our bodies.

"The best means of resisting the devil is, to destroy whatever of the world remains in us, in order to raise for God, upon its ruins, a building all of love. Then shall we begin, in this fleeting life, to love God as we shall love him in eternity.

"We scarce conceive how easy it is to rob God of his due, in our friendship with the most virtuous persons, until they are torn from us by death. But if this loss produce lasting sorrow, that is a clear proof that we had before two treasures, between which we divided our heart.

"(7.) If, after having renounced all, we do not watch incessantly, and beseech God to accompany our vigilance with his, we shall be again entangled and overcome.

"As the most dangerous winds may enter at little openings, so the devil never enters more dangerously than by little unobserved incidents, which seem to be nothing, yet insensibly open the heart to great temptations.

"It is good to renew ourselves, from time to time, by closely examining the state of our souls, as if we had never done it before; for nothing tends more to the full assurance of faith, than to keep ourselves by this means in humility, and the exercise of all good works.

"To continual watchfulness and prayer ought to be added continual employment. For grace fills a vacuum as well as nature; and the devil fills whatever God does not fill.

"There is no faithfulness like that which ought to be between a guide of souls and the person directed by him. They ought continually to regard each other in God, and closely to examine themselves, whether all their thoughts are pure, and all their words directed with Christian discretion. Other affairs are only the things of men; but these are peculiarly the things of God.

"(8.) The words of St. Paul, 'No man can call Jesus Lord, but by the Holy Ghost,' show us the necessity of eyeing God in our good works, and even in our minutest thoughts; knowing that none are pleasing to him, but those which he forms in us and with us. From hence we learn that we cannot serve him, unless he use our tongue, hands, and heart, to do by himself and his Spirit whatever he would have us to do.

"If we were not utterly impotent, our good works would be our own property; whereas now they belong wholly to God, because they proceed from him and his grace: While raising our works, and making them all divine, he honors himself in us through them.

"One of the principal rules of religion is, to lose no occasion of serving God. And, since he is invisible to our eyes, we are to serve him in our neighbor; which he receives as if done to himself in person, standing visibly before us.

"God does not love men that are inconstant, nor good works that are intermitted. Nothing is pleasing to him, but what has a resemblance of his own immutability.

"A constant attention to the work which God entrusts us with is a mark of solid piety.

"Love fasts when it can, and as much as it can. It leads to all the ordinances of God, and employs itself in all the outward works whereof it is capable. It flies, as it were, like Elijah over the plain, to find God upon his holy mountain.

"God is so great, that he communicates greatness to the least thing that is done for his service.

"Happy are they who are sick, yea, or lose their life, for having done a good work.

"God frequently conceals the part which his children have in the conversion of other souls. Yet one may boldly say, that person who long groans before him for the conversion of another, whenever that soul is converted to God, is one of the chief causes of it.

"Charity cannot be practiced right, unless, First, we exercise it the moment God gives the occasion; and, Secondly, retire the instant after to offer it to God by humble thanksgiving. And this for three reasons: First, to render him what we have received from him. The Second, to avoid the dangerous temptation which springs from the very goodness of these works. And the Third, to unite ourselves to God, in whom the soul expands itself in prayer, with all the graces we have received, and the good works we have done, to draw from him new strength against the bad effects which these very works may produce in us, if we do not make use of the antidotes which God has ordained against these poisons. The true means to be filled anew with the riches of grace is thus to strip ourselves of it; and without this it is extremely difficult not to grow faint in the practice of good works.

"Good works do not receive their last perfection, till they, as it were, lose themselves in God. This is a kind of death to them, resembling that of our bodies, which will not attain their highest life, their immortality, till they lose themselves in the glory of our souls, or rather of God, wherewith they shall be filled. And it is only what they had of earthly and mortal, which good works lose by this spiritual death.

"Fire is the symbol of love; and the love of God is the principle and the end of all our good works. But truth surpasses figure; and the fire of divine love has this advantage over material fire, that it can re-ascend to its source, and raise thither with it all the good works which it produces. And by this means it prevents their being corrupted by pride, vanity, or any evil mixture. But this cannot be done otherwise than by making these good works in a spiritual manner die in God, by a deep gratitude, which plunges the soul in him as in an abyss, with all that it is, and all the grace and works for which it is indebted to him; a gratitude, whereby the soul seems to empty itself of them, that they may return to their source, as rivers seem willing to empty themselves, when they pour themselves with all their waters into the sea.

"When we have received any favor from God, we ought to retire, if not into our closets, into our hearts, and say, 'I come, Lord, to restore to thee what thou hast given; and I freely relinquish it, to enter again into my own nothingness. For what is the most perfect creature in heaven or earth in thy presence, but a void capable of being filled with thee and by thee; as the air, which is void and dark, is capable of being filled with the light of the sun, who withdraws it every day to restore it the next, there being nothing in the air that either appropriates this light or resists it? O give me the same facility of receiving and restoring thy grace and good works! I say, *thine;* for I acknowledge the root from which they spring is in thee, and not in me.'"

26. In the year 1764, upon a review of the whole subject, I wrote down the sum of what I had observed in the following short propositions:

"(1.) There is such a thing as perfection; for it is again and again mentioned in Scripture.

"(2.) It is not so early as justification; for justified persons are to 'go on unto perfection.' (Heb. 6:1.)

"(3.) It is not so late as death; for St. Paul speaks of living men that were perfect. (Phil. 3:15.)

"(4.) It is not absolute. Absolute perfection belongs not to man, nor to angels, but to God alone.

"(5.) It does not make a man infallible: None is infallible, while he remains in the body.

"(6.) Is it sinless? It is not worth while to contend for a term. It is 'salvation from sin.'

"(7.) It is 'perfect love.' (1 John 4:18.) This is the essence of it; its properties, or inseparable fruits, are, rejoicing evermore, praying without ceasing, and in everything giving thanks. (1 Thess. 5:16, &c.)

"(8.) It is improvable. It is so far from lying in an indivisible point, from being incapable of increase, that one perfected in love may grow in grace far swifter than he did before.

"(9.) It is amissible, capable of being lost; of which we have numerous instances. But we were not thoroughly convinced of this, till five or six years ago.

"(10.) It is constantly both preceded and followed by a gradual work.

"(11.) But is it in itself instantaneous or not? In examining this, let us go on step by step.

"An instantaneous change has been wrought in some believers: None can deny this.

"Since that change, they enjoy perfect love; they feel this, and this alone; they rejoice evermore, pray without ceasing, and in everything give thanks. Now, this is all that I mean by perfection; therefore, these are witnesses of the perfection which I preach.

'But in some this change was not instantaneous.' They did not perceive the instant when it was wrought. It is often difficult to perceive the instant when a man dies; yet there is an instant in which life ceases. And if ever sin ceases, there must be a last moment of its existence, and a first moment of our deliverance from it.

'But if they have this love now, they will lose it.' They may; but they need not. And whether they do or no, they have it now; they now experience what we teach. They now are all love; they now rejoice, pray, and praise without ceasing.

'However, sin is only suspended in them; it is not destroyed.' Call it which you please. They are all love to-day; and they take no thought for the morrow.

'But this doctrine has been much abused.' So has that of justification by faith. But that is no reason for giving up either this or any other scriptural doctrine. 'When you wash your child,' as one speaks, 'throw away the water; but do not throw away the child.'

'But those who think they are saved from sin say they have no need of the merits of Christ.' They say just the contrary. Their language   is,   --

> 'Every moment, Lord, I want
> The merit of thy death!'

They never before had so deep, so unspeakable, a conviction of the need of Christ in all his offices as they have now.

"Therefore, all our Preachers should make a point of preaching perfection to believers constantly, strongly, and explicitly; and all believers should mind this one thing, and continually agonize for it."

27. I have now done what I proposed. I have given a plain and simple account of the manner wherein I first received the doctrine of perfection, and the sense wherein I received, and

wherein I do receive, and teach it to this day. I have declared the whole and every part of what I mean by that scriptural expression. I have drawn the picture of it at full length, without either disguise or covering. And I would now ask any impartial person, What is there so frightful herein? Whence is all this outcry, which, for these twenty years and upwards, has been made throughout the kingdom; as if all Christianity were destroyed, and all religion torn up by the roots? Why is it, that the very name of perfection has been cast out of the mouths of Christians; yea, exploded and abhorred, as if it contained the most pernicious heresy? Why have the Preachers of it been hooted at, like mad dogs, even by men that fear God; nay, and by some of their own children, some whom they, under God, had begotten through the gospel? What reason is there for this, or what pretence? Reason; sound reason, there is none. It is impossible there should. But pretences there are, and those in great abundance. Indeed, there is ground to fear that, with some who treat us thus, it is mere pretence; that it is no more than a copy of their countenance, from the beginning to the end. They wanted, they sought, occasion against me; and here they found what they sought. "This is Mr. Wesley's doctrine! He preaches perfection!" He does; yet this is not his doctrine any more than it is yours, or any one's else, that is a Minister of Christ. For it is His doctrine, peculiarly, emphatically His; it is the doctrine of Jesus Christ. Those are his words, not mine: εσεσθε ουν υμεις τελειοι ωσπερ ο πατηρ υμων ο εν τοις ουρανοις τελειος εστιν -- "Ye shall therefore be perfect, as your Father who is in heaven is perfect." And who says, ye shall not; or, at least, not till your soul is separated from the body? It is the doctrine of St. Paul, the doctrine of St. James, of St. Peter, and St. John; and no otherwise Mr. Wesley's, than as it is the doctrine of every one who preaches the pure and the whole gospel. I tell you, as plain as I can speak, where and when I found this. I found it in the oracles of God, in the Old and New Testament; when I read them with no other view or desire but to save my own soul. But whosesoever this doctrine is, I pray you, what harm is there in it? Look at it again; survey it on every side, and that with the closest attention. In one view, it is purity of intention, dedicating all the life to God. It is the giving God all our heart; it is one desire and design ruling all our tempers. It is the devoting, not a part, but all our soul, body, and substance to God. In another view, it is all the mind which was in Christ, enabling us to walk as Christ walked. It is the circumcision of the heart from all filthiness, all inward as well as outward pollution. It is a renewal of the heart in the whole image of God, the full likeness of Him that created it. In yet another, it is the loving God with all our heart, and our neighbor as ourselves. Now, take it in which of these views you please, (for there is no material difference,) and this is the whole and sole perfection, as a train of writings prove to a demonstration, which I have believed and taught for these forty years, from the year 1725 to the year 1765.

28. Now let this perfection appear in its native form, and who can speak one word against it? Will any dare to speak against loving the Lord our God with all our heart, and our neighbor as ourselves? against a renewal of heart, not only in part, but in the whole image of God? Who is he that will open his mouth against being cleansed from all pollution both of flesh and spirit; or against having all the mind that was in Christ, and walking in all things as Christ walked? What man, who calls himself a Christian, has the hardiness to object to the devoting, not a part, but all our soul, body, and substance to God? What serious man would oppose the giving God all our heart, and the having one design ruling all our tempers? I say, again, let this perfection appear in its own shape, and who will fight against it? It must be disguised before it can be opposed. It must be covered with a bear-skin first, or even the wild beasts of the people will scarce be induced to worry it. But whatever these do, let not the children of God any longer fight against the image of God. Let not the members of Christ say anything against having the whole mind that was in Christ. Let not those who are alive to God oppose the dedicating all our life to Him. Why should you who have his love shed abroad in your heart withstand the giving him all your heart? Does not all that is within you cry out, "O who that loves can love enough?" What pity that those who desire and design to please him should have any other design or

desire! much more, that they should dread, as a fatal delusion, yea, abhor as an abomination to God, the having this one desire and design ruling every temper! Why should devout men be afraid of devoting all their soul, body, and substance to God? Why should those who love Christ count it a damnable error, to think we may have all the mind that was in him? We allow, we contend, that we are justified freely through the righteousness and the blood of Christ. And why are you so hot against us, because we expect likewise to be sanctified wholly through his Spirit? We look for no favor either from the open servants of sin, or from those who have only the form of religion. But how long will you who worship God in spirit, who are "circumcised with the circumcision not made with hands," set our battle in array against those who seek a entire circumcision of heart, who thirst to be cleansed "from all filthiness of flesh and spirit," and to "perfect holiness in the fear of God?" Are we your enemies, because we look for a full deliverance from that "carnal mind which is enmity against God?" Nay, we are your brethren, your fellow-laborers in the vineyard of our Lord, your companions in the kingdom and patience of Jesus. Although this we confess, (if we are fools therein, yet as fools bear with us,) we do expect to love God with all our heart, and our neighbor as ourselves. Yea, we do believe, that he will in this world so cleanse the thoughts of our hearts, by the inspiration of his Holy Spirit, that we shall perfectly love him, and worthily magnify his holy name."

BRIEF THOUGHTS ON CHRISTIAN PERFECTION

SOME thoughts occurred to my mind this morning concerning Christian perfection, and the manner and time of receiving it, which I believe may be useful to set down.

1. By perfection I mean the humble, gentle, patient love of God, and our neighbor, ruling our tempers, words, and actions.

I do not include an impossibility of falling from it, either in part or in whole. Therefore, I retract several expressions in our

Hymns, which partly express, partly imply, such an impossibility.

And I do not contend for the term *sinless,* though I do not object against it.

2. As to the manner. I believe this perfection is always wrought in the soul by a simple act of faith; consequently, in an instant.

But I believe a gradual work, both preceding and following that instant.

3. As to the time. I believe this instant generally is the instant of death, the moment before the soul leaves the body. But I believe it may be ten, twenty, or forty years before.

I believe it is usually many years after justification; but that it may be within five years or five months after it, I know no conclusive argument to the contrary.

If it must be many years after justification, I would be glad to know how many. *Pretium quotus arroget annus?*

And how many days or months, or even years, can any one allow to be between perfection and death? How far from justification must it be; and how near to death?

LONDON, Jan. 27, 1767.

PART TWO:

SCRIPTURE DOCTRINE OF CHRISTIAN PERFECTION

by

ASA MAHAN

DEAR BROTHER WARNER,

It is now about forty years since, after the most careful and prayerful examination of the Word of God upon the subject, I embraced the views set forth in my work, entitled "Christian Perfection." All my subsequent examinations, and all my observations of facts, from that period to the present, have tended but in one direction—to confirm and render absolute my confidence in the truth and supreme importance of those views. Our SAVIOUR has, Himself, stated definitely the condition on which the world will come to *know,* that "he came forth from God." "I in them, and thou in me, that they may be made *perfect* in one; and that the world may *know* that thou hast sent me, and hast loved them as thou hast loved me." My life-labours are, therefore, supremely directed to this one end—"the perfecting of the saints."

Yours in the hands of Christ,

ASA MAHAN.

INTRODUCTION

MORE than twenty years ago a good brother said to us, "I have a good book here I will give you, and if you will read it through on your knees it will do you five pounds' worth of good." We wanted to get good, and accepted the book; it was "Christian Perfection, by Dr. Mahan." We read it through on our knees, and got good—good, not to be balanced by five pound notes. We knew something of the experience of Christian Perfection, and this book greatly tended to show its scriptural foundation, and to establish us in the faith. We never read any other book through on our knees, save our Bible; we have thus read that annually every year since, and every year of our life are more fully convinced that it is God's will that His people should be fully saved from all sin, and be "filled with the Holy Ghost." During the last twenty years we have read almost everything on the subject we could lay our hands on, but on the whole, know of no human production which more clearly sets forth the scriptural character of this great grace than does the present work. Meeting with the author, he readily gave us permission to reprint his work, for the edification and salvation of those interested in the subject.

The question is not, "What is the experience of the Church?" but, "What are the provisions of grace?" The experience of the Church may be far too low, and must never be our standard of appeal. God has more light to pour upon the world than we have yet seen; and more grace to bestow than we have yet received. The question with which we should approach God's word is, "What is my Father's will concerning me?" George Fox, the Quaker, preached the Gospel of salvation from sin—Antinomians met him at his open air meetings, and contended that we could never get further in this world than, "Who shall deliver me from the body of this death?" They would proceed to quote passages which they supposed supported their views, but the Quaker stopt them with, "Nay, friend, thou must not take God's Holy Word to prove thy dirty doctrine!" And he was right. God's Holy Word enjoins a holy religion. A good brother says: "The doctrine we contend for is not limited to a bare and questionable place, a doubtful and uncertain existence in the holy records, but is repeatedly and abundantly.—explicitly, and with great clearness—embodied as a cardinal feature throughout the whole system. It breathes in the prophecy—thunders in the law—murmurs in the narrative—whispers in the promises—supplicates in the prayers—sparkles in the poetry—resounds in the songs—speaks in the types—glows in the imagery—voices in the language—and beams in the spirit of the whole scheme, from its Alpha to its Omega—from its beginning to its end. Holiness! Holiness needed! Holiness required! Holiness offered! Holiness attainable! Holiness a present duty—a present privilege—a present enjoyment, is the progress and completeness of its wondrous theme! It is the truth glowing all over—webbing all through revelation; the glorious truth which sparkles, and sings, and shouts in all its history, and biography, and poetry, and prophecy, and precept, and promise, and prayer; the great central truth of the system. The wonder is that all do not see, that any rise up to question, a truth so conspicuous, so glorious, so full of comfort."

The experience of Dr. Mahan, as related towards the end of the work, goes to show that the reception of this grace was to him what the Old Methodists would call the "*Second Blessing*." He was a Professor in a College, and a successful Minister of the Gospel, and yet but a babe in grace. He had pointed many sinners to Christ for justification, and yet often felt as if he would give the world, if he had it, if some one would help him into the enjoyment of that which he dimly saw was in reversion for him.

However, the time of his deliverance came, and now for about forty years he has lived and preached on a higher plane, and has seen a complete revolution of thought on this subject in the Church with which he is associated. His testimony is the more important, in the estimation of some persons, coming as it does from outside Methodism, and yet according with her acknowledged standards. A good brother said to us, some time since, when we had been insisting on the doctrine as a present privilege, to be received at once by faith, that there were some amongst us who were teaching that it was a grace into which we were *to grow*, but he had always believed we were to receive it *at once* as God's gift, and then *grow in it*. That was evidently Mr. Wesley's view of the subject. In the early part of the Methodist Revival, many were brought into the enjoyment of full salvation. Concerning these, he said:

"Not trusting to the testimony of others, I carefully examined most of these myself; and every one (after the most careful inquiry, I have not found an exception either in Great Britain or Ireland), has declared that his deliverance from sin *was instantaneous; that the change was wrought in a moment.* Had half of these, or one third, or one in twenty declared that it was gradually wrought in them, I should have believed this with regard to them, and thought that some were gradually sanctified, and some instantaneously. But as I have not found in so long a space of time a single person speaking thus, as all who believe they are sanctified, declare with one voice *that the change was wrought in a moment,* I cannot but believe that *sanctification is commonly, if not always, an instantaneous work.*"

We heard Dr. Mahan, now in his seventy-sixth year, preaching the doctrine of holiness with uncommon energy of body and mind, and we asked him to give us a line to prefix to this issue of his work, saying if his opinions were still unchanged, and the following day we received the communication which we print.

We have ventured on a large edition, in order to be able to offer it at a low price, and now send it forth in God's name to do His work. We hope to spend our days in sanctified effort to "fill Jerusalem with this doctrine," and for Christ and His Church are yours, in the King's Highway of Holiness.

GEORGE WARNER.
65, Stepney Green, London, E.,
January, 1875.

CHRISTIAN PERFECTION

DISCOURSE I

THE NATURE OF CHRISTIAN PERFECTION

"Be ye therefore perfect, even as your Father in heaven is perfect." ~ *Matt. v*: 48.

Two important features of this passage demand our special attention:
  1. The demand, "Be perfect."
  2. The nature and extent of the command; "even as your Father in heaven is perfect."

In other words, we are here required to be as perfect, as holy, as free from all sin, in our sphere as creatures, as God is in his as our Creator and our Sovereign.

My design in the present discourse is to answer this one question, — What is perfection in holiness? In answering this inquiry, I would remark, that perfection in holiness implies a full and perfect discharge of our entire duty, of all existing obligations in respect to God and all other beings. It is perfect obedience to the moral law. It is "loving the Lord our God with

---

all our heart, and with all our soul, and with all our strength, and our neighbour as ourselves." It implies the entire absence of all selfishness, and the perpetual presence and all-pervading influence of pure and perfect love. "Love is the fulfilling of the law."

In the Christian, perfection in holiness implies the consecration of his whole being to Christ—the subjection of all his powers and susceptibilities to the control of one principle,—"faith on the son of God." This is what the moral law demands of him in his circumstances. Were the Christian in that state in which he should "eat and drink, and do all that he does for the glory of God," in which his eye should be perfectly single to this one object; or in which the action of all his powers should be controlled by faith, which works by love, he would then, I suppose, have attained to a state of entire sanctification—his character would be "perfect and entire, wanting nothing." Every duty to every being in existence would be discharged.

It will readily be perceived, that perfect holiness, as above described, does not imply *perfect wisdom,* the exclusive attribute of God. The Scriptures, speaking of the human nature of Christ, affirm, that he "increased in wisdom." This surely does not imply that his holiness was less perfect at one time than at another. So of the Christian. His holiness may be perfect in *kind,* but *finite* in *degree,* and in this sense imperfect; because his wisdom and knowledge are limited, and in this sense imperfect.

Holiness, in a creature, may also be perfect, and yet progressive—progressive, not in its nature, but in degree. To be perfect, it must be progressive in the sense last mentioned, if the powers of the subject are progressive. He is perfect in holiness, whose love at each successive moment corresponds with the extent of his powers. "If there be first a willing mind, it is accepted according to that a man hath, and not according to that he hath not."

Hence I remark that perfection in holiness does not imply, that we now love God with all the strength and intensity with which redeemed spirits in heaven love him. The depth and intensity of our love depend, under all circumstances, upon the vigor and reach of our powers, and the extent and distinctness of our vision of Divine truth. "Here we see through a glass darkly; there face to face." Here our powers are comparatively weak; there they will be endowed with an immortal and tireless vigor. In each and every sphere, perfection in holiness implies a strength and intensity of love corresponding with the reach of our powers, and the extent and distinctness of our vision of truth in that particular sphere. The child is perfect in holiness who perpetually exercises a filial and affectionate obedience to all the Divine requisitions, and loves God with all the powers which it possesses as a child. The man is perfect in holiness who exercises the same supreme and affectionate obedience to all that God requires, and loves him to the full extent of his knowledge and strength as a man. The saint on earth is perfect, when he loves with all the strength and intensity rendered practicable by the extent of his knowledge and reach of his powers in his present sphere. The saint in heaven will be favored with a seraph's vision, and a seraph's power. To be perfect there, he must love and adore with a seraph's vigor, and burn with a seraph's fire.

To present this subject in a somewhat more distinct and expanded form, the attention of the reader is now invited to a few remarks upon 1Thes. 5:23,—"And the very God of peace sanctify you wholly; and I pray God your whole spirit and soul and body be preserved blameless unto the coming of our Lord Jesus Christ." The prayer of the apostle for Christians here is, in the language of Dr. Scott, that the "very God of peace" "would sanctify them wholly, and in respect to their entire nature, as consisting of a rational and immortal soul, an animal life, with its various sensitive appetites, and a material body; that every sense, member, organ, and faculty might be completely purified, and devoted to the service of God; and that thus they might be preserved blameless till the coming of Christ." In short, the prayer of the apostle is, that all the powers and susceptibilities of our being may not only be purified from all that is unholy, but wholly sanctified and devoted to Christ, and forever preserved in that state. Now, the powers and susceptibilities of our nature are all comprehended in the following enumeration:—the will, the intellect, and our mental and physical susceptibilities and propensities. The question to which the special attention of the reader is invited is this: When are we in a perfectly sanctified and blameless state, in respect to the action of all these powers and susceptibilities?

1. That we be in a perfectly sanctified and blameless state in regard to our wills, implies, that the action of all our voluntary powers be in entire conformity to the will of God; that every choice, every preference, and every volition, be controlled by a filial regard to the Divine requisitions. The perpetual language of the heart must be, "Lord, what wilt thou have me do?"

2. That we "be preserved blameless" in regard to our intellect, does not imply that we never think of what is evil. If this were so, Christ was not blameless, because he thought of the temptations of Satan. Nor could the Christian repel what is evil, as he is required to do. To repel evil, the evil itself must be before the mind, as an object of thought.

To be blameless in respect to the action of our intellectual powers, does imply:

> A. That every thought of evil be instantly suppressed and repelled.
> B. That they be constantly employed on the inquiry, what is the truth and will of God, and by what means we may best meet the demands of the great law of love.
> C. That they be employed in the perpetual contemplation of "whatsoever things are true, whatsoever things are honest, whatsoever things are just, whatsoever things are pure, whatsoever things are lovely, whatsoever things are of good report; if there be

any virtue, and if there be any praise," in thinking of these things also. When the intellectual powers are thus employed, they are certainly in a blameless state.

3. That our feelings and mental susceptibilities be preserved blameless, does not imply that they are, at all times and circumstances, in the same intensity of excitement, or in the same identical state. This the powers and laws of our being forbid. Nor, in that case, could we obey the command, "Rejoice with those that do rejoice, and weep with those that weep." Nor does it imply that no feelings can exist in the mind, which, under the circumstances then present, it would be improper to indulge. A Christian, for example, may feel a very strong desire to speak for Christ under circumstances when it would be improper for him to speak. The feeling itself is proper. But we must be guided by wisdom from above in respect to the question, when and where we are to give utterance to our feelings.

That our feelings and mental susceptibilities be in a blameless state, does imply:

> A. That they all be held in perfect and perpetual subjection to the will of God.
> B. That they be in perfect and perpetual harmony with the truth and will of God as apprehended by the intellect, and thus constituting a spotless mirror, through which there shall be a perfect reflection of whatsoever things are "true," "honest," just," "pure," "lovely," and of "good report."

4. That our "bodies be preserved blameless," does not, of course, imply that they are free from fatigue, disease, or death. Nor does it imply that no desire be excited through our physical propensities, which, under existing circumstances, it would be unlawful to indulge. The feeling of hunger in Christ, under circumstances in which indulgence was not proper, was not

sinful. The consent of the will to gratify the feeling, and not the feeling itself, renders us sinners.

That we be preserved in a sanctified and blameless state in respect to our bodies, does imply:

> A. That we endeavor to acquaint ourselves with all the laws of our physical constitution.
> B. That in regard to food, drink, and dress, and in regard to the indulgence of all our appetites and physical propensities, there be a sacred and undeviating conformity to these laws.
> C. That every unlawful desire be instantly suppressed, and that all our propensities be held in perfect subjection to the will of God.
> D. That our bodies, with all our physical powers and propensities, be "presented to God as a living sacrifice, holy, and acceptable," to be employed in his service.

Such is Christian Perfection. It is the consecration of our whole being to Christ, and the perpetual employment of all our powers in his service. It is the perfect assimilation of our entire character to that of Christ, having at all times, and under all circumstances, the "same mind that was also in Christ Jesus." It is, in the language of Mr. Wesley, "in one view, purity of intention, dedicating all the life to God. It is the giving God all the heart; it is one desire and design ruling all our tempers. It is devoting, not a part, but all our soul, body, and substance to God. In another view, it is all the mind that was in Christ Jesus, enabling us to walk as he walked. It is the circumcision of the heart from all filthiness, from all inward as well as outward pollution. It is the renewal of the heart in the whole image of God, the full likeness of him that created it. In yet another, it is loving God with all our heart, and our neighbor as ourselves."

REMARKS

I. We will, in the first place, notice some of the features of the subject now under consideration, in respect to which all evangelical Christians are agreed.

1. All, I have no doubt, will admit that the *nature* of Christian perfection has been correctly stated in the preceding remarks; that were any individual actually in the state there described, his moral and Christian character would be "perfect and entire, wanting nothing."

2. All agree that this entire perfection in holiness is definitely and positively required of us in the Bible, and that, for not rendering such obedience to God, we are wholly without excuse.

3. All agree that the fact, that one is not thus perfect, should be to him a subject of deep repentance and humiliation, and of unfeigned sorrow and contrition of heart. It is certainly no pleasing feature of Christian character, that we are living in partial disobedience to the reasonable requirements of our God and Savior; and the individual that can contemplate the fact that he is thus living, without deep unfeigned, and unmingled contrition, penitence, and self-abasement, gives fearful evidence that he is a stranger to the love of Christ.

4. All admit that it is the indispensable duty of every Christian to *aim* at entire perfection in holiness, and that the individual, who is not aiming at a full discharge of every duty, is wanting in, at least, one fundamental requisite of Christian character.

5. All agree that, we are not only under obligation to aim at such a state, but to make it the subject of constant and fervent prayer, that God himself will thus sanctify us.

6. All agree that it is practicable for professors of religion, generally, to make far higher attainments in holiness than they

now do, In view of this admission, let me ask the question—Can he be a Christian who is conscious that he is living far below his privileges, and is yet comparatively satisfied with his present state, and is not making vigorous and prayerful efforts to arise to the full standard of practicable attainment? Is he not living in the habitual and allowed neglect of an acknowledged duty?

7. All agree that no line can be drawn this side of entire perfection in holiness, beyond which it is not practicable for the Christian to go.

8. All agree that, at death, or a short period prior to that event, every Christian does arrive at a state of entire sanctification.

Such are the questions connected with this subject, in reference to which all Christians are agreed. We will now,

II. In the second place, consider the question in respect to which they differ. It is in reference to the simple question, *Whether we may now, during the progress of the present life, attain to entire perfection in holiness, and whether it is proper for us to indulge the anticipation of making such attainments?* One part of the Church affirm, that the perfect obedience which God requires of us, we may render to him. The other affirm, that it is criminal for us to *expect* to render that obedience. One part affirm that we ought to aim at entire perfection in holiness, with the expectation of attaining to that state. The other part affirm, that we ought to aim at the same perfection in holiness, with the certain expectation of not attaining to that state. On the one hand, it is affirmed, that we ought to pray that the "very God of peace will sanctify us wholly, and preserve our whole spirit, and soul, and body, blameless unto the coming of our Lord Jesus Christ," with the expectation that God will answer our prayers by the bestowment of that very blessing. On the other hand, it is affirmed, that we ought to put up that identical prayer, with the certain expectation of not receiving the blessing which we "desire of him." On the one hand, it is affirmed that grace is provided in the Gospel to render the Christian, even in this life, "perfect in every good work to do the will of God" On the other hand, it is affirmed, that no such grace is provided.

Such is a fair and unvarnished statement of the questions connected with the subject under consideration, in respect of which Christians agree and disagree.

III. No evil can result from the belief that entire perfection in holiness is attainable in this life, provided the true standard of perfection be kept constantly and distinctly before the mind. No one can show anything intrinsic in this doctrine, thus entertained, at which the Church ought to be alarmed. On the other hand, the belief of this doctrine, under the circumstances supposed, must be of the highest practical utility; because it lays the only adequate foundation for the most vigorous and prayerful efforts after those attainments in holiness, at which all admit we are bound to aim. To aim at a state, with the certain expectation of not reaching it, must be a hard task, truly, and must render all our efforts well nigh powerless. To aim at a state, on the other hand, with the belief that it is attainable, is the indispensable condition of efficient action.

IV. Whatever our present condition and circumstances may be, there is no presumption in our indulging the expectation of attaining to entire perfection in holiness, provided corresponding provisions are made in the Gospel, and God himself has promised thus to sanctify us. If Christ has promised to guard us against all temptation, we ought to expect to be thus kept by him, whatever the temptations may be which beset us. If God, on condition of our trusting him for this very blessing, has promised to "sanctify us wholly," we ought to expect to be thus sanctified. In view of such provisions and promises, there is no more presumption in expecting perfect, than partial sanctification; since our faith, alike in both instances, rests not upon an arm of flesh, but upon the grace and power of God.

V. The question, Whether entire perfection in holiness is attainable in this life, depends exclusively upon the question,

What are the nature and extent of the provisions of the Gospel for our present sanctification, and of the "exceeding great and precious promises" of Divine grace? In pursuing our inquiries in respect to this question, we are to look away from our condition and circumstances as sinners, and from our natural powers as moral agents, to the provisions and promises of the grace of God. If the "riches of Christ's inheritance in the saints" comprehends their entire sanctification in this life, we certainly are under obligations infinite to possess that inheritance in all its fullness. Are you, Christian, prepared to enter upon the investigation of the subject before us, with the simple inquiry, what has God provided for and promised to me, as a Christian? When will the Church be again able to say, "We have known and believed the love which the Father hath unto us?"

VI. Finally, inasmuch as entire perfection in holiness is required of us, not only in the law, but also in the Gospel, and is a ceaseless demand of our being, we are under complete obligation to approach the inquiry, whether the doctrine, that such perfection is attainable in this life, is contained in the Bible? with the hope of finding it there. To this inquiry the attention of the reader will be directed in the following discourse.

DISCOURSE II

PERFECTION IN HOLINESS ATTAINABLE

"Be ye therefore perfect, even as your Father in Heaven is perfect." ~ *Matt.* v: 48

THE object of the preceding discourse was, to illustrate and explain the *nature* of Christian perfection. The object of the present discourse is to answer the inquiry, "*Is such a state attainable in this life?*"—to ascertain the fact, *whether it is practicable for us, as Christians, to consecrate our entire being, with all its powers and susceptibilities, to Christ, and to live under the continual influence of the all-pervading and all-controlling principle of pure and perfect love—"of faith on the Son of God?"*

I use the terms *attainable* and *practicable,* with reference not merely to our power as moral agents, but also with respect to the provisions and promises of Divine grace. If provision is made in the Gospel for the entire sanctification of believers in this life; if God has promised to render those "perfect in every good work to do his will," by whom he is inquired of by faith to do it for them,—then is such a state, in the highest and most common acceptation of the term, attainable; and we are under the most sacred obligation to aim at that state, with the full and joyful expectation of attaining it.

The question now returns, *is* perfection in holiness, in the sense of the term as above explained, attainable in this life? That it is attainable, I argue from the following reasons:

I. The Bible positively affirms that provision is made in, the Gospel for the attainment of that state, and that to make such provision is one of the great objects of Christ's redemption. Rom. 8:3, 4,—"For what the law could not do, in that it was weak through the flesh, God, sending his own Son, in the likeness of sinful flesh, and for sin, condemned sin in the flesh; that the righteousness of the law might be fulfilled in us, who walk not after the flesh, but after the spirit." The phrase "righteousness of the law," obviously means the precepts of the law, or the moral rectitude which the law requires. This I argue, 1st, from the fact that the same phrase is undeniably used in this sense in the preceding part of the epistle, chap. 2:26,—"If the circumcision keep the righteousness [the precepts] of the law." Without the best of reasons, we should not suppose the apostle to use the same phrase, in entirely different senses, in the same epistle. 2nd, Justification, the only other sense ever, I believe, attributed to the phrase under consideration, is never in the Bible called the justification of the law, but is definitely distinguished from it, by being called "justification by faith." 3rd, If justification were the thing primarily referred to in this phrase, still the moral rectitude required by the law, *i.e.,* sanctification, is also implied in it. For, if Christ should justify, and not to the same extent sanctify his people, he would save them *in,* and not *from,* their sins. The phrase righteousness of the law, then, directly and primarily means, or obviously implies, the precepts of the law, or the moral rectitude required by the law. To have this righteousness fulfilled in us, implies, that it be *perfectly accomplished in us,* or, that we are brought into *perfect conformity to the moral rectitude required by the law.* This is declared to be one of the great objects of Christ's death. Such conformity, then, is practicable to the Christian, or Christ failed to accomplish one of the prime purposes of his redemption.

Again, 1 Peter 2:24,—"Who his own self bare our sins in his own body on the tree, that we, being dead to sin, might live unto righteousness." To be dead *to* sin, and alive unto righteousness, implies entire sanctification; or, to be dead *in* sin, does not imply total depravity. That we might be thus dead, and thus alive, Christ "bore our sins in his own body on the tree." Entire sanctification, then, is attainable, or Christ failed, in one important respect, to finish the work which his Father "gave him to do."

> *And he died for all, that they which live should not henceforth live unto themselves, but unto him that died for them, and rose again." In other words, Christ died that his people might be free from all selfishness, and become purely and perfectly benevolent. Did he fail to accomplish his work? ~ 2 Cor. 5:15*

> *Whereby are given unto us exceeding great and precious promises; that by these ye might be partakers of the Divine nature, having escaped the corruption that is in the world through lust. ~ 2 Peter 1:4,*

> *Having therefore these promises, dearly beloved, let us cleanse ourselves from all filthiness of the flesh and spirit, perfecting holiness in the fear of God. ~ 2 Cor. 7:1*

If to "escape the corruption that is in the world through lust," and to be "made partakers of the Divine nature," to "cleanse ourselves from all filthiness of the flesh and spirit," and to "perfect holiness," do not imply entire sanctification, how, I ask, can that doctrine be expressed? That the Christian may be thus sanctified is the declared object for which the promises were given. Who will deny that they are adequate to this object? Unless they are thus inadequate, perfection in holiness is, in this life, practicable to the Christian.

Under this head I might cite many other passages, equally to my purpose; but these must suffice. On these and other kindred passages, I have one remark to make, to which the special attention of the reader is invited. It is this: We have the same evidence from the Bible, that provision is made for the entire *sanctification* of Christians, that we have that provision is made for their entire *justification.* Any principles of interpretation that will show that provision is not made for the former, will be equally conclusive to show that it is not made for the latter.

II. Perfection in holiness is promised to the Christian in the new covenant under which he is now placed. To present this part of the subject distinctly before the reader's mind, we will first inquire what is the old or first covenant.

> *And the Lord said unto Moses, Write thou these words; for after the tenor of these words have I made a covenant with thee and with Israel. And he was there with the Lord forty days and forty nights; he did neither eat bread nor drink water. And he wrote upon the tables the words of the covenant, the ten commandments.* ~ *Exod. 34:27, 28*

> *And it came to pass at the end of forty days and forty nights, that the Lord gave me the two tables of stone, even the tables of the covenant." "So I turned, and came down from the mount, and the mount burned with fire; and the two tables of the covenant were in my hands.* ~ *Deut. 9:11, 15*

The first, or the old covenant, then, is the *moral law,* that law by which we are required to "love the Lord our God with all our powers, and our neighbor as ourselves." This covenant, as we learn from Heb. 9:1-4, had annexed to it the types and shadows of the ancient dispensation. "Then verily the first covenant had" attached to it "ordinances of Divine service, and a worldly sanctuary," etc.

What the *new covenant* is, we learn from Jer. 31:31-34, and Heb. 8:8-11,

> *"Behold the days come, saith the Lord, when I will make a new covenant with the house of Israel, and with the house of Judah; not according to the covenant that I made with their fathers, in the day that I took them by the hand to bring them out of the land of Egypt (which my covenant they brake, although I was a husband unto them, saith the Lord); but this shall be the covenant that I will make with the house of Israel: After those days, saith the Lord, I will put my law in their inward parts, and write it in their hearts; and I will be their God, and they shall be my people. And they shall teach no more every man his neighbor, and every man his brother, saying, Know the Lord; for they shall all know me, from the least of them unto the greatest of them, saith the Lord; for I will forgive their iniquity, and I will remember their sins no more."*

The following blessings, specifically promised in this covenant, demand our special attention:

1. A confirmed state of pure and perfect holiness, such as the first covenant, or moral law, demands—"I will put my law *in* their inward parts, and write it in their hearts."
2. The pardon of all sin, or perfect justification—"I will forgive their iniquity, and I will remember their sins no more."
3. The perpetual fruition of the Divine presence and favor—"I will be their God, and they shall be my people."
4. The general spread of the Gospel among mankind—"All shall know me."

We will now notice the *relations* of these two covenants.

I. The same standard of character, perfect holiness, is common to both.

II. What the old covenant *requires* of Christians, the new *promises* to them. For example,

1st, The old covenant *requires perfect* holiness. Its language is, "Thou shalt be perfect with the Lord thy God;" "He that keepeth the whole law, and yet offendeth in one point, is guilty of all."

On the other hand, the new covenant *promises* to the believer perfect holiness.

> *But this shall be the covenant that I will make with the house of Israel: After those days, saith the Lord, I will put my law in their inward parts, and write it in their hearts; and I will be their God, and they shall be my people. ~ Jer. 31:32*

See also Heb. 8:10. Here, as above remarked, the very thing which the moral law requires is positively promised to the believer.

> *Then will I sprinkle clean water upon you, and ye shall be clean: from all your filthiness, and from all your idols will I cleanse you. A new heart also will I give you, and a new spirit will I put within you; and I will take away the stony heart out of your flesh, and I will give you a heart of flesh. And I will put my spirit within you, and cause you to walk in my statutes, and ye shall keep my judgments, and do them. ~ Ezek. 36:25-27*

Is it in the power of language to express the doctrine of entire sanctification, if it is not here expressed?

> *In those days, and at that time, saith the Lord, the iniquity of Israel shall be sought for, and there shall be none; and the sins of Judah, and they shall not be found; for I will pardon them whom I reserve. ~ Jer. 50:20*

146

What other thought, let me ask, is such language adapted to convey but this,—a state of entire sanctification?

> *And the Lord thy God will circumcise thine heart, and the heart of thy seed, to love the Lord thy God with all thine heart, and with all thy soul, that thou mayest live.* ~ *Deut. 30:6*

Here the perfect holiness required by the law is promised in the very words of the law itself.

Again, 2nd, The old covenant or moral law requires not only *perfect*, but *perpetual* holiness.

> *Cursed is every one that continueth not in all things which are written in the book of the law to do them.* ~ *Gal. 3:10*

The new covenant, on the other hand, promises not only perfect but perpetual holiness.

> *And I will give them one heart, and one way, that they may fear me for ever, for the good of them, and of their children after them. And I will make an everlasting covenant with them that I will not turn away from them, to do them good; but I will put my fear in their hearts, that they shall not depart from me.* ~ *Jer. 32:39, 40*

If, to give to Christians one heart and one way, that they may fear God for ever, and never depart from him, does not imply, not only perfect, but perpetual holiness, we may truly say that language cannot express that idea.

> *Neither shall they defile themselves any more with their idols, nor with their detestable things, nor with any of their transgressions.* ~ *Ezek. 37:23*

Every one will perceive, that if the Holy Spirit has not here given us the promise, not only of perfect, but perpetual holiness, he has made as near an approach to it as is in the power of language to make, and that, if he had designed to express that promise, no stronger language could possibly have been used.

The same truth is taught with equal distinctness in Isa. 59:21, and Luke 1:74, 75,

> *"As for me, this is my covenant with them, saith the Lord: My Spirit which is upon thee, and my words which I have put in thy mouth, shall not depart out of thy mouth, nor out of the mouth of thy seed, nor out of the mouth of thy seed's seed, saith the Lord, from henceforth and for ever."*

> *"That he would grant unto us, that we, being delivered out of the hands of our enemies, might serve him without fear, in holiness and righteousness before him, all the days of our life."*

I cite but one other passage under this head—a passage, which, if we had none others of the kind in the Bible, would place the doctrine under consideration upon an eternal rock.

> *And the very God of peace sanctify you wholly; and I pray God your whole spirit, and soul, and body, be preserved blameless unto the coming of our Lord Jesus Christ. Faithful is he that calleth you, who also will do it.* ~ *1Thes. 5:23, 24*

Here we have,

1. A prayer for perfect and perpetual holiness, dictated by the direct inspiration of the Spirit of God. Who can believe that the Holy Spirit has dictated a prayer which is

not "according to the will of God," and which he requires us to believe that God will never answer by the bestowment of the blessing desired of him?

2. We have the positive declaration of God himself, that this blessing, when asked in faith, shall be granted "Faithful is he that calleth you, who also will do it."

On the promises of Scripture, as thus presented, I remark,

I. That we have evidence just as conclusive, that perfect and perpetual holiness is *promised* to Christians, as we have that it is *required* of them. Any principles of interpretation that would prove that the former is not promised, would be equally conclusive to show that the latter is not required.

II. We have the same evidence from Scripture, that all Christians may, and that some of them will, attain to a state of entire sanctification in this life, that we have that they will attain to that state in heaven. No passages can be adduced which more positively affirm the latter than the former. Any principles of interpretation that will show that such passages as I have cited, and shall hereafter cite, do not prove the practicability of perfect holiness here, will annihilate all evidence that heaven itself is a state of perfect and perpetual purity.

An objection, deserving a passing notice, is sometimes brought to the view of the new covenant here given. This covenant, it is said, is applicable to the Jews only. To this position I reply,

1st, That to the converted Jew, at least, entire sanctification is undeniably attainable. Why deny it to other Christians?

2nd, Christ is the mediator of the new covenant, does he, as mediator, sustain one relation to the Jewish, and another to the Gentile Christian? Has he not "broken down the wall of partition between them," and made both one?

3rd, In Eph. 3:6, and elsewhere, we learn that the Gentiles have become "fellow-heirs," and "of the same body," and partakers of the same promise with the Jews.

4th, The promise, from Thessalonians, above cited, is expressly addressed to all Christians, without discrimination.[9]

III. I infer that a state of perfect holiness is attainable in this life, from the commands of Scripture, addressed to Christians under the new covenant. I refer here, not merely to the fact, that perfect holiness is required of Christians, but to the *manner* and *circumstances* in which these commands are given. A general sends to a subordinate officer a dispatch containing several distinct and specific requisitions. The officer selects one of these requisitions, given in the same manner and circumstances as all the rest, and affirms, that his commander never expected obedience to this command, and that it would be criminal to suppose he did. What would be thought of such a conclusion? In the light of this illustration let us first contemplate the command of Christ, *"Be ye therefore perfect, even as your Father in heaven is perfect."* (Matt. 5:48) To every other precept found in this discourse, all admit that obedience is not only required, but expected. On what authority, I ask, is this one precept selected

---

[9] I have recently learned that certain objections to the views of the "two covenants," presented in this volume, have been started by some, on account of the declaration of Paul, Heb. 8:13,—"In that he saith a new covenant, he hath made the first old. Now, that which decayeth and waxeth old is ready to vanish away." If the old covenant is the moral law, does not the apostle, it is asked, here affirm its abrogation? In reply, I would remark, that the old covenant, as shown in this discourse, is the moral law, with the types and shadows of the ancient dispensation annexed to it. It includes, therefore, not only the "ten commandments," but all the precepts of the Pentateuch, together with the whole ritual of Moses. All these together, considered as a system of moral influences for the moral renovation of man, constituted the old covenant. The moral law, as embodied in the ten commandments, was, by way of eminence, called *the covenant,* because it embodied the most essential elements of that covenant. Now, the moral law, considered as a rule of action, constitutes an essential element of both covenants, the new as well as the old. In this sense it can never "wax old," nor be abrogated. But, contemplated as a part of the ancient dispensation, and as a part of a system of influences for the moral renovation of man, it has, together with the entire ritual of that dispensation, already "waxed old and vanished away."

from the midst of such requisitions, as a solitary command to which obedience is not expected—a command clothed in similar language, given at the same time, and under the same circumstances as all the others among which it is found?

Again, 2 Cor. 13:11, "*Finally, brethren, farewell. Be perfect, be of good comfort, be of one mind, live in peace; and the God of love and peace shall be with you.*" Why except the first of these precepts, and maintain that obedience to all the rest is expected? How could the expectations of the spirit be more clearly indicated, respecting the precept, "Be perfect," than by clustering it, in this manner, with other precepts, in respect to which we know that such expectations exist?

2 Cor. 7:1, "*Having, therefore, these promises, dearly beloved, let us cleanse ourselves from all filthiness of the flesh and spirit, perfecting holiness in the fear of God.*" Who would dare affirm to the Christian, that what he is here exhorted and commanded to do, he never can nor will do, and that it is heresy for him to expect it?

1Tim. 6:13, 14,—"*I give thee charge, in the sight of God, who quickeneth all things, and before Jesus Christ, who, before Pontius Pilate, witnessed a good confession, that thou keep this commandment without spot, unrebukable until the appearing of our Lord Jesus Christ.*" The command here referred to, as any one will see, who will read the context, includes everything required of Christians. Let us suppose that Timothy had answered this epistle, informing Paul that he had read his charge with solemn interest, and that, by the grace of God, he expected to keep it. What should we think, if, in Paul's second epistle, such a rejoinder as this were found: "Timothy, your letter to me has filled me with amazement and sorrow of heart. You have become a wild fanatic—a *Perfectionist*. How could you have misunderstood me so much, as to suppose that I ever dreamed that you would expect to keep that awful charge?" Why should we be shocked at such a reply? Simply because we cannot believe that such a charge could be dictated by the Spirit of God, not only in the absence of all expectation that it would be kept, but with the intention of impressing the subject with the opposite belief.

IV. I argue, that perfection in holiness is attainable in this life, from the fact, that the attainment of this state *in this life* is the declared object for which the Holy Spirit dwells in the hearts of God's people, and for which all the gifts that Christ bestowed upon the Church when he ascended up on high were conferred.

> *For this cause I bow my knees unto the Father of our Lord Jesus Christ, of whom the whole family in heaven and earth is named, that he would grant you, according to the riches of his glory, to be strengthened with might by his Spirit in the inner man; that Christ may dwell in your hearts by faith; that ye, being rooted and grounded in love, may be able to comprehend, with all saints, what is the breadth, and length, and depth, and height; and to know the love of Christ, which passeth knowledge, that ye might be filled with all the fulness of God. Now unto him that is able to do exceeding abundantly above all that we ask or think, according to the power that worketh in us, unto him be glory in the Church by Christ Jesus throughout all ages, world without end. Amen. ~ Eph. 3:14-21*

Also

> *And he gave some, apostles; and some, prophets; and some, evangelists; and some, pastors and teachers; for the perfecting of the saints, for the work of the ministry, for the edifying of the body of Christ; till we all come in the unity of the faith, and of the knowledge of the Son of God, unto a perfect man, unto the measure of the stature of the fulness of Christ; that we henceforth be no more children, tossed to and fro, and carried about with every wind of doctrine, by the sleight of men, and cunning craftiness, whereby they lay in wait to deceive;*

but, speaking the truth in love, may grow up into him in all things, which is the head, even Christ: from whom the whole body, fitly joined together and compacted by that which every joint supplieth, according to the effectual working in the measure of every part, maketh increase of the body unto the edifying of itself in love. ~ Eph. 4:11-16

To be "filled with all the fulness of God" implies, unquestionably, that we be put in possession of all the moral perfections of God, as far as finite can resemble infinite; which can be nothing less than entire perfection in holiness. The same thing is, with equal manifestness, implied in the phrases "unity of the faith," "unto a perfect man," and "unto the measure of the stature of the fulness of Christ." Verses 14-16, chap. 4, make it undeniably evident that these passages are to be understood with reference to this life. Now, that Christians may attain to this state of perfect holiness, is the declared object for which the Holy Spirit is here represented as dwelling in the hearts of God's people, and for which the ministry of reconciliation, etc., was conferred upon the Church, by our Savior, when he "ascended up on high, and gave gifts unto men." Thus Christ expressly adapted means to an end, which means are inadequate to that end? If not, perfection in holiness is not only to be regarded as attainable, but to be expected, in this life.

V. As a fifth argument in favor of the attainableness of entire sanctification in this life, we will now consider the prayer dictated by our Savior to his disciples, together with the one put up by him, in behalf of the Church, on the evening preceding his crucifixion. Who can believe that Christ has dictated a standing petition for the Church, which he requires her to believe that it is not for the glory of God to answer? Matt. 6:10, *"Thy will be done on earth as it is in heaven."* That this is a prayer for perfection in holiness, none, I presume, will deny.

From the fact that Christ dictated this petition, I infer,

1st, That the object of this petition is agreeable to the will of God, and, consequently, that when the Church puts up the petition in faith, she will be heard, and will have the petition which she desired of him.

2nd, That, in the petition, we have the pledge of Christ, that it shall be granted when asked in faith, just as the petition, "Thy kingdom come," contains a pledge that that kingdom shall come.

Again,

> *Neither pray I for these alone, but for them also which shall believe on me through their word; that they all may be one; as thou, Father, art in me, and I in thee, that they, also, may be one in us; that the world may believe that thou hast sent me. And the glory which thou gavest me I have given them; that they may be one, even as we are one; I in them, and thou in me; that they may be made perfect in one; and that the world may know that thou hast sent me, and hast loved them, as thou hast loved me. ~ John 17:20-23*

On this passage I remark,

1st, That the union here prayed for is a union of perfect love— "As thou, Father, art in me, and I in thee." In other words, perfection in holiness is the object of this prayer.

2nd, The salvation of the world is declared to be suspended upon the existence of this love among believers— "That the world may believe and know that thou hast sent me."

Consequently, we must admit that this love, and consequent union, will exist among believers, <u>or</u> maintain,

1st, That Christ, at that solemn hour, prayed for that which he requires us to believe that it is not for the glory of God to bestow upon his children.

2nd, That the world are never to believe in Christ.

Christian, ponder this prayer, and then ask yourself if you can believe, or dare affirm, that this love shall never, in this life, exist in your heart.

VI. I argue, that perfection in holiness is attainable in this life, and that the sacred writers intended to teach the doctrine, from the fact, that inspired men made the attainment of this particular state the subject of definite, fervent, and constant prayer.

> *Epaphras, who is one of you, a servant of Christ, saluteth you, always labouring fervently for you in prayers, that ye may stand perfect and complete in all the will of God.* ~ *Col. 4:12*

> *Now the God of peace, that brought again from the dead the Lord Jesus, that great Shepherd of the sheep, through the blood of the everlasting covenant, make you perfect in every good work to do his will, working in you that which is well pleasing in his sight, through Jesus Christ.* ~ *Heb. 13:20, 21*

The prayer of the apostle, in 1 Thes. 5:23, is also distinctly before the reader's mind,—"The very God of peace sanctify you wholly," etc.

On these, and kindred passages, I remark—

1. Such prayers are in perfect conformity with the prayer of Christ himself in behalf of his Church, as recorded in John 17:20-23, and cited above. They are also in conformity with the standing petition which Christ dictated to his Church—"Thy will be done on earth, as it is done in Heaven."

2. All such prayers were dictated by direct inspiration of the Holy Spirit. Now, in Rom. 8:27, we learn, that the "Spirit maketh intercession for the saints according to the will of God." In 1 John 5:14, 15, we also learn, that this is the confidence that

we have in him [Christ], and if we ask anything according to his will, he heareth us. And if we know that he hear us, we know that whatsoever we ask, we have the petitions that we desired of him." Have we not, then, proof positive, that when we pray, and pray in faith for perfect holiness, that blessing will be bestowed upon us? Is it possible, reader, for us to believe, that Christ himself prayed, and taught his Church to pray, and the Holy Spirit inspired and influenced apostles and saints to pray, for a blessing which the Scriptures require us to believe God will not bestow upon his people?

3. Let us suppose that God has revealed to us the fact, that he has made no provision for the bestowment of a certain blessing upon us; that whatever our prayers, intentions, and efforts actually may be, infinite wisdom has unchangeably determined to withhold the grace necessary to its attainment in this life.

Would it be proper for us, under such circumstances, to pray for that blessing? What would such a prayer be, less than a request that God would reverse the revealed dictates of infinite wisdom? In what other light shall we regard the prayers of inspired men for the perfect holiness of Christians, on the supposition that God had revealed to them the fact, that no provisions were made in the Gospel for the bestowment of that blessing; that he had irreversibly determined not to confer the grace necessary to its attainment, whatever the prayers and efforts of the people actually might be; and that it is a dangerous error for them to suppose the opposite? Is not the fact, that inspired men prayed thus fervently and constantly for this blessing, the highest possible evidence that they regarded the attainment of the blessing as coming within the range of the provisions and promises of Divine grace?

VII. I infer that perfect holiness is attainable in this life, from the many promises of Scripture which are conditioned on this state. For example,

Thou wilt keep him in perfect peace whose mind is stayed on thee, because he trusteth in thee. ~ Isa. 26:3

If therefore thine eye be single, thy whole body shall be full of light. ~ Matt. 6:22

Be perfect, be of good comfort, be of one mind, live in peace; and the God of love and peace shall be with you. ~ 2 Cor. 13:11.

Be careful for nothing; but in everything, by prayer and supplication, with thanksgiving, let your requests be made known unto God. And the peace of God, which passeth all understanding, shall keep your hearts and minds, through Christ Jesus. ~ Phil. 4:6, 7

All the blessings promised in such passages, of which the Bible is full, are conditioned, directly or indirectly, on the existence of perfect holiness in the subject. When, for example, God promises "perfect peace to those whose minds are stayed on him," the condition of the promise is, of course, perfect faith, or confidence; because the want of such confidence would forfeit the blessing, or render the enjoyment of it an impossibility. So also the "single eye," the command, "be perfect," and "be careful for nothing," etc., directly require the same thing, a state of perfect holiness. Does God promise to his people, in this life, blessings of infinite value, upon conditions which he requires them to regard as impracticable? What is this but the most solemn mockery conceivable? A parent continually holds before his children promises of the richest blessings in his power to bestow, but all pledged upon the conditions with which he holds it criminal in them to believe they will ever comply. What would be thought of such a parent? Shall we charge such conduct upon God?

In reply to the above argument, it is sometimes said that Christians do experience the fulfillment of these promises in proportion to their fidelity. Very true, I reply. This fact, however, does not in the least diminish the force of the argument, as above stated. God does hold out the richest blessings upon the definite condition of perfect holiness in us. Now as is true, according to the common theory, he requires us to believe that these blessings are proffered upon a condition with which we shall not comply, what is this, I ask again, but the most solemn mockery conceivable?

VIII. I argue, that perfection in holiness is attainable in this life, from the testimony of Scripture that some did attain to that state. On this subject I remark

1. That from what the sacred writers have left on record in respect to the provisions and promises of Divine grace, from their prayers, exhortations, precepts, etc., in respect of this identical subject; in short, from the fact that this particular subject was the special theme of their meditations, discourses, and prayers, we ought to conclude, in the absence of positive proof to the contrary, that they did attain to this state, just as, in the absence of evidence to the contrary, we ought to conclude that they died in the triumphs of faith.

2. The fact, that some of them are said to have fallen into sin in some particular instances, is no evidence at all that they did not subsequently attain to a state of entire sanctification, any more than the sins of Paul previous to his conversion are proof of his want of holiness subsequent to that event.

3. There is no positive evidence on record that many of those men did not attain to this state, any more than there is that they did not "die in faith."

4. There is, on the other hand, positive evidence that some of them did attain to this state. To show this, I begin with the character of Paul, as drawn by the pen of inspiration. In respect to this apostle, I remark—

1. That there is but one act of his entire Christian life, on record, which is of a doubtful character. I refer to the controversy with Barnabas.

2. With this exception—and whether it be an exception, is, to say the least, doubtful—his character, as presented by the sacred historian, is "perfect and entire, wanting nothing."

3. The testimony of the apostle to his own attainments, shows that he had arrived to a state of entire sanctification.

> *I am crucified with Christ: nevertheless I live; yet not I, but Christ liveth in me; and the life which I now live in the flesh, I live by faith on the Son of God.* ~ *Gal. 2:20*
>
> *Ye are witnesses, and God, also, how holily, and justly, and uublameably, we behaved ourselves among you that believe.* ~ *1 Thes. 2:10*
>
> *I know nothing by myself,* (i.e., I am conscious of no wrong.) ~ *1Cor. 4:4*
>
> *Wherefore I take you to record this day, that I am pure of the blood of all men.* ~ *Acts 20:26*

Now, who would dare to apply such language to himself, who was conscious of being in any other than a state of entire consecration to Christ? How can he be "pure of the blood of all men," who is constantly failing in his duty? And we do fail in our duty to *men,* when we are not wholly consecrated to *Christ.* How can he be conscious of no wrong, and affirm of himself that he lives "holily, and justly, and unblameably," not in the sight of *men* merely, but also in the sight of *God,* who is conscious of daily and hourly departures from the rectitude required by the Gospel? Who, let me ask, in view of the character of Paul, as drawn by the pen of inspiration, and of his own testimony to his own attainments, will dare to lay sin to his charge, or affirm that he did not arrive to a state of perfect consecration to Christ?

Further, the apostle presents himself as an example for the imitation of Christians, requiring and exhorting them to copy that example, without any intimation, that, in so doing, they will not discharge their whole duty.

Those things which ye have both learned, and received, and heard, and seen in me, do; and the God of peace shall be with you. ~ *Phil. 4:9*
Brethren, be ye followers together of me, and mark them which walk so, as ye have us for an ensample. ~ *Phil. 3:17*
Be ye followers of me, even as I also am of Christ; (i.e., Be ye imitators of me, inasmuch as I am an imitator of Christ.) ~ *1Cor. 11:1*

Now, who would dare to address such language to Christians, unless he was conscious of presenting to them a perfect pattern for their imitation? Such, then, was Paul. If he did not claim to have been in a state of entire sanctification I know not by what language such a claim can be expressed.

Again 1 John 3:21, and 4:17, 18,—

"Beloved, if our heart condemn us not, then have we confidence toward God."

"Herein is our love made perfect, that we may have boldness in the day of judgment, because as he is, so are we in this world."

"There is no fear in love, but perfect love casteth out fear."

Who can read such declarations, without the conviction that the apostle is here speaking of what he knew to be true from actual experience? Was he a stranger to a heart that doth not condemn, and its effects, and to perfect love, and its consequences? Is he not testifying as a witness to what his own consciousness affirmed to be a reality?

If the "one hundred and forty and four thousand also, who follow the Lamb whithersoever he goeth," are not declared, Rev. 14:4, 5, to have attained to perfect holiness in this life, I have failed to divine the meaning of the passage. "These are they who were not defiled with women, for they are virgins." "And in their mouth was found no guile; for they are without fault before the throne of God." The phrase "they are without fault" evidently relates to their character as Christians in this life; because the conjunction "for" connects this with the preceding part of the sentence, the meaning of which is perfectly evident; also, because the reason is here assigned for their pre-eminent glory in heaven. All this may be said to be mere hyperbole. I will not, therefore, insist upon it. The same principle, however, would be equally applicable to any phraseology that could have been adopted.

> *Then said I, Woe is me! for I am undone; because I am a man of unclean lips, and I dwell in the midst of a people of unclean lips; for mine eyes have seen the King, the Lord of hosts. Then flew one of the seraphims unto me, having a live coal in his hand, which he had taken with the tongs from off the altar. And he laid it upon my mouth, and said, Lo, this hath touched thy lips; and thine iniquity is taken away, and thy sin is purged.* ~ Isa. 6:5-8

Previous to this event, the prophet had at least some degree of holiness. What was his state subsequently when "his iniquity was taken away, and his sin purged?" was it a little higher degree of holiness than he before possessed? Was it not, as the language used implies, a state of perfect holiness?

Other cases might be cited; but these must suffice.

IX. I argue that perfection in holiness is attainable in this life, from the fact, that no one can point out any incentive to sin, from within or around him, for which a specific remedy is not provided in the Gospel. Do our lusts rebel? We are told, that if "Christ be in us, the body is dead because of sin;" that "the old man is crucified with him;" and that if we will "walk in the spirit, we shall not fulfil the lusts of the flesh." Do the world and Satan entice? We are assured that "this is the victory that overcometh the world, even our faith;" that "stronger is he that is in us, than he that is in the world; and that, when we have "put on the whole armour of God," we shall be able, with the shield of faith, to quench all the fiery darts of the wicked one." In short, from whatever source temptation to sin arises, we are assured that God will not "suffer us to be tempted above what we are able," but will, "with the temptation, make way for our escape." With Christ within us, and these "exceeding great and precious promises" around us, we are commanded to "reckon ourselves dead indeed to sin, and alive unto God through our Lord Jesus Christ." In the presence of such facts and promises, who would dare to say to the Christian, It is impracticable for you to "cleanse yourself from all filthiness of the flesh, and spirit, perfecting holiness in the fear of God?"

X. I argue that perfection in holiness is attainable in this life, from the fact, that no one can lay down any line this side of that state, beyond which it is not practicable for the Christian to go. Who would dare to lay down such a line, and then say to the convert, panting after holiness, "as the hart panteth after the water-brooks," "Hitherto mayest thou come, and no farther?"

XI. As another argument in favor of the attainableness of holiness in this life, I adduce the striking contrast between the language of inspiration and of the Church upon this subject, wherever the Church has denied the doctrine under consideration. I appeal to the conscience and memory of every one who reads these pages, whether from the pulpit, the press, or the private walks of life, as far as this doctrine has been denied, you have ever heard language which corresponds with the plain, positive, and unqualified declarations of the Bible upon this subject, which have now been spread out before you. Why this contrast between the language of inspiration and of the Church? One supposition, and one only, in my judgment, solves the mystery. The Church and the sacred writers hold different sentiments upon this subject.

Let any minister, for example, holding the common sentiments upon this subject, begin, in the simple and unqualified language of inspiration, to pray that his people may be "sanctified wholly, and preserved in that state unto the coming of our Lord Jesus Christ;" let him charge them, "before God and our Lord Jesus Christ, to keep the commandments of God without spot unrebukable, until the appearing of our Lord Jesus Christ;" let him begin to talk of the perfect peace of pure and perfect love; let him tell his people that the blood of Christ "cleanseth from all sin," and that he "bore our sins in his own body on the tree;" that we, "being dead to sin, might live unto righteousness;" that the "righteousness of the law might be fulfilled in us," etc., what would his Church and Congregation think of him? Would they not conclude that he had adopted some entirely new theory in regard to Christian perfection? I ask again, why has the language of the Bible so entirely disappeared, so far as this doctrine is denied? and why is it, that, as soon as this doctrine is adopted, the simple and expressive language of the Bible reappears, as the only language appropriate to express the sentiments of the preacher and the Church.

XII. The convictions of the Church, as universally expressed in her covenants, demand the admission of the attainableness of perfect holiness in this life. I have never, that I recollect, read or heard of such a covenant, which did not pledge its members to a state of entire sanctification. Every one, in the presence of God, angels, and men, and that under the sanction of the most solemn oath, avouches the Lord to be his God, promising to obey him in all things, and none else, to "deny himself of *all ungodliness, and every worldly lust,* and to live soberly, and righteously, and godly, in this present evil world." This is nothing less than a pledge to "be perfect," and no Church dares to pledge her members to do less than this.

Yet, while this pledge is thus solemnly imposed upon all her members, they are required, under sanctions hardly less awful, to believe that this pledge will never be redeemed, and that it is a *crime* to suppose that it may. All this is done in the face of an acknowledged Divine declaration "It is better that thou shouldst not vow, than to vow and not pay." Now, why has the Holy Spirit thus constrained the Church to pledge her members in direct opposition to her creed? To open her eyes to the absurdity and ruinous tendency of her creed, in respect to the subject under consideration. Such is my solemn conviction. The Churches of Christ are bound fundamentally to change their covenants, or admit the doctrine under consideration.

XIII. The tendency of this doctrine, as compared with that of its opposite, is another important reason why we should admit it. To place this part of the subject distinctly before the mind, I remark,

1. That, as it was observed in the preceding discourse, no evil can result from the belief of this doctrine, provided we keep the true standard of holiness distinctly in view. Christ requires us to consecrate to him our entire being. What evil can result from the belief that we may do this, provided we understand what this requirement is? All the evil that has ever arisen, connected with this doctrine, can be demonstrated to have arisen, not from the belief that perfection in holiness is practicable to the Christian, but from a misapprehension of the nature of holiness itself.

2. The belief that perfection in holiness is attainable in this life, involves the very principle that is considered necessary to efficient action on every other subject. Who would expect an army to fight with energy under the impression of inevitable defeat? All acknowledge it to be the duty of the Christian to aim at perfection in holiness. How can he do this efficiently with the persuasion that such perfection is impracticable?

3. Every Christian also admits that no one can be saved who does not aim at perfection. Now, to aim at this state with the belief that it is unattainable, is an absolute impossibility. To *aim* at the accomplishment of an object, is the same thing as to *intend* to accomplish it. How can a man intend to do that which he

regards as impracticable? Let the hunter, for example, if he can, point his weapon at the moon, with the intention of hitting it. He will find the formation of such intention, with his present belief of the power of his weapon, and the distance of the object, an impossibility. Has God required the Christian, upon pain of his eternal displeasure, to aim at perfection in holiness, and then required him to believe a certain fact, the belief of which renders the formation of that intention an impossibility? Who can believe it? The principle before us, no one, I believe, at all acquainted with the laws of mind, will deny. Whatever a man regards as impracticable, or thinks it absolutely certain that he never will perform, the changeless laws of mind render it impossible for him to aim at, or intend to perform it. How can a man throw a stone at the sun, aiming or intending to hit the sun? An individual is shooting at a mark, with the full belief, that no man, whatever his natural powers may be, ever did or ever will hit that mark. It is an absolute impossibility that he ever should, with that belief intend to hit it. For the same reason, while a man regards perfection in holiness as impracticable; while he believes that no man ever did, or ever will, in this life, attain to that state, and that it is criminal to suppose the opposite,—to aim at perfection in holiness, or to intend to be perfectly holy, is, then, an absolute impossibility. Now the Church universally affirms, and ministers everywhere preach the same thing, that no one can be a Christian who does not aim at perfection in holiness, or intend to be perfectly holy. The Church and the ministry, then, almost as universally, hold it criminal for any man not to believe a certain fact, to wit, that such perfection is unattainable, the belief of which fact renders the existence of such intention an absolute impossibility. "Thus have ye made void the law of God by your traditions." If a man must aim at perfection in holiness, or he cannot be saved, he must theoretically or practically believe that such perfection is practicable, or he cannot be saved.

XIV. As a final argument, in favor of the truth of the doctrine under consideration, I notice the absurdity of the common supposition, that the Christian is always perfectly sanctified at, or a few minutes before, death, and never at an earlier period. Two considerations will place the absurdity of this supposition in its proper light:—

1st, the grace which sanctifies the believer amid the gloom and wreck and distraction of dissolving nature, would, if applied, have sanctified him at an earlier period.

2nd, No other reason can be assigned for this grace being thus withheld, but the supposition that God can be better glorified, and his kingdom better advanced by saints *partially,* than wholly, consecrated to their sacred calling. Where is the foundation for such an absurdity in the Bible?

Some objections to the interpretation which has been given to the various passages cited in this discourse demand a passing notice.

I. The fact, it is said, that provision is made in the Gospel for the entire sanctification of Christians; that this state is promised to them in the new covenant, on condition of their faith; and that, in view of these provisions and promises, perfect holiness is required of them, proves merely that such a state is *attainable,* but not that it is actually *attained.* I reply,

1. That my object in citing such passages has been, not to show Christians what they *are,* but what they *may* become; and thus to lay the foundation for the exercise of that faith by which they may come into the full possession of all the "riches of Christ's inheritance in the saints."

2. The manner in which the sacred writers have presented the provisions, promises, and commands of the Gospel, demonstrates the fact that they did expect Christians to "cleanse themselves from all filthiness of the flesh and spirit, and perfect holiness in the fear of God"—an expectation precisely the opposite of what is now commonly entertained upon the same subject.

3. The supposition that such men as Paul, for example, knew that provision was made in the Gospel for their entire sanctification; that it was promised to them in the new covenant, and required of them as Christians; the supposition, I say, that they knew, that by simply trusting Christ for this blessing, they could enjoy it, and yet withheld the faith necessary to its attainment, is absolutely incredible. It is to suppose, that they lived in the habitual and allowed indulgence of known sin. The same remark is equally applicable to real Christians of every age. When they know their privileges they will avail themselves of them. That they may know their privileges, and thus "come out of darkness into God's marvellous light," is the great object of this work, and of all my prayers and efforts.

II. The prayer of Christ, recorded in John 17:20-23, it is objected, is put up in behalf of all Christians without distinction; and this prayer, in all its fullness, must be answered in the experience of each Christian, or Christ prayed in vain. In other words, according to this objection, the union *now* existing among Christians, is all that is implied in such language as the following: "That they all may be one, as thou, Father, art in me, and I in thee;" that "they may be one in us;" that "they may be made perfect in one;" and the effect produced by this union, is all that is meant by the phrases "that the world may believe," and "that the world may know," - "That thou hast sent me."
In reply, I remark,

1. That the supposition that the union, or rather the disunion, now existing among Christians, presents a full reflection of all that is implied in the language above referred to, renders the Bible the most unmeaning book that ever was written.

2. The supposition that Christ prayed for any higher union than now exists, involves all the difficulties embraced in the supposition that he prayed for a perfect union. In both instances alike, according to the above objection, he prayed in vain.

3. If Christ did not here pray for a perfect union among Christians, and consequently for their entire sanctification, it is absolutely beyond the power of language to express such a prayer.

4. Christ here prays as the Mediator of the new covenant, and when the Church comes to her Mediator, in faith, for an answer to this prayer (and the day is no doubt near when she will do it), this prayer, in all its blessed fullness, will be answered.

III. It is further objected, that no particular time is specified when the prayer of Christ, and the promises of the new covenant, etc., are to be fulfilled; consequently, they do not prove the attainableness of entire sanctification in *this life*. I reply,

1. In some of the promises the time of their fulfilment is definitely specified. For example, 1 Thes. 5:23. When can our "whole spirit, and soul, and body, be preserved blameless unto the com
2. ing of our Lord Jesus Christ," if not in this life?

2. If no time were specified, we should involve ourselves in infinite guilt, were we to "limit the Holy One," by fixing a time, at or subsequent to the hour of death. Such a limitation of the promises sanctions those principles of interpretation by which the worst forms of error are sustained from the Bible. Take, for example, the passage," Without holiness no man shall see the Lord." True, says the universalist, and all men will be holy in eternity. Shall we sanction such a principle by our manner of limiting the application of the exceeding great and precious promises of Divine grace?

I close this discourse with a few brief reflections:—

1. We are now prepared for a distinct survey of the foundation on which the doctrine under consideration rests;—a doctrine upheld by the declared provisions and promises of the Gospel; a doctrine sustained by the prayer of Christ as the Mediator of the

new covenant, and by the "prayers of the saints," as dictated by him and by the Spirit of grace; a doctrine which so perfectly corresponds with what God requires of us as Christians, and with all that inspired apostles and prophets taught and wrote upon the subject. Upon what foundation does such a doctrine rest, but upon the "Rock of Ages?"

2. We see the reason of the aspect of living death which the Church now presents to the world. It is simply this: She is in a state of unbelief in respect to the nature and extent of the provisions and promises of Divine grace.

3. We see when it is that the Church will realize, in her own experience, the fulfillment of the promises of the new covenant.
a. When she fully becomes aware of the nature and extent of these promises.
b. When the conditions are fulfilled by her on which the fulfillment of these promises rests, as recorded in Ezek. 36:37:

> *"Thus saith the Lord God—I will yet for this be inquired of by the house of Israel, to do this thing for them." When this is done—and the time is near, I believe, when it will be done— there will then exist upon earth "a holy generation, a royal priesthood, and a peculiar people."*

4. Christian brother, suppose that in view of all the facts, arguments, and Divine declarations, which have now been spread before you, you should reproach your Redeemer with holy boldness, confidently expecting that his "blood shall cleanse you from all sin"—"that the very God of peace shall sanctify you wholly, and preserve your whole spirit, and soul, and body, blameless to the coming of our Lord Jesus Christ"—would that Redeemer, think you, frown you from his presence, for having asked and expected more than he himself has authorized you to ask and expect? On the other hand, should you refuse to "open your mouth thus wide," would he not charge it to your unbelief, and would he not marvel at that unbelief?

DISCOURSE III

OBJECTIONS ANSWERED

"Nicodemus answered, and said unto him, How can these things be? Jesus answered and said unto him, Art thou a master of Israel, and knowest not these things?"
~ John 3:9, 10.

THE evidence by which the attainableness of a state of entire sanctification in this life is sustained, is now, to some extent, before the reader's mind, as the subject presents itself to my own. Notwithstanding the abundance and force of the evidence, some may still be disposed to ask, how can these things be? Are there not many passages of Scripture which positively contradict this doctrine? And are there not many fundamental objections against it? To a consideration of such passages and objections, the attention of the reader is now invited.

I. We will first consider the objections drawn from Scripture. I begin with Romans 7:14-25.

> *For we know that the law is spiritual: but I am carnal, sold under sin. For that which I do I allow not: for what I would, that do I not; but what I hate, that do I. If then I do that which I would not, I consent unto the law that it is good. Now then it is no more I that do it, but sin that dwelleth in me. For I know that in me (that*

is, in my flesh,) dwelleth no good thing: for to will is present with me; but how to perform that which is good I find not. For the good that I would I do not: but the evil which I would not, that I do. Now if I do that I would not, it is no more I that do it, but sin that dwelleth in me. I find then a law, that, when I would do good, evil is present with me. For I delight in the law of God after the inward man: But I see another law in my members, warring against the law of my mind, and bringing me into captivity to the law of sin which is in my members. O wretched man that I am! who shall deliver me from the body of this death? I thank God through Jesus Christ our Lord. So then with the mind I myself serve the law of God; but with the flesh the law of sin. ~ Romans 7:14-25

The bearing of this passage upon the doctrine under consideration, depends upon the question whether the apostle is here describing the state of the *Christian* under the Gospel, or of the *sinner* under the law, and acted upon by legal motives only. In favor of the first supposition, two, and only two, considerations deserving notice, have, to my knowledge, been adduced.

1. The present tense is here used, "I am carnal," etc.; showing, it is said, that the apostle is describing his present character as a Christian. In answer to this, I remark,
1st, that it is perfectly common for the sacred writers to use this tense in describing not only past but future events.
2nd, The present tense was demanded in this instance, inasmuch as the design of the apostle is to describe his own, and the state of every other person, under the exclusive action of legal motives, in opposition to their state under the Gospel. Under the former, he says, "I am [and of course every other man is] carnal, sold [a bond slave] under sin." Under the latter, chap. 8:2, "I am free from the law of sin and death." Thus said Whitefield, as a drunkard was reeling before him, "There is George Whitefield, but for the grace of God." Supposing the

apostle here to be describing his state as a sinner under the law, the present tense is demanded just as much as if he were describing his state as a Christian.

2. The language used by the apostle in this passage, it is said, is applicable to the Christian only. For example, "I delight in the law of God after the inward man." "That which I do I allow not." "What I hate, that I do," etc. To this I answer,
1st, That language equally strong is applied to the sinner in other parts of the Bible.

> *And lo! thou art unto them as a very lovely song of one that hath a pleasant voice, and can play well on an instrument; for they hear thy words, but they do them not. ~ Ezek. 33:32*

> *Yet ye seek me daily, and delight to know my ways, as a nation that did righteousness, and forsook not the ordinances of their God; they ask of me the ordinances of justice; they take delight in approaching to God. ~ Isa. 58:2*

> *He was a burning and a shining light; and ye were willing, for a season, to rejoice in his light. ~ John 5:35*

> *Behold thou art called a Jew, and restest in the law, and makest thy boast of God, and knowest his will, and approvest the things that are more excellent, being instructed out of the law. ~ Rom. 2:17, 18*

Many other passages of similar import might be cited. With what propriety, I ask, can the language used in Rom. 7. be cited as proof, that the sinner cannot there be referred to, when language equally strong is so frequently applied to him in other parts of the Bible?
2nd, Precisely similar language was at this time in common use among the heathen, and by them applied to men as sinners. "He

that sins," says one, "does not what he would; but what he would not, that he does." "I see the good," says another, "and approve it, but follow the bad." "I have forgotten none of the things about which you admonished me; but, although I have a desire to do them, nature struggles against it." "I knew that it was becoming; but, me miserable! I could not do it." Such is the language common with those very heathen converts to whom the apostle was writing, and applied by them to sinners as such. On what principle, I ask, is it asserted, that they would understand this language, in opposition to all previous usage, as applicable to the Christian only?

We will now consider a few of the reasons in favor of the supposition that the sinner under the action of legal influences, and not the Christian under the Gospel, is the subject of the apostle's remarks in this passage:

1. It was so understood by the entire primitive Church for the first two or three centuries after the epistle was written. This, none, I believe, acquainted with the records of the primitive Church will deny. Did the entire Church, who received the passage directly from the apostle, mistake his meaning?

2. The supposition that the Christian is here referred to, places what the apostle says of himself, as a Christian, in this passage and elsewhere, in palpable and irreconcilable contradiction to each other. In the state here described, the apostle says of himself, "I am carnal, sold under sin," that is, a bond slave under the power of sin, as the slave is under the absolute control of his master. We might here ask, Is this the Christian? Again, "The good that I would," i.e., approve, "I do not, but the evil that I would not," i.e., disapproves "that I do." "I find then a law," an invariable order of sequence—for such only is law—"that when I would do good, evil is present with me." Speaking of himself as a Christian, the apostle says, "I keep my body under, and bring it into subjection." Again, "The life that I now live in the flesh, I live by the faith of the Son of God." Are these states compatible? Are they one and the same? Again, the Christian is represented

in the Bible as "overcoming the world." The individual here referred to is invariably overcome by the world. Are these characters identical? Again, in the state here described, the apostle declares himself to be in "captivity to the law of sin and death." In chap. 8:2, he says, that as a Christian he is free from that very law. How can an individual be a captive under a law, and free from that law, at one and the same time? Once more: In the state here referred to, the apostle says, "I am carnal." In chap. 8:9, he declares absolutely, that every real Christian is "not in the flesh," that is, carnal, "but in the spirit." How can these states be identical?

3. If the apostle has described the condition of the Christian under the Gospel, in the passage under consideration, he has defeated his own object, by showing that the Gospel is equally impotent with the law in producing holiness of heart, the opposite of which he designed to show. The law convicts of sin, and then leaves the subject in bondage under sin. What more does the Gospel, if the Christian, also, is "carnal, sold under sin?"

Well might the Jew ask, in view of such a presentation of the power of the Gospel, What advantage hath the Christian, and what profit is there in faith in Christ, as far as holiness is concerned? Do the motions of sin, which are by the law, work in my members to bring forth fruit unto death?" So is the Christian, by the same influence precisely, "brought into captivity to the law of sin, which is in his members." Am I in the flesh?—The Christian, also, is "carnal." Am I in bondage, under the power of sin?—The Christian, also, is a bond slave, "sold under sin." Do I "approve of the things which are more excellent," and delight to know God and the "ordinances of righteousness," and at the same time remain in a state of disobedience to God? The Christian, also, "delights in the law of the Lord, after the inward man," without obeying that law. "The good that he would he does not; but the evil that he would not, that he does." How could the apostle, by such a train of reasoning as this, convince the Jew, that in depending upon the law for *sanctification* as well as for justification, he was a sinner leaning upon a broken reed? and that the Gospel alone not only *justifies* but *sanctifies* the sinner?

4. The apostle, in the passage before us, declares expressly that he refers to his state as a sinner. "In me, that is, in my flesh," that is, in my carnal, unrenewed state, "dwelleth no good thing."

5. The individual here described is, by the apostle's own showing, totally depraved. Notwithstanding all the opposition which the law of God and the law of his mind make to sin, he invariably practices it, on all occasions and under all circumstances. If such a state does not indicate the entire absence of holiness, nothing can do it. The whole matter is summed up by the apostle in verse 25, "*So then, with the mind, I myself serve the law of God; but with the flesh the law of sin.*" That is, in the language of Professor Stuart, "While my mind, *i.e.,* my reason and conscience, takes part with the law of God, and approves its sanctions, my carnal part obtains the predominance, and brings me into a state of condemnation and ruin." For a full and complete illustration of the meaning of the entire passage, the reader is referred to the commentary of Professor Stuart.

I conclude, then, that this chapter, as it refers to another subject, has nothing to do with the question whether entire holiness is attainable in this life.

> For the flesh lusteth against the Spirit, and the Spirit against the flesh; and these are contrary one to the other; so that ye cannot do the things that ye would. ~ Gal. 5:17

The apostle here gives the reason for the declaration found in the verse preceding, "*Walk in the Spirit, and ye shall not fulfill the lusts of the flesh.*" The reason assigned is this. The dictates of the flesh and of the Spirit are in contradiction the one to the other. Obedience to one excludes subjection to the other. Hence, if we

"Walk in the Spirit," we "cannot do the things that we would," *i.e.,* "fulfill the lusts of the flesh."

Strange that an objection to the doctrine of holiness should be drawn from this passage, which, when rightly understood, directly asserts the doctrine; unless the ground is taken that obedience to the command, "Walk in the Spirit," is impracticable.

The common explanation of the passage makes the apostle assign the strange reason for the declaration, "Walk in the Spirit and ye shall not fulfill the lusts of the flesh;" that as the flesh and the Spirit are contrary the one to the other, the Christian cannot do the things that he would, *i.e.,* Cannot walk in the Spirit.

> *Not as though I had already attained, either were already perfect.* ~ *Phil. 3:12*

On this passage I remark,—
1st, from a comparison of this passage with the phrase in verse 15, "Let us therefore, as many as be perfect," it is evident the apostle considered himself in one sense perfect, and in another imperfect. Why, then, is the inference directly drawn that, in verse 12, he affirms his imperfection in holiness, when the opposite conclusion is as fully sustained by verse 15?
But, 2nd, The apostle, as is perfectly evident from the context, is not here speaking of sanctification at all. There are three senses, somewhat differing the one from the other, in which the verb here rendered *perfect*, as well as the adjective from which it is derived, are used in the Bible,—

    1. To designate moral perfection, or entire sanctification in holiness, as in Matt. 5:48—"Be ye therefore perfect."

    2. *Maturity* in Christian knowledge and virtue, 1 Cor. 2:6, "We speak wisdom to them that are perfect."

    3. Exaltation to a state of reward or happiness in a future world, in consequence of a life of devotion to the Divine service in the present world.

Thus, in Heb. 2:10, Christ, as the Captain of our salvation, is said to have been made "perfect," that is, advanced to a state of glory through [or on account of] sufferings." "Among the Greeks," says Professor Stuart, speaking upon the passage last referred to, "this verb was employed to designate the condition of those who, having run in the stadium, and proved to be victorious in the contest, were proclaimed as successful combatants, and had the honors and rewards of victory bestowed upon them." Such persons were said to be perfect, or to have been perfected. Now, that the apostle uses the term "perfect" in this last sense exclusively in Phil. 3:12, is demonstrably evident from the fact that he was writing to Greeks, and uses it with reference to the very custom, in reference to which they had been accustomed to use the term in this one sense only. He represented himself as running in a race; but not as yet being "perfect;" that is, as not having been advanced to a state of glory in consequence of having victoriously finished his course. It is, then, in reference to having finished his course and received the consequent rewards, and not in reference to moral perfection, that the apostle uses the term "perfect" in the passage under consideration. This the apostle himself directly affirms. He uses the phrases, "not as though I had already attained, either were already perfect," and "I count not myself to have apprehended," with express reference, not to present holiness at all, but with exclusive respect to the "resurrection of the dead," and "the prize of the high calling of God in Christ Jesus," *i.e.,* to the glory and blessedness consequent on having victoriously finished his Christian race. Hence, Professor Robinson, in his Lexicon on the New Testament, thus explains the phrase, "either were already perfect"—"Not as though I had already completed my course, and arrived at the goal, so as to receive the prize." In respect to holiness, an individual who is running the Christian race, is perfect, who puts forth his entire energies in that course. In respect to a state of glory and blessedness, he is perfect, when, and only when, he has finished his course, and received the consequent reward. It is with exclusive reference to the latter, and not to the former, that the apostle affirms, that he had not "attained, and was not perfect." The passage, then, has no reference at all to the question whether perfection in holiness is attainable in this life.

> *If we say that we have no sin, we deceive ourselves, and the truth is not in us.* ~ *I John 1:8*

The phrase "have no sin" may relate to our present or to our past chapter. Thus, when a man says, "I am a sinner," he may mean, I am now actually sinning, or I have sinned, and on that account sustain the character of a sinner. In which sense does the apostle here use the phrase, "If we say we have no sin?" Does he refer to our character in view of what we are now doing, or of what we have done in past time? To the latter, I argue, for the following reasons:

1st, The denial here spoken of stands opposed to the phrase "confessing our sins" in the following verse. Confession relates to past, and not to present sin; it being absolutely impossible for a person to commit a sin, repent of it, and confess it, at one and the same moment; which must be the case if confession relates to sins which we are now committing.

2nd, In verse 10 the apostle repeats the thought contained in the phrase under consideration, in a manner which leaves no doubt in respect to his meaning, "If we say we have not sinned, we make him a liar." This declaration is added, to give emphasis to the affirmation, "if we say we have no sin, we deceive ourselves," and is only another form of stating the same thing.

3rd, The context plainly shows that the apostle is speaking of another thing, altogether, than the question whether a man ever attains to a state of entire holiness in this life. In the verse preceding, he says, "If we walk in the light as he is in the light, we have fellowship one with another, and the blood of Jesus Christ his Son cleanseth us from all sin." He then adds, "If we say we have no sin," to be cleansed from, to be forgiven, that is, if we deny our need of the redemption of Christ, "we deceive ourselves, and the truth is not in us." Now, what class of persons existed at the time, to whom this declaration was applicable? I answer, it was the unconverted Jew, who maintained, that in consequence of his obedience to the law, he was free from all sin, and did not need the redemption of Christ. Such persons the apostle addresses by saying, "If we deny our need of Christ's redemption, by affirming our freedom from sin, we deceive ourselves; and not only so, by saying that "we have not sinned," i.e., affirming that "we have no sin," we also make God a liar. The passage, then, refers exclusively to sinners who deny their need of Christ's redemption, by saying that they "have not sinned," and not to such men as John Wesley and James B. Taylor, who believed, that, by the grace of Christ applied to "cleanse them from all sin," they had "been made perfect in love." To be made thus perfect, is what we are here taught to expect, as the consequence of "walking in the light," and "confessing our sins." The passage, then, instead of contradicting the doctrine under consideration, when rightly explained, altogether favors the doctrine. What else can be the meaning of the declarations,—"If we walk in the light, as he is in the light, we have fellowship one with another, and the blood of Jesus Christ his Son cleanseth us from all sin?" Also, "If we confess our sins, he is faithful and just to forgive our sins, and to cleanse us from all unrighteousness?"

James 3:2; "*In many things we offend all*." Here, it is said, we have the positive testimony of inspiration, that in many respects all Christians sin.

If so, the doctrine under consideration must be given up, of course. But what is the meaning of the above declaration? To answer this, it is necessary to explain the verse preceding, "My brethren, be not many masters, knowing that we shall receive the greater condemnation." The term "masters" may mean, simply, religious teachers, or it may mean slanderers, or critics on the manners and morals of others. The Greeks and Romans, as Calvin remarks, in speaking upon the term, "were at that time accustomed to call persons of the class last mentioned, masters, because they set themselves up as masters in morals." In this sense, not only Calvin, but Schleusner explains the term. It is used in the same sense as the term *judge* is in Matt. 7:1, the same identical sin being prohibited in the phrase "judge not," as in the prohibition, "Be not many masters." That the term *masters* is to be understood in this passage in this sense, as designating, not religious teachers, but slanderers, or critics on the manners of others, I argue,

1st, From the fact that the abuse of the tongue is the exclusive subject of discourse in the whole passage with which the term is connected.

2nd, The apostle declares absolutely, that, if we are "masters," we shall receive greater condemnation, which is only conditionally true of religious teachers, that is, if they sin. The apostle, as Calvin observes, forbids "that there should be many masters," because many are everywhere disposed to rush into this business. Understanding the term "masters" here, in this, its true sense, the declaration, "In many things we offend all," may be readily explained. It contains the reason why we "shall," if we are "masters," "receive the greater condemnation." The reason is this: as masters, "we all offend in many things," that is, are great offenders. The term here rendered "many things," is often used adverbially in the Bible, as explained above, Thus, the apostle says, "I wept *much.*" Again, "He *straitly* charged them," *i.e.,* earnestly. "And he besought him *much.*" "I *greatly* desired him to come to you." In all these passages, the term rendered "many things" in the passage under consideration, is used. Now, when the apostle says that "we all offend greatly," or are aggravated offenders, he does not affirm this of us all as *Christians,* but as *masters;* just as in the phrase, "we shall receive greater condemnation," he affirms that as *masters,* and not as Christians, we shall be thus condemned. If we are masters, we are to receive greater condemnation; because we then are *aggravated offenders,* the only reason conceivable why we should be thus condemned.

The common explanation of the passage makes the apostle render the strangest reason conceivable for the fact that masters "will receive the greater condemnation," to wit, that all men sin in many things. How does the fact, that all men sin in many things, prove, that those who are guilty of particular sins shall receive severer punishment than others? Or that religious teachers, even, if they sin, will be thus punished? Suppose a person should reason in a similar manner in respect to any other crime—murder, for example. "All men sin in many things; therefore, the murderer shall receive the greater condemnation." This would be just as reasonable as in reference to the sin of evil speaking, or the sins of religious teachers.

Further, according to the common explanation of the passage, "masters" are to be punished more than they deserve. Two men, we will suppose, commit to-day the same sin. One immediately dies without repentance. The other subsequently becomes a "master," or slanderer. The former, according to the Bible, will be punished for that sin, all that it deserves. The latter, according to the present explanation of the passage, is, for that identical sin, to receive still "greater condemnation," *i.e.*, to receive greater punishment than the sin deserves. The meaning of the passage, together with the context, it may be thus expressed: Do not multitudes of you, my brethren, be "masters" or slanderers. If we are, we shall receive greater condemnation; because, in that case, we all offend in many things, that is, are aggravated offenders. On the other hand, "if any man offend not in word, the same is a perfect man." The object of the apostle is, to contrast our character and prospects as "masters," with our state when our tongue is subject to the law of life. In the former case we are to "receive greater condemnation," because we are then all of us great offenders. In the latter, we are perfect. Nothing, then, was farther from the intention of the sacred writer, than the design of denying the doctrine of holiness, as maintained in these discourses.

Matt. 6:12, "*And forgive our debts, as we forgive our debtors.*" From the fact, that this petition is found in the Lord's prayer, it is argued, that Christians will always have sins to confess, or will never arrive at a state of perfect holiness in this life. This principle, if admitted, would prove that the kingdom of God will never come, and that the Christian will never be in a state in this life in which he will not be subject to injuries from others. The time will arrive, when the kingdom of God will have come, and when "they will not hurt nor destroy in all God's holy mountain." At that time the above petitions will be inappropriate; because the prayers of all the saints in this respect will have been fully answered. So of the petition under consideration. The Savior says, "After this *manner* pray ye;" that is, if ye have, among other things, sins to confess, confess them in this manner. It was no part of his design to affirm or deny that we shall ever be in a state in which our "heart will not condemn us."

Heb. 12:6, "*Whom the Lord loveth he chasteneth, and scourgeth every son whom he receiveth,*" From the fact, that all Christians are chastened of God, it is inferred that they never become perfect in holiness in this life; because they would not then need chastisement. I reply, that the case of the earthly parent, cited by the apostle to illustrate his meaning, proves precisely the opposite to what the objection supposes. An earthly parent induces obedience in his child by the rod; but the rod, properly applied, brings the child into a state in which the rod is no more needed. So of the rod in the hand of our heavenly Father. Its object is to render us "partakers of his holiness." Till this end is accomplished the rod will be used. When this end is accomplished it will no longer be needed. That the Christian will never come into this state in this life, it was no part of the apostle's object to affirm.

These are all the passages that I have met with from the New Testament, which have been supposed to deny the doctrine under consideration. A very few passing remarks are called for, upon certain passages in the Old Testament, which are commonly adduced for the same object as the passages noticed above. Two preliminary observations are deemed requisite to a correct understanding of these passages, in respect to the subject before us.

1. Whatever is said of the character of saints, under the old dispensation, cannot be applied to Christians under the new, unless such application was manifestly intended by the sacred writer. The ancient saints, we are told, "received not the promises, God having reserved some better things for us, that they without us should not be made perfect."

2. When the sacred writers would express a fact which is true of the majority of men, though not of every individual, they make use, in most instances, of universal terms.

One example will illustrate both of the above principles. Jer. 9:4, *"Take ye heed every one of his neighbour, and trust ye not in any brother; for every brother will utterly supplant, and every neighbour will walk with slanders."* Who supposes that this passage is applicable to all Christians, or even to real saints at the time the prophet wrote—to the prophet himself, for example? Now, in the light of this example, let us contemplate two similar passages.

> *For there is not a just man on earth, that doeth good and sinneth not.* ~ Eccles. 7:20

On this passage I remark,—
1. If it is to be understood in an unlimited sense, no reason can be assigned why it should be applied to Christians in the full possession of the blessings of the new covenant. It was made with reference to men in the state then present, and not with reference to their condition under an entirely different dispensation.
2. The context shows that it is only in a general, and not in an unlimited sense, that this passage is to be understood. In the verse preceding the writer says,—"Wisdom strengtheneth the wise more than ten mighty men that are in the city." We are here exhorted to use prudence in our transactions with men. The reason is then assigned—"There is not a just man upon

earth, that doeth good and sinneth not;" *i.e.,* in all your transactions with men, act upon the prudential maxim, that no man can be trusted. As a prudential maxim, the declaration under consideration is true,—true not in a universal, but general sense; just as the declaration of the prophet, above cited, is true in a similar sense. In this sense only each of the writers under consideration evidently designed to be understood.

Again,

> *Who can say, I have made my heart clean; I am pure from my sin?* ~ *Prov. 20:9*

The first remark upon the passage last cited is equally applicable to this. The true meaning of this passage, however, is, in my judgment, generally overlooked. The, design of the sacred writer, as I suppose, is this: to ask the question,—"Who, in looking over his past life, can deny the fact that he is a sinner, and is clear from all the sin charged upon him?" When an individual, in the language of the Bible, would affirm his innocency of any crime, or sin, he was accustomed to affirm that he "had cleansed his hands," or "washed them in innocency;" *i.e.,* had kept himself pure. So of the sacred writer in the passage before us "Who can say, I have made my heart clean; I am pure from my sin?" *i.e.,* Who can say, I have preserved my heart free from all sin, and my hands from all the iniquity that may be laid to my charge? This question is asked with reference to the entire past life, and not with reference to the fact whether any individual does, at any period of life, attain to a state of entire sanctification.

Job 9:20, "*If I say, I am perfect, that also will prove me perverse.*" How does this declaration, which Job applies to himself, and to no other person, prove that all other saints, and Christians even, are imperfect, any more than the confession of David proves that all are guilty of adultery? The inference is just as legitimate in one case as in the other.

1 Kings 8:46, "*If they sin against thee (for there is no man that sinneth not).*" This passage, simply affirms, that all men do, at some period of their lives, sin, and not that no man, at any period, arrives at a state of entire holiness. The former, and not the latter, is the thought that would naturally suggest itself to the speaker, under the circumstances in which he was then placed.

The imperfection of good men, whose lives are recorded in Scripture, is also adduced to prove that perfection in holiness is impracticable in this life. In reply, I remark, that all that is recorded, is the simple fact, that such men were, at particular times, guilty of particular sins. How does this prove that, subsequently, they did not attain to perfection in holiness? How, for example, does the fact, that Paul disputed with Barnabas, the only sin, if it be a sin, of Paul's Christian life, I believe, on record, how does this fact, I say, prove, that, when Paul afterwards said, "The life which I *now* live in the flesh, I live by the faith of the Son of God," he was not in a state of entire sanctification?

Having noticed all the objections derived from Scripture to the doctrine under consideration, it remains to notice some others arising from the supposed tendencies of the doctrine itself.

I. This doctrine, it is said, is, or in its legitimate tendencies, leads to, Perfectionism.[10] If any individual will point out anything intrinsic, in the doctrine here maintained, at all allied to *that* error, I, for one, will be among the first to abandon the position which I am now endeavoring to sustain. Perfectionism, technically so called, is, in my judgment, in the nature and necessary tendencies of its principles, worse than the worst form

---

[10] [A form of error which arose, before the institution at Oberlin was founded, in two theological seminaries of the United States— one in Troy, New York, under the care of Dr. Beman and the Rev. E. Kirk; the other in Newhaven, Connecticut. A species of absolute Antinomianism, the extravagance and evil of which is sufficiently obvious, and which, it will be clearly seen, has no relation to the form of Christian truth and experience presented in these discourses, except that of contrariety and counteraction.]

of infidelity. The doctrine of holiness, now under consideration, in all its essential features and elements, stands in direct opposition to Perfectionism. It has absolutely nothing in common with it, but a few terms derived from the Bible.

1. Perfectionism, for example, in its fundamental principles, is the abrogation of all law. The doctrine of holiness, as here maintained, is perfect obedience to the precepts of the law. It is the "righteousness of the law fulfilled in us."

2. In abrogating the moral law, as a rule of duty, Perfectionism abrogates all obligation of every kind, and to all beings. The doctrine of holiness, as here maintained, contemplates the Christian as a "debtor to all men," to the full extent of his capacities, and consists in a perfect discharge of all these obligations,—of every obligation to God and man.

3. Perfectionism is a "rest" which suspends all efforts and prayer, even, for the salvation of the world. The doctrine of holiness, as here maintained, consists in such a sympathy with the love of Christ, as constrains the subject to consecrate his entire being to the glory of Christ, in the salvation of men.

4. Perfectionism substitutes the direct teaching of the Spirit, falsely called, in the place of the "word." This expects such teachings only in the diligent study of the Word, and tries every doctrine by the "law and the testimony,"—"the law and the testimony," expounded in conformity with the legitimate laws of interpretation.

5. Perfectionism surrenders up the soul to blind impulse, assuming, that every existing desire or impulse is caused by the direct agency of the Spirit, and therefore to be gratified. The doctrine of holiness, as here maintained, consists in the subjection of all our powers and propensities to the revealed will of God.

6. Perfectionism abrogates the Sabbath, and all the ordinances of the Gospel, and, in its legitimate tendencies, even marriage itself. The doctrine of holiness, as here maintained, is a state of perfect moral purity, induced and perpetuated by a careful observance of all these ordinances, together with subjection to other influences of the Gospel, received by faith.

7. Perfectionism renders, in its fundamental principles, all perfection an impossibility. If, as this system maintains, the Christian is freed from all obligation, is bound by no law,—in short, if there is no standard with which to compare his actions (and there is none), if the moral law, as a rule of action, is abrogated,—moral perfection can no more be predicated of the Christian than of the horse, the ox, or the ass. The doctrine of holiness, on the other hand, as here maintained, contemplates the moral law as the only rule and standard of the moral conduct, and consists in perfect conformity to the precepts of this law.

Perfectionism, in short, in its essential elements, is the perfection of licentiousness. The doctrine of holiness, as here maintained, is the perfect and perpetual harmony of the soul, with "whatsoever things are true, whatsoever things are honest," "just," "pure," "lovely," and of "good report," "and *if* there be any virtue, and if there be any praise," with these things also.

What agreement, then, has the doctrine of holiness, as here maintained, with Perfectionism? The same that light has with darkness. A man might, with the same propriety, affirm that I am a Unitarian, because I believe in one God, while I hang my whole eternity upon the doctrine of the Trinity, as to affirm that I am a Perfectionist, because I hold the doctrine of holiness as now presented.

II. This doctrine, it is said, will lead to spiritual pride. I answer,—
1. An individual holding the sentiment under consideration, who has the true standard of holiness before his mind, and is conscious of coming "short of the glory of God," will be weighed down in deep humiliation and self-abasement, under the conviction that he not only is not what he ought to be, but what he might become. On the other hand, the man holding the common views will be greatly comforted, under a consciousness

of moral imperfection, with the thought that he, in common with holy Paul, and David, and Isaiah, and all the purest saints that ever lived, through the "law in his members warring against the law of his mind, is in captivity unto the law of sin and death."

2. If an individual should attain to a state of entire consecration to Christ, spiritual pride would, of course, be wholly excluded. I shall recur to this subject again in a subsequent discourse.

III. It is further objected, that the belief of this doctrine will lead individuals to suppose themselves perfect, when they are not, and thus leave them in delusions fearfully dangerous. I answer,—

1. This will not be the case, if as remarked in a former discourse, the true standard of holiness be kept before the mind.

2. If no doctrine is to be proclaimed which hypocrites will abuse, we must certainly find some other doctrine than this that none are entirely sanctified in this life.

IV. I have never yet seen any person that was perfect. I answer,—

1. The reason may be, and I have no doubt is, the unbelief of the Church in respect to the nature and extent of the provisions and promises of Divine grace.

2. If, brother, your confidence in the provisions and promises of Divine grace is at all weakened, or your judgment of their nature and extent is at all influenced by the actual attainments of Christians at the present time, you ought to know that your faith rests upon "things seen," and not upon the Word of God. Where is the authority for determining the meaning of God's declarations by the attainments of those who, by their unbelief, perhaps, are "making void the law of God?"

3. The objection under consideration lies with equal force against the Divine declaration, that the "earth shall yet be full of the knowledge of the Lord as the waters cover the sea." No such event has ever yet taken place. What should we think of the Christian, who, for this reason, should affirm that such an event

never will take place? The question before us is, not what Christians have attained, but what God has promised.

REMARKS

1. The reader is now prepared to determine the fact, where the weight of evidence lies, in respect to the momentous question, "Is perfection in holiness attainable in this life"? On the one hand, we have a long array of Devine declarations in respect to the provisions of the Gospel and the design of the redemption of Christ. We have also a similar array of "exceeding great and precious promises," the meaning of which cannot easily be misapprehended by the honest inquirer after truth. In addition to all these, we have the express commands of Scripture addressed to us as Christians, together with the prayer of Christ, and of inspired men, who spake and prayed as they were "moved by the Holy Ghost," all bearing upon this one point. On the other hand, we have a small number of passages, a careful analysis of which clearly shows to have no relevancy to the subject whatever—passages the most important of which (such, for example, as Rom. 7, Gal. 5:17, Phil. 3:12, and 1 John 1:8) have long since been given up as proof texts upon this subject, by many, who deny the doctrine maintained in these discourses. Under such circumstances, how is it possible for us to doubt, not only where the weight of evidence, but where the *truth* lies?

2. Here, also, I may be permitted to allude to the manifest carelessness with which the Church generally has made up her judgment upon the doctrine under consideration, and to the necessity of a careful and prayerful re-examination of the whole subject. In reading the works of the ablest divines upon this subject, I have been forcibly struck with their manner of treating it, as indicating the fact, that their opinions were formed, and their proof texts selected, almost at random, without reference to fundamental principles. How else can we account, for example, for the strange phenomenon that a declaration, which Job made with exclusive reference to himself, has been so universally cited as proof that the man who

189

embraces the views maintained in these discourses is not only deceived, but shows himself, by the sentiment which he has embraced, to be perverse. How else can we account for the general adoption of the maxim, as if it were a revealed truth, that, if a man should become entirely sanctified, he would be taken directly to heaven, and not be permitted to live on earth a moment? Sin, or at least some degree of it, is regarded as an essential element of Christian character, as a life-preserver, notwithstanding the Divine declaration, that, "he that would love life, and see good days, must refrain his tongue from evil, and his lips that they speak no guile," and that implicit obedience to all God's commandments is the only surety for long life.

3. Permit me, in conclusion, to allude to the state of mind necessary to a correct investigation of this subject. It is a supreme and ardent desire after holiness, and a knowledge of the means of attaining it. "If thine eye be single, thy whole body shall be full of light." Without this state of mind, we are unprepared, not only for this, but for every inquiry in respect to the Scriptures.

Reader, is this your state? Is the inquiry after the way of holiness the great and absorbing inquiry of your heart? "Blessed are they that hunger and thirst after righteousness; for they shall be filled."

THE NEW COVENANT

" Behold, the days come, saith the Lord, when I will make a new covenant with the house of Israel and with the house of Judah: not according to the covenant that I made with their fathers, in the day when I took them by the hand to lead them out of the land of Egypt; because they continued not in my covenant, and I regarded them not, saith the Lord. For this is the covenant that I will make with the house of Israel after those days, saith the Lord; I will put my laws into their mind, and write them in their hearts; and I will be to them a God, and they shall be to me a people; and they shall not teach every man his neighbour, and every man his brother, saying, Know the Lord; for all shall know me, from the least to the greatest. For I will be merciful to their unrighteousness, and their sins and their iniquities will I remember no more. In that he saith, A new covenant, he hath made the first old." ~ Heb. viii. 8-13.

" And to Jesus, the Mediator of the new covenant." ~ Heb. xii. 24.

THE great difficulty, which a vast majority of Christians feel, in respect to holy living, is the want of the constant presence and influence of a filial, affectionate, confiding, and obedient spirit towards God,—a spirit which perpetually cries, Abba, Father, and consists in the spontaneous flow of the heart's purest and best affections towards Christ. If the mind could always be in this state, how easy it would be to avoid all sin, and perfectly to obey all the Divine requisitions! This spirit Christians often resolve to cherish. They find their resolutions, however, wholly inefficient to move the heart. To remedy the difficulty, they resort to their Bibles and to prayer, and renew their resolutions with increasing earnestness. Still the heart remains comparatively unmoved; and whatever effect is produced by such means, very soon passes away, "like the morning cloud," leaving in the heart the same "aching void" as before. Now, while the Christian is thus "resolving, and re-resolving," and constantly sliding back to the cheerless state from which he started, while, in spite of his efforts, he is perpetually sinking deeper and deeper in the "mire and deep waters," suppose the Divine Redeemer should pass along, and say to his weary and desponding disciple, If you will at once cease from all these vain efforts, and yield yourself up to my control, relying with implicit confidence in my ability and faithfulness, I will enter into a covenant with you, that I will, myself, shed abroad in your heart that "perfect love which casteth out all fear,"—that filial and affectionate spirit which you have vainly endeavoured to induce in your own mind. I will so present the truth to your apprehension that your heart's purest and best affections shall constantly and spontaneously flow out toward me. I will secure you in a state of perfect and perpetual obedience to every command of God, and in the full and constant fruition of his presence and love. All this I will do in perfect consistency with the full, and free, and uninterrupted exercise of your own voluntary agency. Such a message would be to the believer, "afflicted, tossed with tempest, and not comforted," as life from the dead. This, Christian, is precisely what the Lord Jesus Christ offers to do for you, as the Mediator of the new Covenant. With the Psalmist you can say, "I will run in the way of thy commandments, when thou shalt enlarge my heart." Christ is now ready thus to enlarge your heart, that, under the spontaneous flow of pure and perfect love, you may do the whole will of God. Till your faith is fastened upon Christ, as the life and light of the soul, as the "quickening spirit," who alone is able to breathe into your heart the breath of spiritual life, all your efforts after holiness will be vain.

My object, in the present discourse, is to present to your contemplation and faith this new covenant, and Christ as the Mediator of this covenant. In illustrating this subject, the attention of the reader is invited to a consideration of the following propositions:—

I. The nature of the new covenant, as distinguished from the first, or the old covenant.
II. The relation of these two covenants.
III. The object of Christ in the provisions of Divine grace.
IV. The conditions on which he will fulfil in us what he has promised as the Mediator of the new covenant.

I. The nature of the new covenant, as distinguished from the first or the old covenant.

The old covenant, as was shown in a preceding discourse, is the moral law, the covenant originally made with Adam, re-announced at Mount Sinai, and which now exists between God and all unfallen spirits.

The new covenant, on the other hand, is the covenant of grace, obscurely disclosed to our first parents, in the promise, "The seed of the woman shall bruise the serpent's head," more distinctly unfolded in the promise to Abraham, and brought out in all its fulness in the new dispensation. As the Mediator of this covenant, Christ, as shown in the text, and in a preceding discourse, promises to believers, on condition of their faith in him, the following blessings:

1. A confirmed state of pure and perfect holiness, such as is required by the moral law.

2. The full pardon of all sin, or entire justification.
3. The perpetual fruition of the Divine presence and favour.
4. The consequent universal prevalence of the Gospel.

Such are the "riches of the glory of Christ's inheritance in the saints." Such is the "completeness of the saints in him," as the Mediator of the new covenant. We will now,

II.[11] Consider the relation of these two covenants. This subject was alluded to in a preceding discourse. My object now is to present the whole subject with greater distinctness and fullness than I then could do for the want of space. I remark,
1. As then observed, the same standard of character, perfect holiness, is common to each of these covenants.
2. In the first covenant, holiness is *required* of the creature. In the new covenant, the same thing is promised to the believer.
3. The condition on which the blessings promised under the first covenant are secured is, Do and live. "Moses describeth the righteousness which is of the law, that the man that doeth these things shall live by them." The condition of the new covenant is, Believe and live. "Now, the just shall live by faith." "But the righteousness which is of faith speaketh on this wise: Say not in thine heart, Who shall ascend into heaven? (that is, to bring Christ down from above;) or, Who shall descend into the deep? (that is, to bring up Christ again from the dead). But what saith it? The word is nigh thee, even in thy mouth, and in thy heart; that is, the word of faith which we preach. That, if thou shalt confess with thy mouth the Lord Jesus, and shalt believe in thy heart that God hath raised him from the dead, thou shalt be saved. For with the heart man believeth unto righteousness; and with the mouth confession is made unto salvation."
4. The "surety" of the first covenant is the creature himself. The "surety" of the new covenant is Christ. In other words, the salvation of a creature under the former depends upon the faithfulness of the creature himself. The salvation of a creature

[11] Most of the distinctions here made between the two covenants were suggested to my mind by my beloved associate, the Rev. C. G. Finney.

under the latter depends upon the faithfulness of Christ. Hence Christ is said, Heb. v. 22, to have been "made a surety of a better testament" [covenant]. In Heb. viii. 6, as the Mediator of the new covenant, Christ is also declared to be the "Mediator of a better covenant, which was established upon better promises."

5. The first covenant is adapted to the condition of creatures only who have never sinned. The new covenant is adapted, by infinite wisdom and love, to the condition of sinners involved in infinite guilt, and hopelessly lost, as far as any efforts of their own are concerned, under the power of sin.

6. The exclusive influence of the first covenant upon sinners is to increase their guilt and aggravate their depravity. The new covenant redeems these very sinners from the curse of the law, and "delivers them from the bondage of corruption into the glorious liberty of the children of God." Hence the first covenant is said to "gender to bondage;" i.e., sinners under its influence are left in hopeless bondage, under the power of sin; while all who are under the full influence of the new covenant, are free, i.e., are delivered from the power of sin, and introduced into a state of purity and blessedness.

> *For these are the two covenants; the one from the Mount Sinai, which gendereth to bondage, which is Agar. For this Agar is Mount Sinai in Arabia, and answereth to Jerusalem which now is, and is in bondage with her children. But Jerusalem, which is above, is free, which is the mother of us all.* ~ Gal. iv. 25-26,

7. The first covenant is a dispensation of justice. The new is a dispensation of mercy, under the influence of which the sinner is brought to the "blood of sprinkling which speaketh better things than the blood of Abel." The former influences the subject by commands and prohibitions, rewards and penalties; the latter subdues and melts the heart of the rebel by the power of love.

8. Finally, whatever the old covenant, or the moral law, *requires* of the creature, the new covenant, as shown in a former discourse, *promises* to the believer. The first covenant, for

example, requires of the creature perfect and perpetual holiness. The new covenant promises to the believer perfect and perpetual holiness. I will first cite a few of the passages quoted in that discourse, to sustain the above declaration, and will then offer some general remarks to show that the construction there put upon them is correct.

And I will give them one heart and one way, that they may fear me for ever, for the good of them and of their children after them; and I will make an everlasting covenant with them, that I will not turn from them to do them good; but I will put my fear in their hearts, and they shall not depart from me. ~ Jer. xxxii. 39, 40

Then will I sprinkle clean water upon you, and ye shall be clean; from all your filthiness, and from all your idols, will I cleanse you. A new heart, also, will I give you, and a new spirit will I put within you; and I will take the stony heart out of your flesh, and I will give you a heart of flesh. And I will put my spirit within you, and cause you to walk in my statutes, and ye shall keep my judgments and do them. ~ Ezek. xxxvi. 25

And the Lord thy God will circumcise thy heart, and the heart of thy seed, to love the Lord thy God with all thy heart, and with all thy soul. ~ Deut. xxx. 6

In those days, and at that time, saith the Lord, the iniquity of Israel shall be sought for, and there shall be none, and the sins of Judah, and they shall not be found. ~ Jer. i. 20

And the very God of peace sanctify you wholly; and I pray God your whole spirit, and soul, and body, be preserved blameless unto the coming of our Lord Jesus Christ. Faithful is he that calleth you, who also will do it. ~ I Thess. v. 23, 24

That Christ, as the Mediator of the new covenant, does, in these and kindred passages, promise to the believer all that the law requires of him, will appear perfectly evident from the following considerations:

1. This sentiment is in accordance with the most direct and obvious import of the phraseology employed in such passages,—that meaning I refer to, which most naturally suggests itself to plain and unlettered men, reading the sacred text without note or comment, and with their judgments unbiased by preconceived opinions. For such minds the Bible was written; and its import to them, in the state referred to, is in accordance with the "mind of the Spirit."

2. This is the construction which would, by all mankind, be put upon the same language, if found in any other book but the Bible.

3. Let any minister, in any congregation in the land, use this identical language in the same full and unqualified manner in which the sacred writers use it, and their hearers will, with one voice, charge him with holding the doctrine of Christian Perfection, as maintained in these discourses; so obvious is the import of such phraseology, when presented without qualification.

4. All Christians admit that entire justification is promised in the new covenant, that the Bible teaches that heaven is a place of perfect holiness, and that Christ was free from all sin while on earth. Now, the same identical principles of interpretation, by which either of the above doctrines can be proved from the language of the Bible, demand the admission of the doctrine under consideration, in all its fullness. If the language employed in the above passages does not sustain this doctrine, neither of the above doctrines can be sustained by the language of inspiration. Every candid reader of the Bible, who will carefully study the sacred volume, with his eye upon the phraseology there employed, in reference to all these doctrines, will find the above affirmations fully sustained.

5. The principles of interpretation by which it can be shown that the phraseology of the passages before us does not sustain the

doctrine under consideration, would be equally conclusive against any other phraseology which the sacred writers could have employed, when from such phraseology this doctrine should be inferred.

6. This is the very sentiment which is invariably impressed by the Spirit of God upon the young convert in the warmth of his early love. The language and sentiment of every such heart is—

"Lord, I make a full surrender;
Every thought and power be thine—
Thine entirely—
Through eternal ages thine."

With the young convert, this is not a poetical hyperbole, but the real sentiment and conviction of the heart. Now, present to such a mind, in the unsophisticated warmth of its "first love," the exceeding great and precious promises of the new covenant, and how would he interpret them? Who can doubt that he would understand them in conformity with the pure sentiments and convictions impressed upon his mind by the Spirit of God, in his conversion? Such are the promises of the new covenant, of which Christ is the Mediator. In looking to Christ for the fulfilment of these promises, would he not charge upon us the sin of unbelief, should we expect less from him than that he should "redeem us from all iniquity," and render us "perfect and complete in all the will of God?" We come now to consider,—

III. The object of Christ in the provisions of Divine grace. It is, to lay the foundation and provide the means for the fulfillment, in believers, of all that is promised in the new covenant; to wit, the full and entire pardon of all their sins, their redemption from all iniquity, their perfection in holiness, and their perfect and perpetual blessedness, in an eternal fruition of the Divine presence and favor.

Who his own self bare our sins in his own body on the tree, that we, being dead to sin, might live unto righteousness; by whose stripes ye were healed. ~I Pet. ii. 24

Even as Christ also loved the Church, and gave himself for it, that he might sanctify and cleanse it with the washing of water by the word, that he might present it to himself a glorious Church, not having spot, or wrinkle, or any such thing; but that it should be holy and without blemish. ~ Eph. v. 25-27

Who gave himself for us, that he might redeem us from all iniquity, and purify unto himself a peculiar people, zealous of good works: ~ Tit. ii. 14

For God so loved the world, that he gave his only begotten Son, that whosoever believeth in him should not perish, but have everlasting life. For God sent not his Son into the world to condemn the world, but that the world, through him might be saved. ~ John iii. 16, 17

For what the law could not do, in that it was weak through the flesh, God sending his own Son in the likeness of sinful flesh, and for sin, condemned sin in the flesh; that the righteousness of the law might be fulfilled in us, who walk not after the flesh, but after the Spirit. ~ Rom. viii. 3

And ye know that he was manifested to take away our sins; and in him is no sin. ~ I John iii. 5

Such is the design of Christ, in all the provisions of Divine grace. It is to lay a broad foundation for the fulfillment, on his part, as the Mediator of the new covenant, of all the blessings promised in that covenant. This was the work which Christ undertook to accomplish, as the incarnate, atoning Savior; and, blessed be God, the work which he assumed in our behalf he finished.

"I have finished the work which thou gavest me to do."

"When Jesus, therefore, had received the vinegar, he said, It is finished; and he bowed his head, and gave up the ghost."

Having finished this work, he now presents himself to us, as "able to save them to the uttermost that come unto God by him, seeing he ever liveth to make intercession for us." We are permitted, by faith, to "behold his glory, the glory as of the only begotten of the Father, full of grace and truth." "And of his fulness we may all receive, and grace for grace." Listen, hearer, to the gracious words which proceeded out of his mouth, as our high priest and intercessor, as the "Mediator of the new covenant."

"I am the resurrection and the life; he that believeth in me, though he were dead, yet shall he live; and whosoever liveth and believeth in me, shall never die."

"Come unto me, all ye that labour, and are heavy laden, and I will give you rest. Take my yoke upon you, and learn of me; for I am meek and lowly in heart; and ye shall find rest unto your souls. For my yoke is easy, and my burden is light."

"I will give to him that is athirst of the fountain of the water of life freely."

We will now consider,—

IV. The conditions on which Christ will fulfil in us what he has promised, as the Mediator of the new covenant. These conditions are distinctly stated in

> *Thus saith the Lord God, I will yet, for this, be inquired of by the house of Israel, to do it for them.* ~ *Ezek. xxxvi. 37*

The things promised, permit me to remind the reader, are these:

—the unlimited pardon of all sin

—entire redemption from the power of sin

—the perfect and perpetual subjection of all our powers to the "whole will of God"

—and the full and eternal fruition of the Divine presence and favour. The condition, on which all this is promised, is, that God be "inquired of," through Christ, as the Mediator of the new covenant, "to do it for us." Now, inquiring of Christ for those blessings, implies,

1. A consciousness of our need of Divine grace, of our infinite guilt and hopeless bondage under sin, of the absolute hopelessness of our securing either of these blessings, through any unaided efforts of our own.

2. Confidence unshaken in Christ's ability and willingness to do all this for us. Suppose Christ should address you as he did one of old, in respect to another subject,

"Believest thou that I am able to do this?"

"Do you believe that I am now standing at the door, and knocking, and that, if you will hear my voice, and open the door, I will come in and sup with you, and you with me," and confer upon you this full and finished redemption? What would be your answer? Could your soul settle down immovably upon the affirmation, "Lord, I believe?"

3. A preference of these blessings above all objects in existence. Suppose God should call upon you to lift your heart to his throne, and ask of him what blessing you pleased. Would your mind fasten upon a heart perfectly pure, together with its consequences, as the "pearl of great price," as the treasure in comparison with which all other objects are, in your estimation, "but loss?" If this is your state of mind, there is but one thing more to be done, which is this

4. An actual reception of Christ, and reliance upon him for all these blessings, in all their fullness, a surrender of your whole being to him, that he may accomplish in you all the "exceeding great and precious promises" of the new covenant. When this is done—when there is that full and implicit reliance upon Christ, for the entire fulfilment of all that he has promised, he becomes directly responsible for our full and complete redemption. "He that believeth in me, though he were dead, yet shall he live. And whosoever liveth and believeth in me shall never die." To us his word stands pledged to "put the laws of God in our minds, and write them in our hearts;" to "circumcise our heart and the heart of our seed, to love the Lord our God with all our heart and with all our soul;" to "sprinkle clean water upon us, so that we shall be clean;" to "give us one heart and one way, that we may fear God for ever; to make an everlasting covenant with us, that he will not turn away from us to do us good, but that he will put the fear of God in our hearts, that we may not depart from him; finally, to "sanctify us wholly, and preserve our whole spirit, and soul, and body, blameless unto the coming of our Lord Jesus Christ." Reader, "Believest thou this?" Can you open your mouth thus wide? Dare you ask, or expect, from your Redeemer, less than this? Methinks I hear that Redeemer asking you the question, "Do you now believe?" "According to thy faith, be it unto thee." Reader, let me ask you again, Do you desire to be imbued with a filial, confiding, and obedient spirit towards God, to be brought into such a state, that your heart's purest and best affections shall spontaneously flow out towards Christ, and the "peace of God, which passeth all understanding, keep your heart and mind through Christ Jesus?" Christ is now present in your heart, and ready to confer all this purity and blessedness upon you, if you can believe that he is able and willing to do it for you, and will cast your entire being upon his faithfulness. To you he says, "If thou canst believe, all things are possible to him that believeth." Come to the fountain, reader, and "wash your garments and make them white in the blood of the Lamb." "Christ bore your sins in his own body on the tree, that you, being dead to sin, might live unto righteousness." Why

should you any longer bear the burden of those sins? especially when Christ, in view of the provisions of his grace, calls upon you to "reckon yourself dead, indeed, unto sin, but alive unto God through Jesus Christ your Lord."

REMARKS

I. We may now understand the reason why Christ himself prayed, and taught his Church to pray, and why the Holy Spirit constantly influences inspired men to pray, for this one specific blessing—entire perfection in holiness; also why this is required of us, as Christians, and such rewards are held before us to induce us thus to consecrate ourselves to Christ. Such prayers, commands, and motives, are all based upon the provisions and promises of Divine grace, which secure to the believer, on condition of his faith, this very blessing; and are designed to raise the Church to a comprehension of the "fulness that she has in Christ," that she may take possession of her purchased and promised inheritance. We are taught to pray for this blessing, and such a state is required of us, because provision is made, in the Gospel, for God to answer such prayers, when we "ask in faith, nothing wavering," and for us to attain to that state, by casting ourselves, in the exercise of simple faith, upon the power and faithfulness of Christ.

II. We learn how to understand and apply such declarations of Scripture as the following:—"Wash you, make you clean;" "Make to yourselves a new heart and a new spirit;" "Let us cleanse ourselves from all filthiness of the flesh and spirit," &c. The common impression seems to be, that men are required to do all this, in the exercise of their own unaided powers; and because the sinner fails to comply, grace comes in, and supplies the condition in the case of Christians. Now, I suppose that all such commands are based upon the provisions of Divine grace. The sinner is not required to "make himself clean," or to "make to himself a new heart," in the exercise of his unaided powers, but by application to the blood of Christ, "which cleanseth from all sin." The grace which purifieth the heart is provided; the fountain, whose waters cleanse from sin, is set open. To this fountain the creature is brought, and because he may descend into it, and there "wash his garments and make them white," he is met with the command, "Wash you, make you clean," "make to yourself a new heart and a new spirit," and "cleanse yourself from all filthiness of the flesh and spirit." The sinner is able to make to himself a "new heart and a new spirit," because he can instantly avail himself of proffered grace. He does literally "make to himself a new heart and a new spirit," when he yields himself up to the influence of that grace. The power to cleanse from sin lies in the blood and grace of Christ; and hence, when the sinner "purifies himself by obeying the truth through the spirit," the glory of his salvation belongs, not to him, but to Christ.

Herein also lies the ability of the creature to obey the commands of God, addressed to us as redeemed sinners. "He that abideth in me, and I in him, the same bringeth forth much fruit; for without me ye can do nothing." "As the branch cannot bear fruit of itself, except it abide in the vine, no more can ye, except ye abide in me." These declarations are literally and unqualifiedly true. We can "abide in Christ," and thus bring forth the fruit required of us. If by unbelief we separate ourselves from Christ, we of necessity descend, under the weight of our own guilt and depravity, down the sides of the pit, into the eternal sepulchre.

III. In view of the provision of Divine grace for our full redemption, and of the promises of Christ, as the Mediator of the new covenant, to that effect, I would remark, that a state of entire sanctification is, and appears to be, the most natural and simple form of Christian experience; the form which we ought to expect to find most common in the Church. If Christ has made provision for our entire sanctification, and promised thus to sanctify us, on condition of faith in him on our part; that any sincere Christian, who is aware of his privileges, should ask for, or expect less from him, is the most unnatural form of Christian experience conceivable, and one whose occurrence, we should think, would be regarded as a strange anomaly among the disciples of such a Savior. So I have no doubt it will be regarded, when Christians come to a full understanding of their "completeness" in Christ.

IV. We are now prepared to contemplate the relation between the views maintained in these discourses, and those very commonly held by Christians upon the same subject. In reference to the standard of moral obligation, there is a perfect agreement. The only existing difference respects the extent of the provisions and promises of Divine grace, in respect to Christians in this life.

V. We are also prepared to estimate the difficulties in which the common theory is involved. I will specify a few of them.

1. The advocates of the common theory maintain, that the sacred writers designed to teach the doctrine, that no individual ever attains to a state of entire sanctification in this life; while it was their object to teach the fact, that Christ was free from all sin, that all Christians are perfectly *justified* here, and will be perfectly *sanctified* in a future state, and that perfect holiness is required of us in this life. Now, if the above positions are true, how can we account for the strange fact, that the same identical principles of interpretation, by which either of the doctrines last mentioned can be proved from the phraseology of the sacred writers, demand, when applied to the phraseology which they employed in expressing the nature and extent of the provisions and promises of Divine grace, the admission of the principle, that entire holiness is attainable in this life a principle precisely opposite to the one which, it is maintained, they intended to teach? Again, how can we account for the fact, in consistency with the common theory, that the sacred writers employed a phraseology which, if found in any other book, or if now used by individuals in the same unqualified manner as used by them, would be universally understood to affirm the doctrine maintained in these discourses? Would the sacred writers have employed such a singular phraseology as this, had it been their object, as the advocates of the common theory affirm, to impress

their readers with the conviction that perfect holiness is, in this life, unattainable? Again, no phraseology conceivable is more perfectly adapted to convey the sentiment maintained in these discourses, than that employed by the sacred writers. To draw any other doctrine from it, it must be narrowed down, and regarded as altogether hyperbolical. Now, how can we account for the strange anomaly, that inspired men adopted a phraseology adapted to convey one sentiment, and that only when, as the common theory affirms, their definite object was, to convey precisely the opposite sentiment? These are some of the difficulties in which the common theory is inextricably involved, as far as the laws of interpretation are concerned.

2. That Christ prayed, and taught his Church to pray, and that the Holy Spirit inspired and influenced the apostles and primitive Christians to pray, continually and fervently, for this one specific object, the entire sanctification of believers in this life, all admit. According to the common theory, it was a prime object of the sacred writers to impress their readers and hearers with the conviction, that such prayers will never be answered by the bestowment of the blessing desired. How can we account for such prayers, in consistency with such an object? Above all, how shall we account for the fact, that Christ and inspired men prayed for one specific blessing, the entire sanctification of believers in this life, when their intention was, to impress us with the conviction, that such a blessing will not be conferred; while they did not pray for another blessing, the partial holiness of the Christian, when their design was to impress us with the conviction, that this blessing is agreeable to the will of God?

3. All admit that the richest blessings are promised to us on the specific condition of perfect holiness. According to the common theory, the sacred writers designed to impress their readers with the conviction that this is a condition with which they will never in this life comply. How, as asked in a former discourse, can such a fact be accounted for, in consistency with the sincerity and love of God?

4. According to the common theory, God requires as, in the most solemn manner conceivable, to be perfectly holy, and then, in a manner equally solemn, requires us to believe, that with such commands we shall not comply. How can such a fact be explained?

5. Certain maxims which have been almost universally regarded as of fundamental importance to efficient action, not only in religion, but other subjects, present difficulties equally inexplicable in consistency with the common theory. For example, "What ought to be done, may be done," i.e., we should expect to do. "God bestows upon every one as much holiness and peace as he sincerely desires and prays for." Suppose, that with these maxims before me, I am met by the command,—"Be ye therefore perfect, even as your Father in heaven is perfect." Suppose, that in view of this command, I lift my heart in honest and fervent sincerity to God, for grace to keep that command. Now, under such circumstances, the advocates of the common theory must either give up the above maxims altogether, or admit the attainableness of entire sanctification in this life.

6. According to the common theory, we are required to aim at perfection in holiness, and, at the same time, as shown in a former discourse, to believe that such a state is unattainable; a belief which renders the formation of the intention required an impossibility.

7. The advocates of the common theory generally admit, that perfection in holiness is *attainable* in this life; but at the same time maintain, that it is never *attained,* and that it is a great error to suppose that it is attained. Now, what evidence can we have, that such state is unattainable, higher than this, that all Christians, in all past ages, have honestly and prayerfully aimed, and all will continue, to the end of time, thus to aim at this state, a fact which all admit, with the absolute certainty of not attaining to it? Should it be said, that such efforts are not made with sufficient vigor; the answer is, that, to put forth efforts with the adequate vigor, is the very thing at which all are aiming. On

the supposition above referred to, how can the position be sustained, that the state under consideration is attainable?

The sinner, it is said, in illustration of the position that perfection in holiness is attainable, but never attained, is able to repent, in the absence of special grace, though he never will do it. To make the cases parallel, let us suppose, that all sinners, in the absence of such grace, are honestly and prayerfully striving after holiness; with the absolute certainty of not, in the circumstances supposed, attaining it. With what propriety, I ask, could it, then, be said, that holiness is practicable to the sinner, in the absence of special grace? What is here supposed of the sinner is actually true of every sincere Christian. Paul, for example, for the space of thirty or forty years, aimed steadily and prayerfully at this one definite state, and that, according to the sentiment under consideration, with the absolute certainty of falling short of his object. The same experiment, and with the same result, every Christian has repeated, and every true Christian will continue to repeat, to the end of time. Yet, it is said, to attain to that state, is to every individual, at every moment, perfectly practicable. What conceivable meaning do such persons attach to the terms "attainable" and "practicable," when so used? The advocates of the common theory are sacredly bound to take the ground, that the state under consideration is not attainable, in any appropriate sense of the term.

VI. We are now prepared to understand the nature and character of the Antinomian, legal, and evangelical spirit.

The Antinomian spirit relies upon Christ for *justification*, in the absence of personal holiness, or sanctification. It looks to him to be saved *in* and not *from* sin.

The legal spirit assumes two forms,—
1. It expects justification and sanctification both through deeds of the law. This is the spirit of the ancient Pharisee and modern moralist.

2. It expects justification from Christ, and sanctification from personal effort. Under the influence of this spirit, an individual will be perpetually and vainly struggling, by dint of resolutions, against the resistless current of carnal propensities. In this hopeless bondage he cries out,—"Who shall deliver me from the body of this death?"

The evangelical spirit looks to Christ alike for justification and sanctification both, and, by implicit faith in him, obtains a blissful victory over "the world, the flesh, and the devil." It is the "spirit of adoption" which cries, "Abba, Father," and in that cry, seeks and obtains deliverance from the "bondage of corruption, into the glorious liberty of the children of God." The Antinomian spirit is the stagnation of the moral powers in a state of spiritual death. The evangelical spirit is their full, and free, and perpetual action, in a state of life and peace. While the legal spirit, in its hopeless struggle with the flesh, cries out, "O wretched man that I am! Who shall deliver me from the body of this death?" the evangelical spirit, in the triumph of faith, exclaims, "I thank God, through Jesus Christ our Lord." The legal spirit crying,

"Where is the blessedness I knew,
When first I saw the Lord?"

looks back to its first love, as the brightest spot in its whole experience, for it was then joined with another spirit than itself. The evangelical spirit, with its eye steadily fixed upon the "bright and morning star," moves peacefully and perpetually onward, in a path which "shines brighter and brighter unto the perfect day." The legal spirit, "vainly puffed up," notwithstanding its perpetual short-comings, "with its fleshly mind," in view of a few fancied attainments, made by dint of resolution, exclaims to the stander-by, "Stand by thyself; I am holier than thou." The evangelical spirit, overwhelmed with a sense of the grace of God in its redemption, exclaims, "Behold what manner of love the Father hath bestowed upon us, that we should be called the sons of God!" "Not for works of righteousness which we have done, but according to his mercy, hath he saved us."

> "Infinite grace to vileness given,
> The sons of earth, made heirs of heaven."

In short, the Antinomian spirit is the spirit of spiritual death. The legal spirit is the "spirit of bondage." The evangelical spirit is the "glorious liberty of the children of God."

VII. We are now prepared for a distinct contemplation of the grand mistake, into which the great mass of Christians appear to have fallen, in respect to the Gospel of Christ. It is this: Expecting to obtain *justification,* and not, at the same time, and to the same extent, *sanctification,* by faith in Christ. Where is the Christian who can say from experience, "This is the victory that overcometh the world, even our faith?" When do we hear the convert, for example, directed to faith in Christ, as the certain means of subduing his temper, subjecting his appetites, crucifying his sinful propensities, overcoming the great enemy, "fulfilling the righteousness of the law," and enjoying perpetual and perfect peace and blessedness in God? An almost entire new leaf will be turned over in Christian experience when the Church knows Christ as such a Savior.

The consequence of the mistake under consideration is what might be expected. The great mass of the Church are slumbering in Antinomian death; or struggling in legal bondage, with barely enough of the evangelical spirit to keep the pulse of spiritual life faintly beating. When will the Church arise from this state of gloom, and death, and barrenness, to an apprehension and enjoyment of her privileges in Christ, as the Mediator of the new covenant?

VIII. We are also prepared to account for a melancholy fact which characterizes different stages of the experience of the great mass of Christians. From the evangelical simplicity of their first love, they pass into a state of legal bondage, and after a fruitless struggle of vain resolutions with the "world, the flesh, and the devil," they appear to descend into a kind of Antinomian death. The reason why Christian experience takes such a course, I suppose to be this: The young convert, in the first instance, is turned away from Christ, to his own resolutions, &c., as the means of continuance in the path of life, and this with the assurance that his carnal propensities will never be fully crucified, till death shall release the captive. Thus, he is very soon conducted into the region of legalism, with the atmosphere around him already charged, to no small extent, with the cheerless, deadening vapors of Antinomianism. Here, after a vain struggle of longer or shorter continuance with sin and sinful propensities, the spirit of Antinomian slumber prevails and death, and not a present Christ, is looked for as the great deliverer from bondage. This direction Christian experience will unchangeably take, till Christians fully understand the import of the question, "Who is he that overcometh the world, but he that believeth that Jesus is the Christ?"

IX. We are now fully prepared to understand the design of Paul in the 7th and 8th chapters of Romans. The whole epistle is mainly directed against two fundamental errors of the Jews, to wit, that justification and sanctification are both to be obtained by deeds of law. The first error he explodes in the preceding chapters, showing the hopeless condemnation of all men under the law, and their entire justification through faith in Christ. In chapters vii. and viii., he pursues a course in regard to *sanctification*, precisely similar to what he had done in the chapters preceding, in regard to *justification*. His object is, to contrast the hopeless bondage and fruitless struggle of the creature after holiness, under the old covenant, or moral law, with his perfect liberty, blessedness, and safety, under the new covenant. As the apostle had himself fully tested the influence of both covenants upon men as sinners, he gives us his own experience; first, as a Pharisee under the old; and secondly, as a Christian under the new, covenant. Under the former, he says, notwithstanding the law is good, and I delight in it "after the inward man," and often resolve to keep its pure requisitions, still

"I am carnal, sold under sin." "The good that I would, I do not, but the evil that I would not, that I do." Under the new covenant, on the other hand, I am "free from the law of sin and death," breathe the "spirit of adoption," am free from all condemnation, possess a hope sure and steadfast, and am an "heir of God, and a joint heir with Jesus Christ." In short, in chapter vii. he gives us a view of the bondage of the legal spirit, in its fruitless struggle against the current of carnal propensities. In the eighth, he gives us the triumph and freedom of the evangelical spirit, through faith in Christ, as the "Mediator of the new covenant."

X. We now see the reason why most professors of religion find their own experience portrayed in the seventh, instead of the eighth, chapter of Romans. One of two reasons must be assigned for this melancholy fact. Either they have never known any other than the legal spirit, or else, "having begun in the spirit," they are engaged in a vain struggle to be "made perfect in the flesh." In other words, they are now in legal bondage. To Christ, as a sanctifying Savior, as the "Mediator of the new covenant," they are, comparatively speaking, strangers. When they thus know Christ, they will find their experience portrayed in another and different chapter than the one now under consideration.

XI. Finally, we may now contemplate the reason why, to most Christians, the idea of arriving at a state of entire sanctification in this life, appears so chimerical. With the views commonly entertained of the power of the Gospel, and of the means of holiness, the thought of arriving at such a state is one of the most chimerical ideas that ever entered the human mind. If there is no other means of coming into that state, but by forcing my way, by dint of personal effort, through the dead sea of my carnal propensities, I may as well give over the struggle first as last. Whatever my natural powers may be, a victory I shall never obtain in this manner. But if, on the other hand, I am permitted to hear the voice of Christ saying, Look to me, and I will enter into a covenant with you, that I will myself "circumcise thy heart to love the Lord thy God with all thy heart and with all thy soul," that I will "redeem you from all iniquity," and cause you to stand "perfect and complete in all the will of God," then I find myself standing in an entirely different relation to the state under consideration. The condition on which this blessedness is promised I can perform. I can as easily look to Christ for *perfect* as for *partial* holiness; and when my faith hangs upon his for a fulfillment of all that he has promised, he has mercifully assumed the responsibility of doing for me according to the faith which his own spirit has induced me to exercise.

Christian, "you have not come unto the mount that might be touched, and that burned with fire, nor unto blackness, and darkness, and tempest, and the sound of the trumpet, and the voice of words; which voice they that heard entreated that the word should not be spoken unto them any more. For they could not endure that which was commanded. And if so much as a beast touch the mountain, it shall be stoned, or thrust through with a dart; and so terrible was the sight, that even Moses said, I exceedingly fear and quake. But ye are come unto Mount Zion, and unto the city of the living God, the heavenly Jerusalem, and to an innumerable company of angels, to the general assembly and Church of the first-born which are written in Heaven, and to God, the judge of all, and to the spirits of the just made perfect; and to Jesus, the Mediator of the new covenant, and to the blood of sprinkling, which speaketh better things than the blood of Abel. See that ye refuse not him that speaketh. For if they escaped not who refused him that spoke on earth, much more shall not we escape, if we turn away from him that speaketh from heaven." To this "blood of sprinkling," let us come and "wash our garments, and make them white," and then lift our hearts to heaven and exclaim, "Unto him that loved us, and washed us from our sins in his own blood, and hath made us kings and priests unto God and his Father; to him be glory and dominion for ever and ever. Amen."

DISCOURSE V

FULL REDEMPTION IN CHRIST

"Wherefore he is able to save them to the uttermost, that come unto God by him, seeing he ever liveth to make intercession for them." ~ *Heb. vii. 25.*

"But whosoever drinketh of the water that I shall give him, shall never thirst; but the water that I shall give him, shall be in him a well of water springing up into everlasting life." ~ *John iv. 14.*

IN remarking upon these passages, the attention of the reader is invited to a consideration of the following propositions, which it will be my object to illustrate and establish.

> I. Christ presents himself to us as a Savior in this sense, that he is both able and willing to meet fully every real demand of our being; in other words, perfectly to supply all our real necessities.
> II. We will notice some of the demands of our nature which Christ pledges himself to meet.
> III. Illustrate the nature of faith in Christ as such a Savior.

IV. I will endeavor to show that the object of Christ, in all his dispensations towards his people, is to induce in them the exercise of this implicit faith towards him.

V. That it is only when this implicit faith is exercised towards Christ, that he can accomplish in us all that he has promised.

VI. That Christians honor Christ most highly, when, and only when, they rely upon him for an entire fulfillment in them of all that he has promised.

I. Christ presents himself to us as a Savior, in this sense, that he is both able and willing to meet fully every real demand of our being; in other words, perfectly to supply all our real necessities. The truth of this proposition I argue,—

1. From the fact that it is positively promised in the text, and elsewhere in the Bible. "He is able to save them to the uttermost that come unto God by him." "Whosoever shall drink of the water that I shall give him shall never thirst;" *i.e.*, all his real necessities shall be perfectly supplied.

> *But my God shall supply all your need according to his riches in glory by Christ Jesus.* ~ *Phil. iv. 19*

> *For the Lord God is a sun and shield; the Lord will give grace and glory; no good thing will he withhold from them that walk uprightly,* ~ *Ps. lxxxiv.11*

> *He that spared not his own Son, but delivered him up for us all, how shall he not with him also freely give us all things?* ~ *Rom. viii. 32*

2. On this condition only can Christ claim to be unto us the object of supreme regard. If there is any real demand of our nature, which he is unable or unwilling to meet, for the supply of that demand, we should look to some other source.

3. Christ is infinite in power and love, and therefore must be both able and willing thus to "supply our need."

II. We will now consider some of the demands of our being, which Christ pledges himself to meet. All the real demands of our nature are comprehended in these two—a state of perfect moral purity and blessedness. That these may be possessed in all their fullness, the following special demands must be met:—

I. As sinners, we need pardon. Till we are conscious that God has forgiven our sins, and fully restored us to his favor, a state of well-being is with us an absolute impossibility. To meet this demand, Christ presents himself to us as our "Advocate with the Father," and as the "propitiation for our sins." "Being justified by faith, we have peace with God through our Lord Jesus Christ." "And not only so, but we also joy in God, through our Lord Jesus Christ, by whom we have now received the atonement."

2. Another demand of our nature is entire deliverance from the power of sin, into a state of conscious perfect moral rectitude. In every condition, actual and conceivable, this is a changeless demand of our being. Until it is met, and perfectly met, the want of it will, of necessity, render our minds "like the troubled sea." To meet this demand, Christ presents himself as able and willing to "redeem us from all iniquity," and render us "perfect and complete in all the will of God."

3. Another demand of our nature is, conscious security against all the temptations to sin, from the "world, the flesh, and the devil." To meet this demand, the Savior pledges himself that "he will not suffer us to be tempted above that we are able, but will with the temptation make a way to escape, that we may be able to bear it." He presents us with the armor of righteousness, assuring us that, if we will "put on the whole armor of God," we shall be "able to stand against all the wiles of the devil."

4. Another fundamental demand of our being is, a love of knowledge. In view of this demand, Christ holds before our

minds the declaration of eternal love—"And this is life eternal, that they might know thee, the only true God, and Jesus, whom he hath sent"—and then presents himself to us as able and willing, through his Spirit, to communicate this knowledge to us.

5. To a state of perfect well-being, the friendship and favor of other minds is an indispensable requisite. To supply this want of our being, he holds before us the Divine declaration,—"I will dwell in them and walk in them;" "and will be a father unto you, and ye shall be my sons and daughters, saith the Lord Almighty." He then lifts our contemplation to the eternal throne, and pledges himself to introduce to us an endless and blissful association with the pure spirits that are congregated there.

6. We have also certain demands through our physical constitution, which need to be met. To meet these, Christ stands ready to do for us the following things:—
1. To render us perfectly contented with our circumstances, whatever they may be.
2. To render us in the highest sense blessed, in what infinite love actually confers upon us. The saint who could sit down to her meal, which consisted barely of a cup of water and a few dry crusts of bread, and lift her heart to heaven with the exclamation, "All this, Lord, and Jesus too," hardly needed another ingredient to her cup of blessedness, to cause it to overflow.
3. To bestow upon us all that will be to us, in our circumstances, a real blessing. "Seek first the kingdom of God and his righteousness, and all these things shall be added unto you."
4. To cause "all things to work together for our good."

7. I notice but one other demand of our nature which is met in Christ, which is this—an assured hope of a peaceful death and a glorious immortality. To meet this demand, he spreads before us the following assurance:—"In my Father's house are many mansions; if it were not so, I would have told you. I go to

prepare a place for you. And if I go and prepare a place for you, I will come and receive you unto myself, that where I am there ye may be also." With what infinite sweetness can we pillow our heads upon such a pledge as this!

Such, Christian, is the fullness that dwells in Christ for you. Such, also, is your completeness in him. In view of this fullness, this perfect completeness, he claims to be the sun and centre of your soul. "To whom shall we go," blessed Jesus, but unto thee? "Thou hast the words of eternal life. And we believe, and are sure, that thou art the Christ, the Son of the living God."

III. We are now prepared for our third inquiry, which is, *The nature of faith in Christ as such a Savior*. It implies,

1. A consciousness of infinite guilt, poverty, and helplessness in ourselves.
2. The apprehension of Christ as a present Savior, able and willing to meet all the demands of our being, as described above.
3. The actual reception of him, and cordial and voluntary surrender of our whole being to his control, that he may accomplish in us all that He has promised to those "who come unto God by him." The individual that knows and believes the "love that the Father hath unto us"—that relies with implicit confidence upon the absolute truth and rectitude of all that Christ has affirmed, and casts all his powers and interests upon his faithfulness, with the peaceful expectation of realizing, in his own experience, a blessed fulfillment of all that he has promised,—such an individual exercises that faith, by which we are told "the just shall live." This leads me to remark,—

IV. That the object of Christ, in his dispensations and teachings, is, to induce in us the exercise of this implicit faith in himself. A bare allusion to a few circumstances in the life of our Savior will afford a sufficient illustration of this part of our subject. For example,

1. The promptness with which he invariably granted the requests of those who cast themselves with implicit faith upon his power and faithfulness, together with the commendation which he always bestowed upon such acts of confidence.

2. The fact that he always required such confidence, as a condition of extending relief, by the exertion of miraculous power. "If thou canst believe, all things are possible to him that believeth."

3. His perpetual reference to the unbelief of his disciples, as the cause of their failure to perform miracles, of their fear in the tempest, and of their carefulness in respect to the supply of their temporal necessities.

4. The repeated assurance that he gave them, that, if they would only exercise this implicit faith in him, "nothing should be impossible to them."

5. The manner in which he sent them forth to preach, and then asking them, at the close of his ministry, whether, in going out under his protection, "as sheep in the midst of wolves," without any provision at all for their wants, they had lacked anything. One object is perfectly visible in all these instances, which was, to break their hold of every other object, and to lead them to hang their entire being, with implicit trust, upon his power and faithfulness. Such was the single object of his entire course of treatment, in respect to his disciples and hearers while on earth. The same object, Christian, he is now pursuing towards you. When unbelief has disappeared from your heart; when you will "credit all that he has said;" when you shall calmly and peacefully repose all your powers and interests upon his faithful word—then his object, in respect to you, is accomplished. Then he will open the fountains of eternal love, and let its life-giving waters flow in upon you for ever. He then can and will accomplish in you all that infinite love desires. "Said I not unto thee, that if thou wouldst believe, thou shouldst see the glory of God?"

V. I am now to show, that it is only when this implicit confidence is exercised towards Christ, as a Savior able and willing to meet all our necessities, that he can accomplish in us all that he has promised. How else, for example, can he preserve us, free from all care, and "keep us in perfect peace?" While the mind reposes with unwavering trust in his ability and faithfulness to meet all its necessities, the necessary result is a state of perfect quietude. Distrust, on the other hand, as necessarily throws the mind into a state of agitation. The little child could be preserved in a state of perfect peace, in the midst of the wildest fury of the hurricane, by the thought that his father held the helm, so long, and so long only, as he reposed implicit confidence in that father's ability and faithfulness to guide the vessel through the storm. So of the Christian: Christ will "keep those in perfect peace" whose minds are stayed on him, because they trust in him. To keep the mind thus, while in a state of distrust, is an absolute impossibility.

For the same reason, it is impossible for Christ to be unto us an object of supreme love and delight, until we are brought to confide in him as being such a Savior as he represents himself to be. Then, and then only, can he stir up the deep fountains of feeling within us, and cause the tide of love and blessedness to roll on for ever.

How, it may further be asked, is it possible for Christ to bring us into a state of perfect obedience to his will, until we are induced to exercise implicit confidence in the absolute wisdom and rectitude of his requisitions? Whatever Christ does for us as a Savior, he does and must do, on one condition only—that confidence implicit is reposed in his ability and faithfulness to meet and supply our necessities. The experience of every individual will present a perfect verification of his declarations,—"I am the resurrection and the life; he that believeth in me, though he were dead, yet shall he live. And whosoever liveth and believeth in me shall never die." On the other hand, "If ye believe not that I am he, ye shall die in your sins."

VI. Lastly, I am to show, that Christians honor Christ the most highly, when, and only when, they rely upon him for an entire fulfillment in them of all that he has promised, *i.e.*, to supply all their real necessities. The more enlarged and confiding their expectations, the higher the honor they confer upon him. This is evident from the following considerations:—

I. They then, and then only, give him full and perfect credit for veracity in the testimony which he has given respecting himself. Such a Savior he represents himself to be. When we trust him with full and perfect confidence as such a Savior, we honor him as a "faithful and true witness." Unbelief, a want of this implicit confidence, casts the highest possible dishonor upon Christ, because it practically affirms, that he is not what he has declared himself to be.

2. In the exercise of this full and implicit confidence in Christ as a perfect Savior, we honor, in the highest possible degree, his benevolence, his mercy, his love. To expect less from Christ than a full supply of all our necessities, is to affirm, that his love is not infinite.

3. In the exercise of this confidence only, we give him credit for being a *perfect* Savior. If there is a solitary demand of our being, which he is not able and willing to meet, he is so far, as a Savior, imperfect.

Do you wish, Christian, to put the highest possible honor upon Christ? "Open your mouth wide," with the joyful confidence that he "will fill it." Cast all your cares upon him. Believe that in him you are "complete," and seek and expect from him the most perfect fullness. When you expect from him less than this, you cast reproach upon his character for veracity and faithfulness, as possessed of infinite love—as an all-powerful and perfect Savior. You affirm, that "in him all fullness" does not dwell. You wound his heart of love. You "grieve his Holy Spirit." You put out the light of your own soul.

REMARKS

I. We may now understand the distinction between perfect and imperfect faith. They are not distinguished, I suppose, by this, that in reference to the same object and the same feature of Christ's character, the mind may be in a state of trust and distrust at one and the same moment. Our faith may be imperfect for two reasons:

1. We may repose confidence in one, and not in every feature of Christ's character as a Savior. For example, the mind, in consequence of ignorance of the perfect fullness of Christ's redemption in all respects, may repose full confidence in Christ as a *justifying*, but not as a *sanctifying* Savior.
2. For the same reason, the mind may repose confidence in Christ, for sustaining grace, in one condition in life, and not in another. We may, for example, expect Christ to bless us in our closets, but not in the midst of our business transactions. The faith of all such persons is imperfect. Perfect faith, on the other hand, is a full and unshaken confidence in Christ, as in all respects, at all times, and in every condition, a full and perfect Savior; a Savior able and willing to meet every possible demand of our being.

II. We also see how it was, that Satan effected the ruin of our first parents. It was by persuading them, that there was one fundamental demand of their being, a love of knowledge, which God did not design to meet; and by inducing them to attempt to supply that demand by transgressing the Divine prohibition. In this state of distrust of God's power or willingness to meet and supply all their necessities, all mankind now are by nature; and this distrust is the sole cause of every act of disobedience on earth.

III. We may now understand one fundamental design of the plan of redemption. It is to restore in man the full, implicit, and universal confidence in the power, wisdom, and love of God, which was exercised by our first parents before the fall, and is now exercised by all holy beings in existence. What God said to Abraham, he says to all the sons of men, who will hearken to his voice, as Abraham did; "I am thy shield, and thy exceeding great reward." When God is chosen by the soul as its eternal portion, in whom every demand of its being is perfectly met, then the work of redemption is accomplished in man, as far as his restoration to the love and favor of God is concerned.

IV. We also see when it is that an individual is brought into a state of entire and permanent holiness—when he is settled into a state of full and perpetual consciousness, that in Christ every demand of his being is met, and when all his powers are sweetly yielded up to his control, that he may thus supply our wants, and accomplish, in and through us, all the good pleasure of his goodness. Of such a person, in such a state, it may truly be said, "There is none occasion of stumbling in him." Nor will there ever be to all eternity. Into this blissful state, Christian, Christ is both able and willing to bring you. Into this state he will bring you, as soon as you will credit his testimony to his own ability and willingness, and will accordingly surrender yourself to his sweet control.

V. We are now presented with another inexplicable difficulty in the way of the theory, that perfection in holiness is unattainable in this life. The advocates of that theory are bound to take the ground, that, in our condition in this life, such perfection (*i.e.*, a state of perfect moral rectitude) would not be, on the whole, a blessing to us, for the glory of God, and the good of the universe; or admit that Christ is able and willing to confer this perfection upon us. If it is a good, Christ stands pledged to confer it upon us. For God has said, that "no good thing will he withhold from them that walk uprightly." "My God shall supply all your need, according to his riches in glory by Christ Jesus." Further, if such perfection would be a good to us, and Christ did not present himself to us as able and willing to meet this perpetual and changeless demand of our being, he would be to us an imperfect Savior.

Again, if such perfection is not in this life a good, for the glory of God, or the well-being of the universe, we are under obligations infinite not to pray for it, or to aim to attain it. To make the present possession of that which, we believe, would not now be a good, the object of prayer and effort, must undeniably be in a high degree criminal. But is not the fact, that a state of moral rectitude would be a good to us, for the glory of God, and the good of the universe, a self-evident truth? Is it not demonstrably evident that it is a good, from the fact that it is required of us in the Bible; that Christ prayed for it in behalf of all Christians, and taught them to pray for it; and that such motives are held before us in the Bible, to induce in us this perfect obedience to God?

Now, which of the above alternatives shall we take? Shall we say, that perfection in holiness is not in this life a good, and, for this reason, as we are bound to do, if the supposition before us is correct, cease to aim at it, or pray for it? Or shall we say, that such perfection is a good, and that Christ, though *able,* is *unwilling* to confer it upon us, and thus impeach his benevolence, his character as a perfect Savior? Or, finally, shall we affirm, that a state of perfect moral rectitude is in this life a good, and that Christ is both *able* and *willing* to confer it upon us, and thus proclaim his absolute perfection as a Savior? One, and only one, of the above alternatives we must take. Which is most honorable to Christ? Which is most conformable to the teachings of inspiration? Which does it become us, as the pupils of the Bible and Spirit of God, as the disciples of such a Savior, to assume?

VI. We see, also, how it is, and by what means that Satan is endeavoring to draw Christians away from Christ. It is by tempting them to believe, that some one or more of the demands of their being are not met in Christ, and thus to draw off their hearts from him to some other object. In every instance in which a Christian falls into sin, he does it under the influence of some such temptation as this. For the time being, he is led practically to distrust the power or willingness of Christ to answer some of the demands of his nature. To meet this demand, the individual trespasses the command of Christ.

VII. We see, also, that the sentiment, that Christ is not both able and willing to render us, in this life, perfect in holiness, and thus meet this great, this fundamental demand of our nature, is directly and most perfectly adapted to induce distrust in him, and throw the mind under the power of the great enemy. No sentiment can be conceived of, which is more perfectly adapted to secure this object, than the one under consideration.

VIII. We may now understand the full meaning of the passage, "Christ is the end of the law for righteousness to every one that believeth." The meaning of the passage I suppose to be this: Christ accomplishes in and for the believer all that the law would have done, had he always perfectly obeyed its requisitions. For example, perfect obedience to the law secures to the subject a full exemption from all condemnation, and a sure title to the protection and favor of God. This the Christian enjoys through faith in Christ. Entire obedience to the law would have rendered his moral character absolutely perfect, and infinitively lovely and excellent in the estimation of God, and of all intelligent beings. A character, equally perfect, lovely, and excellent, the believer receives through implicit faith in Christ. Further, obedience to the law would have rendered the believer perfectly blessed in the love and favor of God. A blessedness equally perfect descends to the believer through faith in Christ. Again, obedience to the law would have secured to the believer a full and perfect supply of every necessity. Every demand of our being is met with equal fullness in Christ. All that the law would have done for the believer, had he perfectly obeyed its requisitions, Christ does for him, and infinitely more.

IX. We are also prepared to answer an objection, which is sometimes brought to the doctrine maintained in these discourses, to wit, that it tends to dishonor the law, by lowering the standard of moral obligation. When I hear this objection, I am often reminded of a declaration made to Paul by a fellow apostle; "Thou seest, brother, how many thousands of Jews there are that believe; and they are all zealous of the law." Whenever the thought is presented, that perfect conformity to the Divine requisitions is not only required, but expected, of us in this life, a great zeal is instantly manifested for the law, as if some fearful sacrilege was done to it by the above supposition. The standard of moral obligation, it is said, will be let down, and Antinomianism, and errors fearfully dangerous, will be introduced. But how a law is honored, by maintaining that the subject will never obey it, is more than I can understand. And what is gained by elevating the standard of theoretical, and lowering that of practical attainment, is equally inexplicable to my mind. Christians should also understand, that, in their zeal to elevate the law, they may limit the grace of God. To place the law far above the provisions and promises of Christ's redemption, confers honor neither upon the law nor Christ. On the other hand, "Christ magnifies the law and makes it honorable," in the highest sense possible, when, as the Mediator of the new covenant, he "puts the law in the minds, and writes it in the hearts," of his people, and brings all the powers of their being into sweet subjection to its requisitions.

X. In the light of this subject you see, Christian, the real cause of every sin you commit; of all your "care and trouble about the many things" of this life; of your want of perpetual peace in God, and of the "aching void" in your heart in its stead; and of the absence of that state of perfect content which arises from the consciousness that all your wants are met in Christ. All this has its origin in one principle exclusively; *unbelief,* a want of confidence in Christ as a full and perfect Savior. Until you become fully sensible of this fact; until you are led to refer all your particular sins, all your carefulness and anxiety about your worldly interest, your want of perfect peace, and every improper feeling that arises in your mind, to one source; *unbelief,* you will never feel as you ought the "exceeding sinfulness of sin."

XI. We may understand the origin and cause of the profound insensibility and hardness of heart, in respect to the love of Christ, of which professors of religion so commonly complain.

Three facts will sufficiently account for this state of gloom and heartfelt despondency:

1. Christians generally are ignorant of the fullness of that redemption which they have in Christ. Unbelief has taken their Lord away from their hearts, and they know not where it has laid him. The secret of having a heart always melted with love and tenderness, is an indwelling Christ, from whose fullness our cup of blessedness may perpetually flow.

2. Another cause of the state under consideration is this; the fact that almost every Christian, in uniting with the Church, took upon him the most solemn covenant and vow to live in a state of entire consecration to Christ, not only in the absence of all expectation that such vow would be kept, but with the definite belief that it would not be kept. With such a vow and such a belief lying together upon your conscience, Christian, cease to wonder that your heart has been hardened into the profoundest insensibility and gloom.

3. Another cause of this state of things is, the daily habit of praying definitely for a state of entire sanctification, with the full belief that God will not answer such requests by the bestowment of the blessing prayed for. Let me beseech you, Christian, as you value the presence and favor of God, as you would not fasten a heart of stone as a perpetual mill-stone to your deathless soul, never to put up such a prayer again. "Be ye not mockers, lest your bands be made strong."

XII. One important aspect of the question at issue between the advocates and opposers of the doctrine of Christian perfection, here presents itself to the contemplation. That Christ is able to render us, in this life, as well as in eternity, "perfect and complete in all the will of God," none, I presume, will deny. The apostle after having prayed for the entire sanctification and perfect blessedness of Christians, thus exclaims:

> "Now unto him that is able to do exceeding abundantly
> above all that we ask or think, according to the power
> that worketh in us, unto him be glory in the Church by

Christ Jesus, throughout all ages, world without end.
Amen. ~ *Eph. iii., 20, 21*

Surely we are not straitened in Christ, as far as power to save is concerned. The great question is, Is he *willing*, as well as able, to render us thus perfect? On this question, the advocates and opposers of the doctrine of Christian perfection are really at issue. On the one hand, it is affirmed that, at all times, and under all circumstances, Christ is both able and willing to meet, and to meet perfectly, every demand of our being, and that, as such a Savior, he is ever present as an object of faith. On the other hand, it is affirmed that there is no moment, during the present life, when he is *willing*, though *able*, to meet one changeless demand of our being, to render us "perfect and complete in all the will of God." Which of the above positions is true, you, reader, are called upon here, in the fear of God, to decide.

XIII. We are now prepared for the contemplation of another, and very interesting aspect of the question, Whether perfection in holiness is attainable in this life. That doctrine has the highest possible internal evidence in its favor, which directly and manifestly falls in with the great design of God in the Gospel; while the doctrine which wants this characteristic is equally destitute of all claim to our belief. Now, every one is aware that the great and fundamental design of the Gospel is, to induce in the Christian the exercise of implicit faith in Christ. Which view of the character of Christ is best adapted to increase in us the exercise of such faith in him; that which presents him to our contemplation as able and willing to meet perfectly every demand of our being, or that which presents him as *able* indeed, but *unwilling*, during the progress of the present life, to meet one fundamental and changeless demand of our nature, *i.e.*, to "sanctify us wholly," and preserve us in that state to his coming and kingdom? Is not the former view of the character of Christ most perfectly adapted to induce the exercise of perfect faith, and the latter as perfectly adapted to induce the opposite state of mind, that is, unbelief?

XIV. I will here notice a remark which is sometimes made in respect to *dwelling* upon the doctrine of Christian perfection. It is not in this manner, it is said, that the Christian makes progress in holiness; but by turning his contemplation directly upon the Divine glory, and thus being changed into the same image from glory to glory, "even as by the Spirit of the Lord." The question is, Does not the doctrine of Christian perfection present one of the essential features of this very glory, upon which we are required to turn our contemplation? What is implied in the general and devout meditation upon this doctrine? It implies three things:

1. Deep and profound meditation upon the pure and perfect law of God, and upon the action of all the powers of our being, in all the circumstances and relations in life, in conformity with that law. By thus meditating upon the Divine statutes, the Psalmist declares that he had become "wiser than his teachers." Who will dare affirm, that such meditations are not in a high degree favorable to holiness? Who will affirm that, in thus meditating upon God's pure and perfect law, we shall see no bright reflections of that glory, in the beholding of which the Christian is changed into the same image?

2. In another view of the subject, dwelling upon the doctrine of Christian perfection implies a devout contemplation of the character of Christ, as a full and perfect Savior, a Savior able and willing to meet all our real necessities. By such contemplations, contemplations in which we are brought to "know and believe the love which God hath to us," we are informed, I John iv., 16, 17, that "our love is made perfect."

3. In yet another view of the subject, dwelling upon the doctrine under consideration implies a frequent and devout contemplation of the provisions of Divine grace for the entire sanctification of believers, and of the designs of God to raise them to this state, whenever they look to him, by faith to do it for them. Such meditations upon God's "thoughts of good, and not of evil," towards his people, tends, in the most powerful manner conceivable, to melt our hearts in love and tenderness

towards God, and to induce in us the most vigorous efforts after that holiness which we are required to perfect. In whatever point of light the doctrine under consideration is contemplated, dwelling upon it has one tendency, and only one: the assimilation of our entire character to that of Christ.

Finally, brethren, seeing we have such a full and perfect redemption in Christ, "what manner of persons ought we to be in all holy conversation and godliness?" For remaining under the power of sin in any form we have no excuse. To "rejoice in the Lord always" we are under infinite obligation. "The joy of the Lord is our strength." To be free from all care; to be perpetually peaceful and blessed in Christ; to "show forth the praises of him who hath called us out of darkness into his marvelous light;" to breathe his spirit, walk in his steps, exemplify his virtues, and have his "joy fulfilled in us,"—is our high privilege and sacred duty. "Behold, I stand at the door, and knock; if any man will hear my voice, and open the door, I will come in to him, and sup with him, and he with me."

DISCOURSE VI

SPECIAL REDEMPTION

"And we have known and believed the love that God hath to us." ~ *I John iv. 16*

"I am crucified with Christ; nevertheless I live, yet not I, but Christ liveth in me: and the life that I now live in the flesh, I live by faith of the Son of God, who loved me, and gave himself for me." ~ *Gal. ii. 20*

"But we see Jesus, who was made a little lower than the angels, for the suffering of death, crowned with glory and honour; that he, by the grace of God, "should taste death for every man." ~ *Heb. ii. 9*

"And he is the propitiation for our sins; and not for ours only, but also for the sins of the whole world." ~ *I John ii. 2*

THERE are three positions, which have been taken by different classes of Christians, in respect to the nature and extent of the redemption of Christ.

1. Christ died for a only part of the human race: the elect. This is called *limited* redemption, or atonement. This doctrine, I would simply remark, is positively contradicted by the passages

---

231

cited above, and stands opposed to the whole aspect of the Gospel, as presented in the Scriptures.

2. Christ died for no individuals of our race in particular, but for all in general. This is called *general* atonement or redemption. This doctrine embodies one important and fundamental element of the grace of the Gospel: the universality of its provisions. It fails, however, to present one of the most interesting and important features of the provisions of Divine grace, as we shall see, when we contemplate,

3. The third position which has been taken in respect to the subject under consideration, which is this, that Christ, instead of dying for no one in particular, died for *every man in particular*. This is positively affirmed in the text: "He tasted death for every man;" "He loved *me*, and gave himself for *me*." The redemption of Christ had as special a regard to each individual, as if that one individual was alone concerned in it. This is what is called *special* atonement or redemption. I use the term "redemption" here, not in its strict theological sense, to designate the accomplishment of the provisions of mercy in the actual salvation of the sinner. In this sense of the term, "redemption" is limited by the reception of grace by the sinner. I use the term to designate the full and special provisions which Christ has made for the salvation of every individual of our race.

My object in the present discourse is, to present to the contemplation of the reader the *special* redemption of Christ; to show what is implied in the fact that Christ, as explained above, "has by the grace of God tasted death for every man." We will then inquire, What is implied in "knowing and believing the love that God hath to us?"

I. What is implied in the fact that Christ has tasted death for every man? It implies,

1. That, in assuming the work of our redemption, Christ had our entire condition and necessities, as sinners and as creatures, distinctly before his mind. Otherwise he could not, with propriety, be said to have tasted death," specifically, "for every

man." The same truth is also implied in the fact, that Christ is omniscient, and must have had his contemplation turned with perfect distinctness upon the entire condition and necessities of every individual, for whose redemption he died.

2. That the object of Christ, in thus tasting death for every man, was, to provide a redemption specifically adapted to the special condition and necessities of each individual for whom he died. For what reason should he taste death particularly for each individual, if this was not his object?

3. That Christ has provided for each individual of our race all the good that infinite wisdom could devise and infinite love desire. In short, he has accomplished a redemption for us, which covers our entire necessities in time and eternity. This he was able to accomplish, when he assumed the work of our redemption, and his infinite love would not permit him to accomplish less than this. This was the work, reader, which Christ undertook for you and me; and having assumed it, he never ceased to travail in the greatness of his strength, till he could say, "It is finished." If you will believe it, such is the "fullness" which you have in Christ.

4. That Christ has rendered the attainment of all this good practicable to us; that is, he has not only provided it for us, but proffered it to us, upon conditions with which we can comply. To suppose that he has offered it upon other conditions, is to accuse him of mocking our misery in the most flagrant manner conceivable, *i.e.*, providing for creatures blessings infinite, and then proffering them upon impracticable conditions. Instead of doing this, Christ has presented the blessings of his redemption to us upon such conditions, that there is an infallible certainty, "that every one that will ask shall receive, that he that will seek shall find, and that to him that knocketh it shall be opened."

The attention of the reader is now invited to a few particular examples, designed still further to illustrate the fullness and specialty of Christ's redemption.

1. He has made full provision, reader, for the entire pardon of every sin that you ever committed. As your mind ranges over

the dark catalogue of past transgressions, remember that those particular sins he "bore in his own body on the tree." For all those sins which rise up in appalling remembrance before you, he was "wounded and bruised," so that by "his stripes you may be healed." He has made such perfect provision for the forgiveness of each and every sin of your entire past existence, that there is no more necessity that you should be excluded from the presence and favor of God, on account of those sins, than there is that the purest spirit before the throne of God should be excluded.

2. Christ has provided means specifically adapted to secure your entire perfection in holiness. He perfectly understood your case when he undertook the work of your redemption. Every obstacle that lies in the way of your perfect sanctification was distinctly before his mind; and he has provided means fully adequate, and specifically adapted, to remedy all the consequences of your sins. However low you may have sunk in sin, he is able to lift you out of the "horrible pit and miry clay." However hard your heart may be, he can take it from you, and give you a heart of flesh in its stead. However firmly fixed your habits of sin may be, he can break them all up. However strong the power of your carnal inclinations, he can subdue them all, and give you a perfect victory over them. Whatever temptations to sin beset you, from within or around you, he can give you strength to endure them. The means to accomplish all this, and specifically adapted to your particular case, are all provided by his infinite love. "If any man be in Christ, he is a new creature. Old things have passed away; behold, all things have become new." Why, then, should you remain under the power of sin? Why should you be appalled by the fixedness of your habits of sin, by the strength of your carnal inclinations, or the multiplicity and power of the temptations which beset you? Christ saw all these when he assumed the work of your redemption. For all these he has provided a specific and all-powerful remedy. Go to Christ, and you will find that in him there is redemption in readiness for you, to render you "perfect and complete in all the will of God." Clad in the armor of

righteousness, which he has provided for you, you will find yourself able to stand against all the wiles of the wicked one.

3. In the redemption of Christ, there is special consolation provided for all the particular afflictions which come upon you. "In all your afflictions Christ was afflicted." If you will carry your wounded spirit to him, he will bind it up, however deep and multiplied the wounds may be. No one of them was forgotten by your Savior, when he undertook the work of "bearing your griefs, and carrying your sorrows." Balm specifically adapted to heal all those wounds is in readiness for you. Whatever the particular affliction may be, which falls upon you at any particular time, remember that that affliction, with all its peculiarities, has been specifically provided for by the love of Christ.

4. Whatever the sphere in life may be, in which you may at any time be called to move, for you Christ has provided special wisdom to meet all the exigencies and responsibilities that fall upon you in that sphere. When you lack wisdom, go to him, and he will "give liberally and not upbraid you." The means to do it are all provided.

5. Christ, in short, has made ample provision for every particular necessity which may come upon you in time and eternity. There is not a solitary want of yours, throughout the endless future beyond you, for which a special supply is not made in the redemption of Christ. For you there is provided a seat in heaven, a robe of righteousness, a harp of gold, a crown of glory, and a special place in the centre of God's heart of eternal love.

Such is the redemption of Christ. I might have illustrated the sentiment of this discourse by referring to other particulars. These are sufficient, however, to present the subject with entire distinctness to the contemplation of the reader. We will now inquire,

II. What is implied in our knowing and believing the love that the Father hath to us? This implies three things,

1. That we apprehend that love as it is, *i.e.*, the infinite love of God in giving his Son to make, by his incarnation and death, such full and special provisions for our necessities.

2. That we credit this love as a reality; in other words, that we give the Lord Jesus Christ full credit for being such a full and special Savior as he represents himself to be.

3. That we receive the Lord Jesus Christ as such a Savior, and yield up our whole being to his control, that he may accomplish in us all the purposes of his infinite and special love.

And now let me ask you, reader, do you believe with all your heart that Christ is in reality such a Savior as he has here been represented? Do you give him full credit for having "loved you and given himself for you," for the purpose of making such full and special provisions for your entire necessities? Do you believe that for you he tasted the bitter cup of death? In every special exigency of your being, can you look to him with the full assurance that this particular exigency, with all its peculiarities, was remembered and provided for by him, when he was "wounded for your transgressions, and bruised for your iniquities?" Can you reckon yourself among the number, who can say, "We have known and believed the love that the Father hath unto us?" Do you believe that Christ has provided redemption for you, a redemption so perfectly and specifically adapted to your particular case, that you can now go to him, and be cleansed from all that is impure and unholy, and so transformed into his likeness that your entire character shall hereafter present a pure reflection of his image. Do you believe that you may bring to him your temper, your appetites, your propensities, your entire habits, and have them all brought into sweet subjection to the will of God? Do you believe that, in him, there is a special balm for every wound; relief from every care; consolation for all affliction; a remedy for every ill; and a full supply for every specific necessity of your entire existence? Unless you believe all this, and your heart is all melted into love and tenderness under the influence of that belief, you have yet to learn the breadth, and depth, and length, and height of the love of Christ.

REMARKS

I. We may now understand the nature of what may be called appropriating faith. It consists in receiving Christ, and relying upon him as our Savior, in reference to all our particular necessities as individuals. As the creatures of God, as sinners against his holy law, we have our particular duties, spheres of action, temptations, trials, afflictions, and necessities. Now, when Christ is contemplated as having provided a redemption for us, specifically adapted to our special exigencies, and is received as a Savior to meet these exigencies, then we exercise towards him appropriating faith. Then we appropriate to ourselves the special redemption that he has provided for us.

II. Here I may be permitted to allude to a very common mistake among Christians, in looking to Christ as a Savior. They appear to look to him as a Savior in general, without any reference to their particular necessities. How seldom do we meet with a Christian, for example, who carries to Christ his temper, his appetites, his habits, and propensities of every kind, which lead him into sin, to have them all corrected and subdued! Where is the Christian, who is accustomed to go to Christ, to be rendered by him all that he requires him or her to be as a father, a mother, a child, a brother, or sister, or in special reference to the business transactions of life? Now, until our faith fastens upon Christ, with reference to specific objects such as these, the power of his redemption will never be experienced. From our sins Christ does not and cannot save us, unless by faith we thus appropriate the provisions of his redemption.

III. In the light of this subject, we may also learn what Christ requires and expects of us as Christians. To present this part of the subject distinctly before the reader's mind, I remark,

1. That Christ designs and expects that our religion shall be carried out, and influence us alike in all the scenes and

transactions of life; that we shall eat, drink, dress, spend our time, talents, and property, transact our business, and move in every sphere in life, with exclusive reference to the same identical objects for which we pray, worship God on the Sabbath, warn sinners to flee from the wrath to come, or partake of the symbols of the body and blood of our Lord. "Whether, therefore, ye eat or drink, or whatsoever ye do, do all to the glory of God." That you may all do this; that Holiness to the Lord may be inscribed upon all that you have, and all that you are, full provision is made in the redemption of Christ. Hence,

2. He requires and expects that you will believe that special grace to do all this is provided for you, and that you will look to him to be rendered thus "perfect and complete in all the will of God."

3. When you are called in providence to move in any particular sphere, he requires and expects that your first object will be, to understand clearly the particular responsibilities, trials, temptations, &c., incident to you in that particular sphere.

4. He requires and expects that you will believe that he, as your Redeemer, has made full and special provision for all your exigencies in that particular sphere; and that, in the exercise of full and implicit faith, you will look to him for grace to meet those exigencies.

Such are some of the requirements and expectations of Christ from us as Christians. Here let me add, that if we do not look to Christ to be saved by him, in every sphere, and in respect of every transaction in life, our faith does not fix upon him at all as a Savior from sin. I would also add, that if Christ does not save us by subduing our tempers, controlling our appetites and propensities, by rendering us in our spheres, as husbands and wives, parents and children, in every sphere, and in all the particular transactions of life, what he requires us to be, he does not save us at all. The man who expects to be a Christian in his closet, and upon the Sabbath, and a man of the world behind his counter, in his shop, or on his farm, will find at last that he has failed of the grace of God.

We also learn the nature of unbelief, in its most common form in the Church. It is withholding from Christ implicit confidence, as a Savior, who has provided special means to do it, and is now able and willing to meet all our particular necessities as individuals.

V. We will now consider some of the most common indications of unbelief. Among these I notice,

1. The impression which individuals have, that there are peculiar difficulties in their case. The redemption of Christ appears fully adequate to the exigencies of every other individual but themselves. Did Christ, reader, in tasting death for you, overlook the special peculiarities of your condition? Or had he, when he cried, "It is finished," failed to make full provision for those peculiarities? Why, then, permit your unbelief to put far from you all the endless provisions of Christ's redemption? If you withhold confidence from Christ as an ever-present Savior, able and willing to meet all the peculiarities of your condition, you do it at the peril, yes, to the certain loss, of your eternal interests.

2. I believe, says another, that Christ has provided full redemption for me; a redemption which perfectly covers all my necessities; but I *cannot* exercise faith in Christ. Christ, then, has purchased full and special redemption for you, but proffered it to you upon conditions with which you cannot comply.

Why let unbelief thus fasten a millstone about that deathless soul of yours?

3. My heart, says another, is so hard and insensible, that nothing in the universe will move or melt it. Did Christ, in tasting death for you, overlook that heart of stone in your bosom? and has he made no special provision to take it out of your flesh, and give in its stead a heart of flesh? Remember, that if you do not carry this very heart to Christ, that he may take it from you, and if you do not exercise special faith in him to do it, he will be no Savior to you in any sense whatever.

4. Another individual complains that his natural temper is so ungovernable, and his habits of sin so omnipotent in their influence over him, that it appears to him that there can be no redemption for him, at least in this life. If Christ has not provided a special and adequate remedy for these evils, and if your faith does not fasten upon that particular remedy, then there is no salvation for you. Christ will "save you from your sins," or not at all. Why let that temper, and those habits, drag you down to death, when Christ has made full and special provision for their perfect subdual?

5. Another individual feels that he cannot be preserved in his particular sphere. "How can a person be kept perfectly free from sin," says one, "in the midst of the numberless temptations incident to a residence in a great city?" If this were so, I would say, "Up, get ye out of this place." It is better for thee to "enter into life," from the obscurest and most barren spot on earth, than to descend into the lake of fire, from the most splendid palace or city. But who is it that has promised that he will not "suffer you to be tempted above that ye are able, but with the temptation will make a way for your escape, that ye may be able to bear it?" Who is the strongest, Christian; "he that is in you," or he "that is in the world?"

"Do you believe," said a mother, "that I can be preserved in a state of perfect peace, in the midst of all the cares and perplexities of this great family?" Christ, according to the suggestions of unbelief in the mind of that individual, had, in the special provisions of his grace for her, overlooked the fact that she was to be the mother of a large family, and had failed to provide a special remedy for all the cares and perplexities incident to her lot in that particular sphere. Sad indeed was her condition, if that were really the case.

6. It does not appear, says another, possible that creatures sunk so low in sin as we are, should be raised to a state of perfect purity. Did you acquire that sentiment, brother, through a full and careful inquiry into the nature and power of the grace of Christ? Did you learn it from a prayerful investigation of the extent of the provisions and promises of Christ's redemption, and of the power of Christ himself as a Saviour? Is that grace,

which has the power to change a rebel into a friend, insufficient, if applied by Christ himself, for the purpose, to change partial into perfect love? What is there to appall us, however deep and settled our habits of sin, if Christ has provided the means, and has undertaken to accomplish a full redemption from all iniquity?

7. If I could only see someone who had attained to a state of entire sanctification, then I would believe the doctrine. It is very doubtful whether, if such a case were actually presented to a person in this state of mind, God would not have occasion to say unto him, "I work a work in your day, which ye will in no wise believe, though a man declare it unto you." Or if he should believe it for that reason, the fact itself would show that his faith rests, as said in a former discourse, upon what he sees, and not upon the Word of God. Which, reader, have you taken as the only infallible rule of faith and practice, the Word of God or the attainments of men?

8. It does not appear to me, that by simply believing in Christ, says another, I could be saved from all sin. In other words, the declaration of Christ, "He that believeth in me, though he were dead, yet shall he live," does not appear to be a reality. Such an individual ought to learn another fact: that he has as yet experienced but very little of the power of faith in his own heart. "Now, the just shall live by faith." "We also believe, and therefore speak."

VI. We may also learn the influence of unbelief. It annihilates wholly the saving influence of the Gospel upon the heart. It places the subject in the same state of absolute hopelessness that he would be in, had no salvation been provided. "If ye believe not that I am He, ye shall die in your sins." Whatever necessity presses upon us, that necessity remains for ever unsupplied till faith fastens upon the special redemption of Christ, as an ever-present and all-powerful remedy.

VII. We may now understand the true remedy for spiritual pride. I recollect having once heard a preacher, in a public address, give this as the all-powerful corrective, "Let a person keep perpetually before his mind the standard of absolute perfection required by the law of God, and let it be his constant aim to ascend to a full discharge of every duty required of him. Now, if, while he is ascending from one degree to another toward the point of perfect holiness, he looks down and reflects upon the attainments he has already made, he will be lifted up with pride. If, on the other hand, in his perpetual ascent, he keeps his eye steadily fixed upon the point above him, he will be kept perpetually humbled in view of constant shortcomings." The remedy was received by the audience with unbounded applause. This reflection, however, forced itself upon my mind, that if the speaker was in the same state of mind in which Christians generally are, he was not a little elevated in his estimation of himself by the beautiful remedy which he had proposed for spiritual pride. And what a thought is this, that a Christian must not obey the commands, "Search your own hearts," "Examine yourselves, whether ye be in the faith; prove your own selves," lest, if he should find that he had attained to any real holiness, he would be lifted with pride, and not exclaim, with adoring gratitude, "By the grace of God I am what I am! "

Now, the apostle has proposed a very different remedy for spiritual pride, from the one under consideration, which is the one commonly proposed, "Where is boasting, then? It is excluded. By what, law? Of works? Nay; but by the law of faith."

Suppose that an individual becomes fully conscious that, in consequence of his own reckless folly, he has involved himself in infinite guilt and hopeless bondage under sin; that Christ, of his self-moved goodness and mercy, has made full provision to meet all his necessities as a sinner; that, by implicit faith in Christ, he enjoys full redemption from the power and consequences of sin; and that the moment his faith loses its hold of Christ, he falls into the same hopeless guilt and bondage as before. When the man finds himself rising in spiritual attainments, under the influence of such a principle, to whom will he spontaneously ascribe the entire glory of his salvation?

"To him that loved us, and washed us from our sins in his own blood." The fact that Christians generally cannot conceive themselves to have ascended in spiritual attainment, at all above the common level, without pride of heart, is to my mind full demonstration of the fact, that they yet need to be taught what are the "first principles" of holy living. "The righteousness which is of faith" excludes all boasting, of every kind.

VIII. You learn, Christian, to what to attribute every act of sin, and all your care, and trouble, and perplexity about the "many things" of this life. All these, together with every wrong feeling which arises in your mind, have their origin in one source exclusively, *unbelief,* a want of confidence in that special redemption of Christ, which, but for unbelief, would meet every possible exigency of our whole existence.

IX. We see, also, how it is that most Christians lose the presence of Christ under the pressure of business, when on a journey, or when brought into any scenes to which they have not before been accustomed. In such circumstances, they do not look to Christ for the special grace which he has provided to meet such exigencies. O that Christians would take this promise with them everywhere, "As thy days, so shall thy strength be!" "Then would their peace be like a river, and their righteousness as the waves of the sea."

X. We also understand the secret of always having a heart melted with love and tenderness. It consists in a full sense of our own infinite guilt and vileness of the boundless love of Christ, in making such full and perfect provision for our entire necessities, and as being ever present in our hearts, to confer upon us the full benefits of this eternal redemption. "Behold what manner of love the Father hath bestowed upon us, that we should be called the children of God!" Such a thought, when it once takes possession of the mind, has omnipotent power to melt the heart, and cause its purest, sweetest, and best affections to roll for ever around one "blissful centre."

XI. We now understand the reason why the Lord Jesus Christ declared "the kingdom of heaven to be like leaven, which a woman took and hid in three measures of meal, till the whole were leavened." The thought here presented, in its application to Christians, is this: When the kingdom of heaven is once set up in the heart of an individual, it will lead directly on to an entire subjection of all the powers and principles of his being to its Divine control. The reason is this: For our entire redemption from sin, into a state of perfect moral purity, the Gospel has made full provision. For every sinful habit and propensity, for every incentive to sin, it presents a specific and all-powerful remedy, through faith in Christ. Who that hates sin, and loves holiness supremely, will remain under the power of the former, and destitute of the fullness of the latter, under such circumstances?

XII. We see also the reason of Christ's declaration, "And this is life eternal, that they might know thee, the only true God, and Jesus Christ, whom thou has sent." Suppose, Christian, that you could apprehend the excellence and love of Christ, as fully as your capacities will permit; suppose you could apprehend the fullness of his special love to you, and to every other individual of our race; that you could apprehend him as ever present with you, to meet your entire necessities in time and eternity; suppose you could apprehend him in all his relations to you, as your God and Savior, and you could be fully assured that, through his love, every attribute of the Godhead stands pledged for your present and eternal well-being: to know Christ in this manner, and to have all the powers of your being moving perpetually under the influence of his infinite love, this would indeed be life eternal. To be in this state is your high and blessed privilege. To present this love to you in all its fullness, God has given you his Holy Spirit. If you will look to that Spirit to be "strengthened with might in the inner man," for this specific object, "that the love of Christ may dwell richly in your heart by faith," you will then be able to "comprehend, with all the saints, what is the breadth, and length, and depth, and height, and to know the love of Christ, which passeth knowledge, that ye may be filled with all the fulness of God."

XIII. Finally, we may, in the light of this discourse, understand the secret of the pre-eminent piety of Paul and of primitive Christians. It is all explained in one single expression of the sacred writer - "Looking unto Jesus, the author and finisher of our faith." At all times, and under all circumstances, they "knew nothing but Jesus Christ, and him crucified." They literally "counted all things but loss, for the excellency of the knowledge of Christ Jesus their Lord." He was their wisdom, "their "righteousness," their "sanctification," and "redemption." He was their consolation in every affliction. He was their perfect pattern, their sole leader and guide. He was their certain victory, in every conflict with the "world, the flesh, and the devil." He was their joy, their hope, their inheritance, their shield, and their "exceeding great reward." He was their "bright and morning star," the magnet of their souls, which held all the powers of their being in a blissful fixedness to one changeless Centre.

Now, Christian, if you will believe it, Christ will be to you all that he was to them. "He is the same yesterday, to-day, and for ever;" and you may share as fully as they did in the infinite fullness of the love and grace of Christ. If, however, you would enjoy this full redemption, all the powers of your being must be brought under the perpetual influence of this one principle: "Looking to Jesus." Do your sins rise up before you, and fill you with apprehensions of coming retributions, "Look to Jesus." Do you desire to be wholly freed from the power of sin, and to have your entire character presented to God, "without spot or wrinkle, or any such thing," "Look to Jesus." Are you burdened with care, or do the storms of affliction gather round you, "Look to Jesus." Is your temper unsubdued, do your appetites and propensities rebel, and call for unhallowed gratification, "Look to Jesus." Do temptations beset you, from within or around you, "Look to Jesus." Do you need wisdom and grace for any exigency whatever, "Look to Jesus." Whatever your condition or necessities may be, hear his gracious voice, "Come unto me, all ye that labour and are heavy laden, and I will give you rest. Take my yoke upon you, and learn of me, for I am meek and lowly in heart, and ye shall find rest to your souls."

"Jesus, we come at thy command,
With faith, and hope, and humble zeal,
Resign our spirits to thy hand,
To mould and guide us at thy will."

DISCOURSE VII

EXCEEDING GREAT AND PRECIOUS PROMISES

"Whereby are given unto us exceeding great and precious promises; that, by these, ye might be partakers of the Divine nature; having escaped the corruption that is in the world through lust." ~ 2 Pet. i. 4.

IN the verse preceding, we are informed that God, in giving us a revelation of Jesus Christ, has furnished us with a knowledge of everything which "pertains to life and godliness." In the text, we are informed, that, in the same revelation, he has given unto us "exceeding great and precious promises;" that these promises are conferred upon us for this purpose, that through them, or by embracing them by faith, we may become "partakers of the Divine nature," and escape the "corruption that is in the world through lust." A promise is a pledge of good. In every promise of Divine grace, Christ discloses to us the good which he stands pledged to confer upon us, on condition that we look to him, by faith, for the blessing presented in the promise. Now, the success of all our efforts after holiness depends upon the use we make of the promises. I propose, therefore, in the following discourse, to illustrate the following propositions:

I. I will present to the contemplation of the reader some of the "exceeding great and precious promises" of Divine grace.

II. Show what is implied in our becoming "partakers of the Divine nature, having escaped the corruptions that are in the world through lust."

III. Show the manner in which the promises must be used, in order that we may obtain the good which they present to us.

I. I am to present to the contemplation of the reader some of the "exceeding great and precious promises" of Divine grace. As much that I should otherwise say upon this part of our subject has been anticipated in preceding discourses, my remarks under this head will be very brief. In presenting the reader with a slight view of these "exceeding great and precious promises," I would remark in general, that Christ has pledged to us an eternal exemption from all that would be to us, on the whole, a real evil, and the possession of everything, in time and eternity, the possession of which would be to us a real blessing. "Not a hair of your head shall perish." "And nothing shall by any means hurt you." "No good thing will be withheld from them that walk uprightly." These promises belong alike to all Christians, in all ages and circumstances. For their fulfillment, they are required, with full and humble confidence, to cast themselves upon the power and faithfulness of Christ. But, to be more particular, I remark,

1. That Christ has promised, to all who will believe in him, an eternal exemption from all the condemnation which they deserve on account of their sins, and which actually will fall upon the wicked. "My sheep hear my voice, and I know them, and they follow me; and I give unto them eternal life; and they shall never perish, neither shall any pluck them out of my hand." "Verily, verily, I say unto you, he that heareth my words, and believeth on him that sent me, hath everlasting life, and shall not come into condemnation, but is passed from death

unto life." "There is therefore now no condemnation to them that are in Christ Jesus."

2. A sure title to all the blessedness enjoyed by the pure spirits around the throne of God. "Ye are come, to an innumerable company of angels, and to the general assembly and church of the first-born which are written in heaven." "I give unto them eternal life, and they shall never perish." "Who shall separate us from the love of God?"

Suppose, reader, that you were introduced within the veil of eternity, and were permitted to look down into the gulf of death, until you should fully apprehend the infinite wretchedness of a lost spirit, as he wanders on, through ceaseless ages, amid the gloom and despair of the eternal sepulcher; suppose you were then permitted to raise your vision to those infinite heights of purity and blessedness to which redeemed spirits in heaven will ascend, as eternity rolls on its endless years. While these depths of gloom and heights of bliss were distinctly before your mind, suppose Christ should pledge himself to you, that he would free you from all exposure to the former, and give you a sure title to the full possession of the latter. What an "exceeding great and precious promise" that would be! Such is the promise of Christ now before you. "Bless the Lord, O my soul, and forget not all his benefits."

3. Entire freedom from all sin, and the transformation of our entire character into a likeness to his own. "I," says Christ, "will sprinkle clean water upon you, and ye shall be clean; from *all* your filthiness, and from *all* your idols will I cleanse you." "And thou shalt call his name Jesus; for he shall save his people from their sins." "But we all, with open face beholding, as in a glass, the glory of the Lord, are changed into the same image from glory to glory, even as by the Spirit of the Lord." This is held before us as a promise. Such a change Christ stands pledged to produce in us if we will believe in him.

4. He promises to subdue our lusts and propensities, to guard us against all temptation to sin from within or around us, and to give us a full and perfect victory over "the world, the flesh, and the devil." "If Christ be in you, the body is dead because of sin." "Walk in the spirit, and ye shall not fulfil the lusts of the flesh." "If any man be in Christ, he is a new creature; old things are passed away; behold all things have become new." "This is the victory that overcometh the world, even our faith." "Fear not, I have overcome the world." "He is able to succour them that are tempted." "Who will not suffer you to be tempted above that ye are able; but will with the temptation make a way to escape, that ye may be able to bear it."

5. Consolation in every affliction. "The Spirit of the Lord God is upon me; because the Lord hath anointed me to preach good tidings to the meek; he hath sent me to bind up the broken-hearted, to proclaim liberty to the captives, and the opening of the prison to them that are bound; to comfort all that mourn; to appoint unto them that mourn in Zion, to give unto them beauty for ashes, the oil of joy for mourning, the garment of praise for the spirit of heaviness." "Come unto me, all ye that labour and are heavy laden, and I will give you rest."

6. The constant fruition of the Divine presence and love, and all the blessedness which he himself enjoys, as far as our capacities will permit. "We will come and make our abode with him." "I will dwell in them, and walk in them." "Peace I leave with you, my peace" *i.e.*, the peace which I enjoy, "I give unto you." "That they might have my joy fulfilled in themselves." "The peace of God, which passeth all understanding, shall keep your heart and mind through Christ Jesus."

7. The privilege of going to God, at all times and under all circumstances, in prayer, with the use of Christ's name, and with the certain pledge that whatsoever we thus ask, that will be a good to us, shall be granted. "If ye abide in me, and my words abide in you, ye shall ask what ye will, and it shall be done unto

you." "If ye shall ask anything in my name, I will do it." "Ask and it shall be given you, that your joy may be full."

8. The constant presence and illumination of the Holy Spirit. "He shall abide with you for ever." "He shall lead you into all truth." "He shall take of mine and show them unto you."

9. Not merely grace to make us holy and keep us from all sin, but an infinite reward for every expression of love that he shall receive from us, and every act of obedience that we shall render to him. "And every one that hath forsaken houses, or brethren, or sisters, or father, or mother, or wife, or children, or lands, for my name's sake, shall receive a hundred fold, and shall inherit everlasting life. And whosoever shall give to drink unto one of these little ones a cup of cold water only, in the name of a disciple, verily I say unto you, he shall in no wise lose his reward." Such is the infinite and incomprehensible love and grace of Christ. By his grace we are rendered holy, and are then to be rewarded infinitely for being what the grace of Christ has rendered us.

10. Great success in our efforts to advance his cause. "He that abideth in me, and I in him, the same bringeth forth much fruit." "Verily, verily, I say unto you, He that believeth on me, the works that I do shall he do also; and greater works than these shall he do; because I go to my Father." Christ has not only promised to render us thus successful, but to bestow an infinite and eternal reward upon us for all that we accomplish for him. "They that be wise shall shine as the brightness of the firmament, and they that turn many to righteousness, as the stars for ever and ever."

11. Christ promises to us a peaceful death, and a glorious immortality. "Mark the perfect man, and behold the upright; for the end of that man is peace." "I will come again and receive you to myself, that where I am, there ye may be also. "We know that when he shall appear, we shall be like him; for we shall see him as he is." "And there shall be no more curse; but the throne of

God and of the Lamb shall be in it; and his servants shall serve him; and they shall see his face; and his name shall be in their foreheads."

Such are the promises of Christ to his people. And, reader, are not these promises "exceeding great and precious?" To you they all belong; and Christ invites you to come to him, and receive your purchased and promised inheritance. We will now inquire,

II. What is implied in our being "made partakers of the Divine nature, having escaped the corruption that is in the world through lust." This implies two things,

1. That we become entirely emancipated from the power of sin. No person, not thus emancipated, but still, in any degree, under the power of sin, could be said to have "*escaped* the corruption that is in the world through lust."

2. It implies that we, to the full extent of our powers, be rendered partakers of the holiness and blessedness of God. This is the only sense in which any intelligent being can be a partaker of the Divine nature. "But he," says the apostle, "for our profit, that we might be partakers of his holiness." To be partakers of the Divine holiness, and consequently of the Divine blessedness, is of course the same thing as to be rendered partakers of the Divine nature.

That we might thus escape the corruptions that are in the world, and be "made partakers of the Divine nature," is the declared object for which the "exceeding great and precious promises" were given. When we come to Christ by faith for a fulfilment of these promises, his power stands pledged to fulfil in us the glorious object for which they were given. I am now,

III. To show the manner in which we are to use the promises, in order that we may obtain the good which they present to us. As the design of the promises is to free us from the "corruptions that are in the world," and render us "partakers of the Divine nature," they are addressed and adapted to every possible condition in which we may be placed, and as a remedy for every evil, natural and moral, in which we may be involved. They descend to the sinner in the lowest depths of guilt and depravity, for the purpose of lifting him out of the "horrible pit and miry clay," and rendering him a partaker of the "Divine nature." They meet the Christian, in a state of partial holiness, for the purpose of raising him to a state of "perfect love," and then of carrying him upward and onward, from glory to glory, through time and eternity. Now, to use the promises so as to become possessed of the blessings which they proffer to us, four things are necessary,

1. That we know our need.

2. That we apprehend the particular promise of Christ, which was designed to meet that particular necessity.

3. That we repose full confidence in Christ's ability and faithfulness to fulfill the promise which he has spread before us.

4. That we cast our whole being upon him, for the specific purpose of securing a fulfillment of the particular promise before us. For example, the sinner is brought to feel himself to be in a lost condition. Here he is met with the declaration of Christ, "I came to seek and to save that which was lost;" together with the promises, "Look to me and be ye saved;" "Whosoever cometh to me I will in no wise cast out." Let the sinner cast himself at once upon Christ, for the definite purpose of securing a fulfillment of those specific promises. Are you in darkness, reader? Go directly to Christ for the fulfillment of the promise, "I will lead the blind by a way which they know not." Is your heart hard and unfeeling? Go to Christ with the definite promise, "I will take the heart of stone out of your flesh, and will give you a heart of flesh," and cast yourself upon his faithfulness for the fulfillment of that promise. Are your appetites, or your propensities the "occasion of stumbling" to you? Carry these particular objects to Christ, and plead the definite promises, "If Christ be in you, the body is dead, because of sin," and "If any man be in Christ he is a new creature; old things have passed away; behold all things have become new." Do temptations beset you? Go to Christ with the promise, "Who will not suffer you to

be tempted above that you are able; but will with the temptation make a way for your escape, that ye may be able to bear it." Are you about to enter into new and untried scenes, or spheres of action? Go to Christ with the specific promises, "Lo, I am with you always," and "My grace is sufficient for thee." Are you "hungering and thirsting after righteousness?" This promise you may now plead with Christ, "They shall be filled." Does the water of life begin to flow in your heart? This promise now rises before you, "Whosoever drinketh of the water that I shall give him, shall never thirst; but the water that I shall give him, shall be in him a well of water springing up into everlasting life." In short, whatever your condition or state of mind may be, remember that you are addressed by your Savior with some specific promise, perfectly adapted to your peculiar case. Your life depends upon your casting yourself at once upon the faithfulness of Christ, for a fulfillment of that promise. In so using the "exceeding great and precious promises," you may, with absolute certainty, be rendered a "partaker of the Divine nature, having escaped the corruption that is in the world through lust."

REMARKS

I. We will notice the great truth, of which we need to have a full and distinct apprehension, in order that all the promises may rise before our minds as living realities. It is the infinite love of God in the gift of Christ for our redemption. In Christ, "all the promises are yea and amen." "He that spared not his own Son, but delivered him up for us all, how shall he not with him freely give us all things?" For the want of such an apprehension of the love of Christ, the promises are, to the great mass of the Church, almost as a "dead letter."

II. We notice one of the first lessons which should be taught to the young convert. He should first of all use the promises as a sovereign remedy to every ill that may press upon him. Let his eye be directed to these; let him become accustomed to apply to them in every possible exigency, and he will ascend upwards upon them, as upon Jacob's ladder, from glory to glory, to eternal heights of purity and blessedness.

III. We see how it is that the peace of the young convert is very commonly destroyed, and his growth in grace prevented, by the instructions which he receives from older Christians. When the convert, alarmed at the discovery of inward corruptions, and of the numerous occasions of stumbling, in himself, arising from his temper, his appetites, his habits of sin, as well as the hardness of his heart, comes for counsel to those who ought to be able to point him at once to the remedy, and thus lead him to the "fountain of living waters," there is commonly a direct attempt to comfort him in his present state. He is told that such discoveries of inward corruption are the highest evidence of our conversion, that he must not be alarmed when he "finds the Canaanite in the land," that these foes will never be dislodged from his bosom till his dying day, and that Christ will very soon teach him the "plague of his own heart," by letting him slide down from the warmth and blessedness of his first love, into the valley of spiritual death, misnamed the valley of humiliation. Well might the convert reply to such guides, "Miserable comforters are ye all." If, now, he will turn from all such directions to the "exceeding great and precious promises" of Christ, and with humble confidence cast himself upon his faithfulness, then shall his "righteousness go forth as brightness, and his salvation as a lamp that burneth." Then shall he prove, by blessed experience, the truth of the promise, "Even the youths shall faint and be weary, and the young men shall utterly fall; but they that wait on the Lord shall renew their strength; they shall mount up on wings as eagles; they shall run and not be weary; they shall walk and not faint."

IV. We may understand the object which the Christian should have in view, in searching his own heart. It should be the same as the physician has in examining the symptoms of his patient; *i.e.*, to determine the nature of the disease, for the purpose of applying the appropriate remedy. So the Christian should examine himself to determine what he is, and what he needs, for the purpose of looking away to some definite promise as the remedy to that necessity. How profitable seasons of fasting and prayer would be, if spent in this manner with the Physician of souls. The want of this definite object is the great reason, I suppose, why such seasons are so generally almost profitless to Christians.

V. We see why it is that Christians apply to Christ for sanctification, &c., almost without success. Their object is commonly general and undefined, and no thing specific is presented. Let an individual, on the other hand, who finds his temper, his appetites, his propensities, or worldly pursuits, the occasion of falling, take one or more of these definite objects to Christ, and cast himself, in view of some definite promise, upon his faithfulness, to have that particular cause of sin removed; let him thus bring all his powers and propensities to Christ, and how soon would all his faculties and susceptibilities be so sweetly and perfectly subjected to the will of God, that all occasion of stumbling would be taken away! In all instances, reader, when you go to Christ with some definite object, resting also upon some definite promise, you are sure to be heard.

VI. We see how it is that Satan often destroys the confidence of Christians in the promises, in their application to themselves. It is by directing their attention to some promise that is not applicable to their present state, and pressing them to attempt to believe in that. Said one, I often thought of the promise, "Blessed are they that mourn, for they shall be comforted;" and, because I was not in the state upon which that promise was conditioned, I thought there was no other promise in the Bible that belonged to me, or upon which I could lay hold. Before that individual could mourn, it was necessary for her to "look on him whom she had pierced." Quite another promise belonged to her in the state referred to, to wit, "Look to me and be ye saved." By casting herself upon this, she would soon have been brought into a state to which the promise first referred to was addressed. As long as Satan can keep the mind from the promises addressed to our particular state, and fixed upon others inapplicable, he will hold us, in spite of ourselves, in unbelief.

VII. We see why it is that, to most professors, the thought of being entirely sanctified in this life appears so chimerical. Their minds have ranged, in the darkness of unbelief, amid their own wrongdoings and shortcomings; and not upon the boundless provisions, and "exceeding great and precious promises" of Divine grace, till they have apprehended the riches of the glory of Christ's inheritance in the saints. If Christ has made provision for our entire holiness, and has promised, on the condition of simple faith in his word, that he will himself sanctify us wholly, and preserve our whole spirit, and soul, and body, blameless unto his coming and kingdom, how reasonable to expect that his power shall effect what his love has provided and his truth has promised!

VIII. We see why it appears to most persons so impossible to exercise that faith which would result in a state of entire sanctification. They do not believe that provision is made in the Gospel for the attainment of that state, or that Christ has promised it to us, on condition of our faith in him for that blessing. If Christ has made such provisions, and given such promises, it would be difficult, if not impossible, to account for the existence of that faith in an individual which induces partial and not perfect holiness, when he has those provisions and promises distinctly before his mind.

IX. In what sense all Christians are expected and required to be witnesses for Christ. They are expected and required so to trust Christ in respect to the fulfillment of all his promises, that they can say, from blessed experience, that in all those promises Christ is a faithful and true witness. Take the following promise as an example: "Thou wilt keep him in perfect peace, whose mind is stayed on thee, because he trusteth in thee." Now, we are expected and required to "stay ourselves upon God" in such a manner that we can affirm, from experience, that the effect of trusting in God is all that it is here affirmed to be. So of every other promise in the Bible. If we cannot thus testify for God, we are found to be false witnesses for him. It is in giving such testimony that we are chiefly to glorify Christ, and benefit our fellow-men. How melancholy is the fact, that most professors, instead of being able to speak for Christ, as his faithful and true witnesses, can only give an opinion, that if they should embrace the promises, they would find them true; which is no more than the impenitent can say, and, of course, is no testimony at all.

X. We see that if, as is commonly supposed, God has so arranged the dispensations of his providence and grace, that no one will attain to a state of entire sanctification in this life, he has made such arrangements that he shall never have a witness on earth that can bear full testimony to the truth of his promises. Many of these promises are, as we have seen in a former discourse, conditioned on the existence of this state in the subject. How infinitely absurd is the supposition that God has made definite arrangement, by which he is never to have a witness on earth who can bear full testimony for him! "Ye are my witnesses, saith the Lord." See to it, Christian, that you, by availing yourself of proffered grace, become perfectly qualified to bear full testimony for God. How reasonable is the supposition that God should make full provision for the perfect qualification, *i.e.*, sanctification, of his own witnesses! How perfectly unreasonable the opposite supposition!

XI. We may also perceive the perfect absurdity of the supposition, that if a Christian were entirely sanctified, he would not be permitted longer to live on earth; but would be taken directly to heaven. In other words, if an individual were fully qualified to bear testimony for Christ, he would not allow him to testify at all.

XII. We perceive the infinite obligation resting upon us, to be entirely free from care and perplexity, and to be always, and under all circumstances, in a state of perfect peace and blessedness. We have only to rest down upon the "exceeding great and precious promises," and every care, every perplexity, and every burden is necessarily rolled from our minds. We are led into the "banqueting-house" of the Redeemer, "where his banner over us is love." We are conducted forth "into the green pastures, and beside the still waters." We range along the banks of the river of life, and our peace and blessedness will be like the broad, and deep, and crystal flow of that river.

Reader, what is the character of your religion? Is it a life-giving and a peace-giving religion? Your body, you say, is the "temple of the Holy Spirit." What are the fruits of the spirit that actually dwells in that temple? Are they, "love, joy, peace, long-suffering, gentleness, goodness, faith, meekness, temperance?" "If any man have not the spirit of Christ, he is none of his."

XIII. In the light of this subject, we are also led to contemplate and adore the infinite love of God to us. This love is manifested in the bestowment upon creatures, infinite in guilt and vileness, of the highest blessing that infinite wisdom could conceive, that infinite love could desire, and infinite power confer—the eternal possession of the "Divine nature", the holiness and blessedness of God. Reader, dwell upon this thought. In it learn to comprehend your own privileges, and the boundless love of God. For the bestowment of this blessing, full provision is made in the Gospel. For its full accomplishment in you, the Son of God is "standing at the door," and the Spirit of grace is now in your heart. If you will open the door, the Son of God will enter in and confer this blessed inheritance upon you.

XIV. Finally, we perceive the infinite obligation that rests upon us, not to remain under the power of any sin; but to have our temper, our appetites, our propensities, habits, and all the powers and susceptibilities of our being, subdued and brought into sweet and perfect subjection to the will of Christ, so that there shall be "none occasion of stumbling in us." For the accomplishment of this, full provision is made in the Gospel of the grace of God, and we have only to cast ourselves upon Christ for the fulfillment of the "exceeding great and precious promises" which he has given us, and all this blessedness is ours.

It is your blissful privilege, reader, in the use of these promises, to be made a "partaker of the Divine nature, having escaped the corruption that is in the world through lust." Remember what God has said, "Now the just shall live by faith; but if any man draw back, my soul shall have no pleasure in him." "See that ye refuse not him that speaketh. For if they escaped not who refused him that spake on earth, much more shall not we escape, if we turn away from him that speaketh from heaven."

DISCOURSE VIII

THE DIVINE TEACHER

"Now the Lord is that Spirit: and where the Spirit of the Lord is, there is liberty. But we all, with open face beholding, as in a glass, the glory of the Lord, are changed into the same image, from glory to glory, even as by the Spirit of the Lord." ~ 2 Cor. iii. 17-18

IN the verses preceding, the apostle speaks of the veil that was over the mind of the Jew, in the reading of the Scriptures, and which prevented his understanding their true import. In the text he speaks of the privileges which Christians enjoy through the illumination of the Holy Spirit. "Where the Spirit of the Lord is, there is liberty;" *i.e.*, there is a full and direct aspect of truth, and a full experience of its renovating power. "But we all, with open face, beholding, as in a glass, the glory of the Lord, are changed into the same image, from glory to glory, even as by the Spirit of the Lord." Every real Christian can call to mind seasons when he had such views of truth as are here referred to, views which melted his whole soul into love and tenderness, and brought all the powers of his being into sweet subjection to the will of God. Could these visions be rendered perpetual in the mind of the Christian, his heart would never wax cold or unfeeling; nor would there ever be any rival to Christ in his heart, to dispute with him the empire of the soul. In the absence of such views, darkness enters and spreads itself over the mind, and temptations to sin have a sovereign power. Now, to impart these visions of truth, to render them perpetual, and thus preserve the mind under the uninterrupted influence of the love of Christ, and give to that love the highest possible efficacy over the heart, is the appropriate office of the Holy Spirit. This is the part which he now acts in the plan of redemption. Christ is of God made unto us "wisdom, and righteousness, and sanctification, and redemption." The office of the Holy Spirit is to present Christ to our minds in such a manner that all these objects shall be fully accomplished in us.

The attention of the reader is now invited to a few general observations, designed to illustrate the office of the Holy Spirit in the work of redemption, as above presented. To accomplish this object, I remark,

I. The Holy Spirit enlightens the intellect, and carries on the work of sanctification in the heart, by the presentation of truth to the mind; and the truth presented does not respect himself, but Jesus Christ. "The sword of the Spirit is the word of God." "Howbeit, when He, the Spirit of truth, is come, he will guide you into all truth; for he shall not speak of himself; but whatsoever he shall hear, that shall he speak; and he will show you things to come. He shall glorify me; for he shall receive of mine, and shall show it unto you." The Holy Spirit sustains to Christ the same relation that a teacher does to the particular science which he teaches. His object is not to present himself to the pupil, but the science. So the Spirit shows not himself, but Christ, to our minds. We feel and recognize the presence of the Spirit, only as Christ is presented to our minds, and thus the "love of God is shed abroad in our hearts by the Holy Ghost, which is given unto us."

II. In thus accomplishing the work of redemption, the Holy Spirit sustains to Christians and sinners entirely different relations. To the latter, he sustains the exclusive relation of a reprover of sin, his object being conviction, for the purpose of leading the sinner, humbled and penitent, to Christ. "And when he is come, he will reprove the world of sin, and of righteousness, and of judgment."

To the Christian, on the other hand, the Christian, I mean, in a state of love and obedience to God, he sustains the relation of a teacher, a comforter, an indwelling light in which the glory and love of Christ are continually reflected upon the eye of the mind. "He shall take of mine, and shall show it unto you." "He shall testify of me." "But the Comforter, which is the Holy Ghost, whom the Father will send in my name, he shall teach you all things, and bring all things to your remembrance, whatsoever I have said unto you." "He dwelleth in you, and shall be in you."

III. The Holy Spirit, in the relation last described, is given to Christians after they believe in Christ, and in consequence of their faith in him.

> *Then Peter said unto them, Repent and be baptised, every one of you, in the name of Jesus Christ, for the remission of sins, and ye shall receive the gift of the Holy Ghost. ~ Acts ii. 38*

> *In whom also, after that ye believed, ye were sealed with the Holy Spirit of promise. ~ Eph. i. 13*

> *Turn you at my reproof; behold, I will pour out my Spirit upon you; I will make known my words unto you. ~ Prov. i. 23*

As these passages respect all Christians alike, they refer, not to the miraculous, but common influences of the Spirit, as an indwelling light in the hearts of God's people.

IV. The design of God, in the gift of his Spirit, is that he be to Christians, not as a "stranger or a sojourner, that turneth aside to tarry but for a night," but as the perpetual light of their souls, of whose illumination they are never to be destitute.

If ye love me, keep my commandments; and I will pray the Father, and he shall give you another Comforter, that he may abide with you for ever; even the Spirit of truth; whom the world cannot receive, because it seeth him not, neither knoweth him; but ye know him; for he dwelleth with you, and shall be in you. ~ *John xiv. 15-17*

Hence it is said of Christians, that their "bodies are the temples of the Holy Ghost," and that they themselves are "the temples of the living God." As the visible manifestation of the Divine glory never departed from the Holy of Holies in the ancient temple, so God designs that the light of his Spirit shall never depart from the more sacred temple of the heart, and nothing but sin can quench his Divine illuminations there. To enjoy these perpetual Divine illuminations, Christian, to have those full and unceasing visions of the glory of Christ, by which you may be able to "comprehend the breadth, and depth, and length, and height, and to know the love of Christ, which passeth knowledge," is your high privilege and most sacred duty.

V. We will now consider the state of those who thus enjoy the perpetual illumination of the Holy Spirit.

1. They have all those full, and direct, and perpetual visions of the love of Christ, which are necessary to their highest purity and blessedness. "Where the Spirit of the Lord is, there is liberty." "But we all, with open face beholding, as in a glass, the glory of the Lord, are changed into the same image, from glory to glory, even as by the Spirit of the Lord." "He that is spiritual" *i.e.*, taught by the Spirit "judgeth all things," has a distinct perception of all truth which it concerns him to understand. "He shall guide you into all truth."

2. All the wisdom that is necessary, that they, as the servants of Christ, may in every sphere and condition in life, glorify him in the most effectual manner. This is implied in the promise, "he shall lead you into all truth." It is also included in the promise,

"If any man lack wisdom, let him ask of God, who giveth unto men liberally, and upbraideth not, and it shall be given him."

3. They have such views of Christ as impart to them full and unfailing consolation in every affliction. In special reference to this part of his office, he is called the "Comforter."

4. Such a full and perpetual fruition of the presence and love of Christ as constitutes the richest foretaste of future blessedness. The gift of the Spirit, for this reason, is called the "earnest of our inheritance, until the redemption of the purchased possession."

5. The Spirit is given to such, as Heaven's signet; as God's seal to their title to the eternal inheritance which Christ has purchased for them. "Grieve not the Holy Spirit of God, whereby ye are sealed unto the day of redemption." "Ye are sealed with the Holy Spirit of promise."

Such are your privileges, Christian, in the gift of the Holy Spirit. All truth is perfectly known to him. "The Spirit searcheth all things, yea, the deep things of God." Every truth that you need to understand, he is able to present to your mind, in such a manner, that, from it, you shall receive the highest possible influence. He is equally able to present those truths, and those aspects of truth, which are perfectly adapted to your necessities in every condition in life. To you he is given as the last and richest gift of your God and Savior, to be in you as a perpetually indwelling light, through which you are to be "filled with all the fulness of God." Christ has promised, that "whosoever believeth in him shall not walk in darkness; but shall have the light of life." By availing yourself of the illumination of the Holy Spirit, this promise may be fully accomplished in your own blessed experience. Remember this, also, that without this Divine illumination, you will and you must walk in darkness. Those life-giving aspects of truth, presented to the mind by the Spirit, you can obtain from no other source whatever. "Even so the things of God knoweth no man, but the Spirit of God." "The natural man," the man that trusts to his own wisdom, without the aid of Divine illumination, "receiveth not the things of the Spirit of God; for they are foolishness unto him; neither CAN HE KNOW THEM, because they are spiritually discerned."

VI. We will now consider the conditions on which we can enjoy the perpetual illumination of the Holy Spirit."

1. His perpetual presence and illumination must be sought by prayer and "faith on the Son of God." "How much more shall your Father, which is in heaven, give the Holy Spirit to them that ask him!"

2. Your motives in seeking his illumination must be identical with those of the Spirit as your teacher. His appropriate office is, to "take of the things of Christ and show them unto you;" to impart to you that knowledge which is necessary to your highest holiness, blessedness, and usefulness, as a Christian. When you ask of God for the indwelling light of his Holy Spirit, ask it for this exclusive purpose, that you may know Christ, and fully experience the renovating power of his love upon your heart, that you may "know the things which are freely given you of God," and understand, as the servants of Christ, all the responsibilities devolving upon you, in every relation and condition in life.

3. Seek the illumination of the Holy Spirit, with a full consciousness and acknowledgement of your own blindness and ignorance, and entire dependence upon his teaching. "Except ye be converted, and become as little children, ye shall in no case enter into the kingdom of heaven." "If any man would be wise among you, let him become a fool, that he may be wise;" that is, let him acknowledge his total darkness and ignorance in himself, and seek for Divine illumination as the only source of true wisdom.

4. Seek the illumination of the Spirit in the diligent use of all appropriate means—the study of the Scriptures, attendance upon the instructions and ordinances of God's house, and in

social converse and prayer with such as are themselves spiritually taught. In the use of such means, with such a Spirit and object, your cup will be always full. It will overflow for ever.

REMARKS

I. In the light of this discourse, a few important passages of Scripture admit of a ready explanation. For example,

> *In that hour Jesus rejoiced in spirit, and said, I thank thee, O Father, Lord of heaven and earth, that thou hast hid these things from the wise and prudent, and hast revealed them unto babes; even so, Father, for so it seemed good in thy sight. ~ Luke x. 21*

"The wise and prudent" are those who proudly depend upon their own wisdom, and are regarded as wise by the world around them. "Babes" are such as acknowledge their blindness and ignorance, and look to Christ as the Divine illumination. How appropriate the joy and gratitude of Christ, that the former were left in darkness, and the latter Divinely illumined.

> *Jesus said unto them, If ye were blind, ye should have no sin; ~ 1 John ix. 41*

that is, if you would acknowledge your blindness, and come to me for Divine illumination, your sins would be wholly removed from you: but now ye say: "We see; therefore your sin remaineth;" that is, you deny your ignorance and dependence upon me; therefore your character remains unchanged, and your sins rest upon you.

> *But, as it is written, Eye hath not seen, nor ear heard, neither have entered into the heart of man, the things which God hath prepared for them that love him. ~ I Cor. ii. 9*

This passage is very commonly considered as applicable only to the condition of saints in heaven. The context shows, however, that it is applied exclusively to the condition of Christians on earth. "But God hath revealed them unto us by his Spirit." Such are your privileges now, Christian, through the love of Christ reflected upon your heart by the Holy Spirit, which is given unto you.

II. We may now understand one, at least, of the ways in which the "Spirit beareth witness with our spirit, that we are the children of God." When, for example, the Christian asks for wisdom from above, or for Divine illumination in respect to any question of truth or duty, and receives from the Spirit an answer to his request; in that answer, the Spirit of God bears witness with his Spirit that he is a child of God. Such is the testimony that he is perpetually bearing in the heart of all who are humble and contrite in spirit, and tremble at God's word. Reader, do you know what it is to have the witness of the Spirit in your own heart?

III. We are also fully prepared to answer the question, In what consists the grand secret of holy living? It is an indwelling Christ, whose image is perpetually reflected upon the eye of the mind, by the illumination of the Holy Spirit. Reader, is your piety of such a character as this?

IV. In what sense only is the Holy Spirit a sanctifier? "Christ is of God made unto us wisdom, and righteousness, and sanctification, and redemption." The Spirit sanctifies by presenting Christ to the mind in such a manner, that we are transformed into his image. The common error of Christians, in respect to this subject, seems to be this looking away from Christ to the Holy Spirit for sanctification, instead of looking for the Spirit to render Christ their sanctification.

V. For not having Christ perpetually dwelling in your heart, reader, as your wisdom, righteousness, sanctification, and redemption, you are without excuse. For this special purpose, the Holy Spirit is given to you. In his light it is your blessed privilege perpetually to walk. "How much more shall your Father which is in heaven give the Holy Spirit to them that ask him?" "Ask, and it shall be given you." "For every one that asketh receiveth."

VI. We see, in the light of this subject, the true ground of the expectation, that, in our efforts after holiness, we may attain to a state of entire consecration to Christ. "Work out your own salvation with fear and trembling; for it is God which worketh in you both to will and to do of his own good pleasure." Our hope of attaining to this state rests not at all upon a view of our own natural powers as moral agents, but upon the provisions of Divine grace for our "redemption from all iniquity," and our perfect "completeness in all the will of God," together with the Divine aid that is promised to succeed all sincere efforts made in simple faith in Christ, for the attainment of that state. In the redemption of Christ, as we have seen in former discourses, full provision is made for the entire sanctification of every believer. The Holy Spirit is given for the express purpose of so presenting the Lord Jesus Christ to our minds, that we may experience in our hearts the full power of his redemption. The Spirit, it should be remembered, has a perfect understanding of all truth pertaining to our salvation. He has, at all times, direct access to our hearts, and is perfectly able to present the image of Christ to our minds in such a manner, that it shall exert upon us the highest possible transforming power. He is always in us, a perpetually indwelling light, whose highest illuminations we can always enjoy, by opening our hearts with simple faith and prayer to receive it. With such provisions and such a helper, to what state ought we to expect to attain? Who is strongest, Christian, let me put the question again, "he that is in you, or he that is in the world?" Which has the greatest power, the Spirit of the living God, together with an indwelling Christ, or your fleshly lusts and propensities? Shall the followers of Christ proclaim the fact, that the Spirit and grace of Christ are less strong in their hearts, than the "world, the flesh, and the devil?" that that grace which changed an enemy into a friend, is not adequate to render that friend "perfect and complete in all the will of God?" "Tell it not in Gath! publish it not in the streets of Askelon! lest the daughters of the uncircumcised triumph!"

VII. We are now prepared, in the light of this and of the preceding discourse, to understand the great and fundamental errors of the Perfectionists, a sect which rose some years ago in the state of New York, and subsequently spread to a small extent over various parts of the country. The following are some of the tenets of this sect:

They maintained,
1. That in the Gospel there is a total abrogation of the moral law as a rule of action, and that Christians are for ever freed from all obligation to God, or any other being.
2. That, by one act of faith, the Christian is brought into such a state, that it is absolutely impossible that he should ever afterwards commit sin.
3. That the Spirit now communicates truth to Christians by direct revelation; and hence the study of the Scriptures, the ministry of reconciliation, prayer, the Sabbath, and all the ordinances, and the Church itself, they wholly dispensed with.
4. For the teachings of the Spirit they substituted impressions and impulses, maintaining that every existing desire or impulse is produced by the direct agency of the Spirit, and therefore to be gratified. Hence,
5. Many of them maintained the abrogation of marriage, even, and became the advocates of gross licentiousness from principle, and all this under the profession of absolute perfection in holiness. The reader will at once perceive, that no system could possibly be devised, which placed the subject more perfectly under the power of the great enemy, than this. The sect, containing in itself the principle of disunion and disorganization, very soon burst asunder, and now lie in scattered fragments in various parts of the country. Its entire history has been the perfect opposite of that union which Christ prayed might exist among believers, and which perfect love must and will produce. In the rise and subsequent

disorganization of the sect, however, the great enemy has gained one important object. Whenever the true doctrine of holiness is urged upon Christians, and Christ held up as a sanctifying Savior, he can raise the cry of Perfectionism, and thus prevent many from receiving the substance, because a few have grasped a shadow. If, in this attempt, reader, you permit him to gain an advantage over you; if, because you have turned the grace of God into lasciviousness, you will reject that grace itself, you foolishly jeopardize your immortal interests.

VIII. The reader will now clearly perceive that the sentiments maintained in these discourses have no alliance whatever with Perfectionism. The two systems, in their essential features and elements, are the direct opposites of each other. An individual holding the sentiments here maintained, cannot become a Perfectionist, without a full and total renunciation of all the principles which he previously held. This every one will perceive who candidly examines the two systems.

IX. There is one error of the Perfectionists, into which Christians not infrequently fall; against which I wish, in a special manner, to guard the reader. It is this: considering impulses and impressions as the teachings of the Spirit. An individual has upon his mind an undefined impression, that he ought, for example, to speak in meeting, or to pursue some particular course of conduct. In following that impression, he conceives himself to be following the leadings of the Spirit. In refusing to follow it, he supposes him self to grieve or quench the Spirit. Now, the principle that I maintain is this; that such impressions are of no authority whatever. The man who is led by the Spirit, is filled, not with impressions and impulses, but with light. He will always be able to give such reasons for his conduct as will commend themselves to his own and the conscience of every other man. Suppose, reader, that you should come to me for instruction or advice in respect to any question of truth or duty; what you would expect of me would be, that I should present such considerations to your mind, as would enable you to form an intelligent judgment in respect to the question before you.

Much more should you expect the same thing, when you pray for Divine teaching. Remember that it is when, and only when, you are led by such considerations, that you are led by the Spirit of God. The individual who turns away from the Spirit, as a teacher and guide, and gives himself up to the control of impulses and impressions, regarding these as the teachings of the Spirit, will very soon find himself in the "snare of the devil."

X. We may also understand, in the light of this discourse, the nature of spiritual-mindedness. It is a mind, all of whose powers and susceptibilities are under the sweet, and perpetual, and all-pervading influence of the "things of the Spirit," the truths revealed and presented by the Spirit. All such persons are "led by the Spirit of God," and "they are the sons of God."

XI. You may now, reader, answer the question, whether you are really spiritually-minded or not. Do you, in your own experience, reap the blissful fruits of the Spirit? "The fruit of the Spirit," remember, "is in all goodness, and righteousness, and truth." Again, "The fruit of the Spirit is love, joy, peace, long-suffering, gentleness, goodness, faith, meekness, temperance; against such there is no law." Is this the character of your religion? Is this the fruit of the Spirit that dwells in you? "If any man have not the Spirit of Christ, he is none of his;" and of the Spirit of Christ, these are the appropriate and invariable fruits.

XII. We see when and how it is that Christians "quench" and "grieve the Holy Spirit of God, whereby they are sealed unto the day of redemption." It is when they turn away from the glory and love of Christ, upon which the Spirit is endeavoring to fix their supreme affection and regard, and give their hearts to other and inferior objects. When you do this, reader, you not only grieve the Holy Spirit of God, but you put out the light of your own soul.

XIII. Finally. We are now prepared to look once more at the question, whether the great doctrine maintained in these discourses accords with the mind of the Spirit, by whose inspiration the Scriptures were written. Here permit me to present a few considerations, bearing upon this question, in addition to those already presented, and which naturally suggest themselves from the train of thought which we have pursued.

1. The first that I notice is a fact which can hardly have failed to impress the mind of the attentive reader of these discourses. It is this: Whenever I have had occasion to give a full and definite expression of my sentiments upon this subject, no phraseology conceivable has been found to be so perfectly adapted to that object, as the simple, unadorned, and most frequent phraseology of the Holy Spirit, as found in the sacred Scriptures. Can it be, reader, as asked in a former discourse, that the Holy Spirit has dictated a phraseology so perfectly adapted to convey one sentiment, and only one, when his design was to convey precisely the opposite sentiment?

2. It was just as easy for Christ to make such provisions, and to give the Holy Spirit to Christians in such measures, as to render their *perfect* as practicable as *partial* holiness. Of what conceivable use can sin be as an element of Christian character, that Christ should have left it as an inseparable element of that character?

3. That Christ should have made provision for the entire sanctification of believers, and given his Spirit in such measure to them as to render that state attainable, best accords with his infinite love, and the absolute perfection of all his other attributes and works. Why should he leave this, the last and greatest of all his works, thus imperfect?

4. This view of the subject best accords with the relations which Christians sustain to Christ and the world around them. They are Christ's witnesses, to testify to the world, from their own experience, to the truth of the "exceeding great and precious promises" of Divine grace; promises, many of which are, as we have seen, conditioned upon a state of entire consecration to Christ. How infinitely absurd, as shown in a former discourse, is

the supposition that Christ has so arranged the dispensations of his grace and Spirit, that he shall never have a witness upon earth, who can bear full testimony to the truth of his promises!

Christians are also constituted of Christ "the light of the world," by reflecting upon it his image. "God, who commanded the light to shine out of darkness, hath shined in our hearts, to give the light of the knowledge of the glory of God, in the face of Jesus Christ." Who can believe that Christ has definitely arranged the dispensations of his grace and Spirit, so that his own image, as reflected through the character of his own people, shall always be presented to the world in a deep and dark eclipse?

Again, Christians are Christ's representatives, his ambassadors, laborers together with God in the great work of saving lost men. Who can conceive a greater absurdity than this, that God has so arranged his dispensations toward his people, that all who are co-operating with him in this work, shall be but partially devoted to the duties of their sacred calling.

Once more, Christians are the "members of Christ's body, of his flesh, and of his bones." Reader, can you believe that Christ has made no provision, but that the members of his own body shall be in a state of disease and moral death? Dare you cast such an imputation upon the Lord Jesus Christ?

5. This doctrine leads the soul directly to Christ as a certain remedy for sin, and for all temptations to sin, and tends to induce the most vigorous efforts after pure and perfect holiness. The opposite doctrine tends directly to weaken confidence in Christ as a Savior from sin, and to paralyze efforts after holiness.

6. This doctrine meets perfectly a changeless demand of our being, a state of perfect moral rectitude, and tends to inspire the mind with life and peace. The opposite doctrine fails to meet that demand, and thereby covers the mind, that is hungering and thirsting after righteousness, with thick gloom. What can be

more gloomy to such a mind than the thought that he is to be perpetually wounding his Savior, in the house of his friends?

7. Finally, this doctrine has all the internal evidence in its favor that the Bible itself, or any doctrine of the Bible, that can be named, has. What higher internal evidence can be adduced, in favor of any doctrine, than this; that it tends directly to moral virtue, and meets fully the changeless laws of our being; while the tendency of the contrary doctrine is precisely the opposite in both the respects above named? Say the opposers of this doctrine, If it is untrue, its tendency must be bad. The same might, with equal propriety, be said of the Bible, and of every doctrine of the Bible. When we speak of the tendency of a doctrine, we then look away from the question whether it is true or false, to what is intrinsic in the doctrine itself. When we try the doctrine under consideration by this principle, we find it to have all the evidence in its favor that any Divine truth can have.

No, reader; in embracing this doctrine, we have not "followed cunningly-devised fables." We have followed the plainest teachings of the Spirit and Word of God. In taking our stand upon this doctrine, we are standing upon the "foundation of the apostles and prophets, Jesus Christ himself being the chief cornerstone." In looking with humble faith to "the very God of peace," that he may "sanctify us wholly, and preserve our whole spirit, and soul, and body, blameless unto the coming of our Lord Jesus Christ," we only look to him for a fulfillment of one of his own "exceeding great and precious promises," "Faithful is he that calleth you, who also will do it."

Reader, "believest thou this?" And will you now come to Christ, to have this promise, in all its fullness, accomplished in your own blessed experience? "Now the just shall live by faith, but if any man draw back, my soul shall have no pleasure in him." "Wherefore, seeing we are compassed about with so great a cloud of witnesses, let us lay aside every weight, and the sin that doth so easily beset us, and let us run with patience the race that is set before us, looking unto Jesus, the author and finisher of our faith; who, for the joy that was set before him, endured the cross, despising the shame, and is set down at the right hand of the throne of God."

CONCLUSION

In drawing my remarks to a close, I will, in conformity with the desires of my own mind, and the suggestions of some brethren, in whose judgment I place much confidence, give the reader a short account of the manner in which I was led, by the Spirit of God, as I believe, to adopt the sentiments maintained in these discourses. In regard to my early experience as a Christian, I would say, that that experience had two prominent characteristics, a desire, inexpressibly strong, to be freed from all sin in every form, and to be entirely consecrated to the love and service of God, in all the powers and susceptibilities of my being. Nor can any one conceive the gloom and horror that covered my mind, when older Christians assured me, and, as I supposed, with truth, that that was a state to which I should never, in this life, attain; that my lusts would not be perfectly subdued or subjected to the will of Christ, and that one of the brightest evidences of my conversion and growth in grace was new discoveries of the deep and fixed corruptions of my heart, corruptions from which I was never to be cleansed till death should deliver me from my bondage. Notwithstanding all the impediments thrown in the way of my progress in holiness, I continued to press forward for a succession of years, till I could say, in the language of another, "I do know that I love holiness for holiness' sake."

In this state, I commenced my studies as a student in college. Here I fell, and fell, by not aiming singly at the "prize of the high calling," but at the prize of college honors. I subsequently entered a theological seminary, with the hope of there finding myself in such an atmosphere, that my first love would be revived. In this expectation, I grieve to say, I was most sadly disappointed. I found the piety of my brethren apparently as low as my own. I here say it, with sorrow of heart, that my mind does not recur to a single individual connected with the "school of the prophets," when I was there, who appeared to me to enjoy daily communion and peace with God.

After completing my course under such circumstances, I entered the ministry, proud of my intellectual attainments, and armed, as I supposed, at every point, with the weapons of theological warfare, but with the soul of piety chilled and expiring within me. Blessed be God, the remembrance of what I had been remained, and constantly aroused me to a consciousness of what I was. I looked into myself, and over the Church, and was shocked at what I felt and what I saw. Two facts in the aspect of the Church and the ministry, struck my mind with gloomy interest. Scarcely an individual, within the circle of my knowledge, seemed to know the Gospel as a *sanctifying* or *peace-giving* Gospel. In illustration of this remark, let me state a fact which I met with in the year 1831 or 1832. I then met a company of my ministerial brethren, who had come together from one of the most favored portions of the country. They sat down together, and gave to each other an undisguised disclosure of the state of their hearts; and they all, with one exception, and the experience of that individual I did not hear, acknowledged that they had not daily communion and peace with God. Over these facts they wept, but neither knew how to direct the others out of the thick and impenetrable gloom which covered them; and I was in the same ignorance as my brethren.

I state these facts as a fair example of the state of the Churches, and of the ministry, as far as my observation has extended; and that has been very extensive. I here affirm that the great mass of Christians do not know the Gospel, in their daily experience, as a life-giving and peace-giving Gospel. When my mind became fully conscious of this fact, I was led to compare my own, and the experience of the Church around me, with that of the apostles and primitive Christians, and with the "path of the just," as portrayed in the sacred Scriptures. I found the two in direct contrast with each other. Hence the great inquiry arose in my mind, *What is the grand secret of holy living?* How shall I attain to that perpetual fullness and peace in Christ, which, for example, Paul enjoyed? Till this secret was fully disclosed to my mind, I felt that I was, and must be, disqualified, in one fundamental respect, to "feed the flock of God." While the Gospel was not life and peace to me, how could I present it in such a manner that it would be life and peace to others. I must myself be led by the Great Shepherd into the "green pastures and beside the still waters," before I could lead the flock of God into the same blissful regions. For years, this one inquiry pressed upon my thoughts; and often as I have looked over a company of inquiring sinners have I said within myself, I would gladly take my place among those inquirers, if any individual would show me how to come into possession of the "riches of the glory of Christ's inheritance of the saints." But clouds and darkness covered my mind in respect to this, the most momentous of all subjects.

In this state of mind, I became connected with the Institution at Oberlin, and continued to press my inquiries with increasing interest upon this one subject, till the fall of 1836. At that time, during a series of religious meetings held in the Institution, a large number of the members of the Church arose and informed us that they were fully convinced that they had been deceived in respect to their character as Christians, and that they were now without hope, and appeared as inquirers, to know "what they should do to be saved." At the same time, the great mass of the remainder disclosed to us the cheerless bondage in which they had long been groaning, and asked us if we could tell them how to obtain deliverance. I now felt myself, as one of the "leaders of the flock of God," pressed with the great inquiry above referred to, with greater interest than ever before. I set my heart, by prayer and supplication to God, to find the light after which I had been so long seeking.

In this state I visited one of my associates in the Institution, and disclosed to him the burden which had weighed down my mind for so many years. I asked him if he could tell me the secret of the piety of Paul, and tell me the reason of the strange contrast between the apostle's experience and my own. In laboring for the salvation of men, I observed, that my feelings often remained unmoved and unaffected, while Paul was constantly "*constrained*" by the love of Christ. Our conversation then turned upon the passage, "The love of Christ constraineth us," &c. While thus employed, my heart leaped up in ecstasy indescribable, with the exclamation, "I have found it." I have now, by the grace of God, discovered the secret after which I have been searching these many years. I understood the secret of the piety of Paul, and knew how to attain to that blissful state myself. Paul's piety all arose from one source exclusively; a sympathy with the heart of Christ in his love for lost man. To attain to that state myself, I had only to acquaint myself with the love of Christ, and yield my whole being up to its sweet control.

Immediately after this, I came before the Church, and disclosed to them what I then saw to be the grand defect in my ministry:

1. Christ had been but as one chapter in my system of theology, when he should have been the sun and centre of the system.

2. When I thought of my guilt, and need of justification, I had looked to Christ exclusively, as I ought to have done; for sanctification, on the other hand, to overcome the "world, the flesh, and the devil," I had depended mainly on my own resolutions.

Here was the grand mistake, and the source of all my bondage under sin. I ought to have looked to Christ for sanctification, as much as for justification, and for the same reason. The great object of my being now was to know Christ, and in knowing him to be changed into his image. Here was the "victory which overcometh the world." Here was the "death of the body of sin." Here was "redemption from all iniquity," into the "glorious liberty of the children of God." At this time, the appropriate office of the Holy Spirit presented itself to my mind with a distinctness and interest never understood nor felt before. To know Christ was the life of the soul. To "take of the things of Christ and show them unto us;" to open our hearts to understand the Scriptures; to strengthen us with might in the inner man, that we might comprehend the "breadth and depth, and length and height, and know the love of Christ, which passeth knowledge," and thus be "filled with the fulness of God," is the appropriate office of the Spirit. The highway of holiness was now for the first time, rendered perfectly distinct to my mind. The discovery of it was to my mind as "life from the dead." The disclosure of that path had the same effect upon others who had been, like myself, "*weary*, tossed with tempest, and not comforted." As my supreme attention was thus fixed upon Christ; as it became the great object of my being to know him, and be transformed into his likeness; and as I was perpetually seeking that Divine illumination by which I might apprehend him, an era occurred in my experience, which I have no doubt will ever be one of the most memorable in my entire past existence. In a moment of deep and solemn thought, the veil seemed to be lifted, and I had a vision of the infinite glory and love of Christ, as manifested in the mysteries of redemption. I will not attempt to describe the effect of that vision upon my mind. All that I would say is, that, in view of it, my heart melted, and flowed out like water. The heart of stone was taken away, and a heart of love and tenderness assumed its place. From that time I have desired to know nothing but Jesus Christ and him crucified." I have literally "esteemed all things but loss for the excellency of the knowledge of Jesus Christ my Lord;" and the knowledge of Christ has been eternal life begun in my heart.

Now, when the Lord Jesus Christ was thus held up among us, by myself and others, a brother in the ministry arose in one of our meetings, and remarked that there was one question to which he desired that a definite answer might be given. It is this: "When we look to Christ for sanctification, what degree of sanctification may we expect from him? May we look to him to be sanctified wholly, or not?" I do not recollect that I was ever so shocked and confounded at any question, before or since. I felt, for the moment, that the work of Christ among us would be marred, and the mass of minds around us rush into Perfectionism. Still the question was before us; and to it we were bound, as pupils of the Holy Spirit, to give a scriptural answer. We did not attempt to give a definite answer to it during that time. With that question before us, brother Finney and myself came to New York, and spent most of the winter together in prayer and the study of the Bible. The great inquiry with us was, "What degree of holiness may we ourselves expect from Christ, when we exercise faith in him, and in what light shall we present him to others as a Savior from sin?" We looked, for example, at such passages as this, passages of which the Bible is full, "And the very God of peace sanctify you wholly; and I pray God, your whole spirit, and soul, and body, be preserved blameless unto the coming of our Lord Jesus Christ. Faithful is he that calleth you, who also will do it?" We looked at such passages, I say, and asked ourselves this question; Suppose an honest inquirer after holiness comes to us, and asks of us, "What degree of holiness is here promised to the believer?" May I expect, in view of this prayer and promise, that God will sanctify me wholly, and preserve me in that state till the coming of our Lord Jesus Christ? What answer shall we give him? Shall we tell him that merely *partial*, and not perfect holiness is here promised, and that the former, and not the latter, he is here authorized to expect? After looking prayerfully at the testimony of Scripture, in respect to the provisions and promises of Divine grace, we were constrained to admit, that but one answer to the above question could be given from the Bible; and the greatest wonder with me is, that I have been so long a "master of Israel, and have never before known these things." Since that time we have never ceased to proclaim the redemption of Christ as a full redemption. Nor do we expect to cease proclaiming it as a full and finished redemption, till Christ shall call us home. For myself, I am willing to proclaim it to the world, that I now look to the very God of peace to sanctify me wholly, and preserve my whole spirit, and soul, and body, blameless unto the coming of our Lord Jesus Christ. I put up this prayer with the expectation that the very things prayed for will be granted. Reader, is that confidence misplaced? In expecting that blessing, am I leaning upon a broken reed, or upon the broad promise of God?

There is one circumstance connected with my recent experience, to which I desire to turn the special attention of the reader. I would here say that I have for ever given up all idea of resisting temptation, subduing any lust, appetite, or propensity, or of acceptably performing any service for Christ, by the mere force of my own resolutions. If my propensities, which lead to sin, are crucified, I know that it must be done by an indwelling Christ. If I overcome the world, this is to be the victory, "even our faith." If the great enemy is to be overcome, it is to be done "by the blood of the Lamb."

Believing, as I now do, that the Lord Jesus Christ has provided special grace for the entire sanctification of every individual, for the subjection of all his propensities, for a perfect victory over every temptation and incentive to sin, and for rendering us, in every sphere and condition of life, all that he requires us to be; the first inquiry with me is, In what particular respects do I need the grace of Christ? What is there, for example, in my temper that needs correcting? Wherein am I in bondage to appetite, or to any of my propensities? What are the particular responsibilities, temptations, &c., incident to each particular sphere and condition in life in which the providence of God has called me to act? What is the temper that I ought there to manifest, so that I may everywhere, and under all circumstances, reflect the image of Christ?

Thus, having discovered my special necessity, in any one of the particulars above referred to, my next object is, to take some promise applicable to the particular exigency before me, and go directly to Christ for the supply of that particular necessity. By having the eye of faith perpetually fixed upon Christ in this manner; by always looking to him for special grace in every special exigency; yes, for "grace to help in every time of need," how easy it is to realize in our own blessed experience the truth of all the "exceeding great and precious promises" of Divine grace! How easy it is to have the peace of God, which passeth all understanding, "keep our hearts and minds through Christ Jesus." "Our peace is then as a river, and our righteousness as the waves of the sea." The mind seems to be borne upward and onward, as upon an ocean of light, peace, and blessedness, which knows no bounds.

> "O glorious change! 'tis all of grace,
> By bleeding love bestowed
> On outcasts of our fallen race,
> To bring them home to God;
> Infinite grace to vileness given,
> The sons of earth made heirs of heaven."

And now, reader, "my heart's desire and prayer to God" for you is, that you may know this full redemption. If you will cease from all efforts of your own, and bring your sins, and sorrows, and cares, and propensities which lead into sin, to Christ, and cast them all upon him; if, with implicit faith, you will hang your whole being upon him, and make it the great object of life to know him, for the purpose of receiving and reflecting his image, you will find that all the "exceeding great and precious promises" of his Word are, in your own blissful experience, a living reality. The waters that Christ shall give you "shall be in you a well of water springing up into everlasting life." You shall have a perpetual and joyful victory over "the world, the flesh, and the devil." Everywhere, and under all circumstances, your peace in Christ shall be as a "river, and your righteousness as the waves of the sea." "O taste and see that the Lord is good." "There is no want to them that fear him." And, reader, when your cup is once filled with the love of Christ, you will then say with truth, "The half has not been told me." "Eye hath not seen, nor ear heard, nor have entered into the heart of man, the things which God hath prepared for them that love him."

John Wesley was born in Epwoth, Lincolnshire, England on June 28, 1703 to Samuel and Susanna Wesley, and died at the age of 87 on March 2, 1791. He was an open air preacher and with his brother Charles founded Methodism. He was a prolific writer and leaves many writings supporting Biblical holiness.

Asa Mahan was born in Vernon, New York on November 9, 1799, the son of Samuel (1760-1840) and Anna Dana (1778-1842) Mahan. The Mahans were a respected service-oriented family of New England background. Like his parents, Asa Mahan experienced a religious conversion as a young man and retained a preoccupation with personal salvation and sin.

INDEX

R

redeem 16, 47, 52, 54, 198, 199, 213, 216

redemption 41, 45, 57, 74, 79, 93, 142, 178, 189, 198, 201, 202, 204, 209, 222, 226, 227, 230, 231, 232, 233, 234, 235, 236, 237, 238, 239, 240, 241, 242, 243, 244, 245, 254, 262, 265, 268, 269, 272, 279, 281, 283

repentance....................104, 137, 181

resurrection......13, 82, 177, 200, 220

righteousness .. 11, 15, 18, 19, 41, 42, 43, 48, 49, 50, 53, 54, 77, 79, 83, 85, 97, 99, 105, 122, 142, 143, 148, 163, 172, 174, 186, 190, 194, 199, 202, 210, 216, 217, 225, 235, 243, 245, 251, 254, 255, 262, 263, 268, 272, 274, 283

S

salvation ... 10, 34, 35, 39, 41, 44, 45, 54, 58, 59, 64, 79, 84, 111, 118, 127, 128, 129, 154, 177, 186, 194, 204, 232, 240, 241, 242, 255, 269, 279, 284

sanctification ...50, 51, 52, 53, 69, 79, 90, 91, 92, 108, 129, 132, 138, 139, 140, 141, 142, 143, 144, 146, 147, 149, 153, 158, 159, 160, 163, 166, 167, 168, 170, 175, 176, 184, 185, 204, 205, 206, 207, 208, 209, 210, 211, 212, 227, 229, 234, 241, 245, 256, 257, 258, 262,⬚ 268, 269, 273, 279, 280, 282

Scripture.... 2, 5, 6, 7, 10, 11, 13, 15, 18, 28, 35, 45, 52, 54, 55, 62, 63, 68, 77, 92, 93, 94, 101, 118, 149, 150, 156, 158, 170, 185, 189, 203, 267, 281

second blessing...........................108

sin ... 8, 11, 12, 13, 14, 15, 16, 22, 26, 35, 36, 37, 38, 40, 42, 44, 46, 47, 48, 49, 50, 52, 53, 54, 55, 56, 57, 58, 59, 60, 61, 62, 65, 66, 67, 68, 69, 71, 73, 74, 77, 78, 79, 82, 83, 86, 87, 89, 91, 92, 93, 94, 95, 98, 99, 100, 103, 105, 110, 114, 118, 119, 122, 127, 128, 129, 131, 142, 143, 145, 158, 159, 161, 163, 167, 169, 170, 171, 173, 174, 175, 178, 179, 180, 181, 184, 185, 188, 192, 194, 195, 197, 198, 199, 201, 202, 203, 205, 208, 211, 212, 216, 224, 226, 230, 233, 234, 237, 238, 240, 241, 242, 243, 244, 245, 249, 250, 251, 252, 253, 255, 256, 259, 261, 262, 264, 267, 270, 273, 274, 275, 276, 279, 281, 282, 283, 284

T

temptation 35, 45, 58, 89, 90, 91, 102, 116, 139, 162, 216, 224, 240, 250, 254, 282

theology 17, 18, 279

tradition 6, 12

Trinity 187

W

Wesley, John..... 2, 5, 24, 25, 26, 34, 65, 85, 99, 120, 129, 136, 179, 284

wisdom.. 8, 72, 75, 79, 100, 101, 132, 135, 156, 176, 195, 220, 222, 233, 235, 245, 259, 262, 264, 265, 266, 267, 268

worship............................ 9, 122, 238

For additional copies of this book and a list of other titles available from Apprehending Truth please visit our website:

http://www.publishers.apprehendingtruth.net

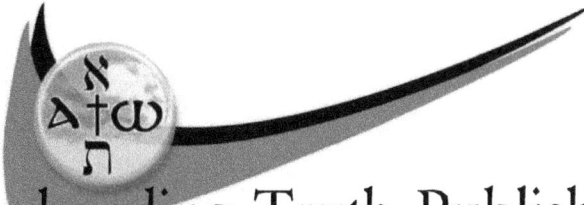

Apprehending Truth Publishers
Proclaiming Truth in the Age of Deceit
AD LEGEM MAGIS ET AD TESTIMONIUM

Published by
Apprehending Truth
Woodville, Mississippi
2011

Apprehending Truth Publishers is a division of Apprehending Truth Ministry.
http://www.ApprehendingTruth.net

www.ingramcontent.com/pod-product-compliance
Lightning Source LLC
Chambersburg PA
CBHW031945090426
42739CB00006B/87